GOOD COUNSEL

GOOD COUNSEL

An environment for growth in wisdom, age and grace

Conducted by The Sisters of the Divine Compassion

by
Sr. Mary Basil Hayes, R.D.C.

edited by
Sr. Mary Doretta Cornell, R.D.C.

DIVINE COMPASSION PUBLICATIONS

Published by   Divine Compassion Publications
                  52 North Broadway
                  White Plains, New York 10603

Manufactured: the United States of America

ISBN 0-9629104-9-X

Foreword

The History of Good Counsel, White Plains and White Plains of Pace University

Having read the manuscript of this combined history of Good Counsel College, The College of White Plains, and The College of White Plains of Pace University, I feel privileged to offer an introduction that may provide the perspective of an admiring "outsider-insider". Sister Basil Hayes demonstrates the craft of a historian as she uses sources skillfully to provide impeccable accuracy and detail. Her weaving together of the story of a religious congregation and the evolution of a fine liberal arts college demonstrates a deep humanity that shares with the reader the glories of success and the anxieties of occasional frustrations.

The accounts of historic events and the visits by cardinals and bishops and distinguished lay people demonstrate the interweaving of the values of inspiring people into the life of a developing college. Each account of a building constructed or acquired or refurbished is an interesting tale woven into a structured history. The role of the founding members of the Congregation and the contributions of the presidents of the College are vignettes that only an author at once subjective and caring might produce.

This history gives me, as the one who was President of Pace University when our two institutions united to become one, a pride in association and a genuine admiration for the remarkable people who have become a strong part of the larger University. A fine small liberal arts college has given depth and scholarship to the University, which in turn has provided the strength and assurance of continuity that its size, management and scope of professional schools make possible.

There is interest in this history for alumni, young and old, for faculty and benefactors, and for dedicated and devoted members of the Congregation of the Divine Compassion.

History is the story of people. This is a warmhearted account of admirable people and their institution. It deserves reading.

Edward J. Mortola
February 20, 1987

Introduction

The History of Good Counsel College by Sister Mary Basil Hayes with a foreword by Dr. Edward J. Mortola, chancellor of Pace University, tells the story of the founding, growth, and development of a liberal arts college in White Plains. The problems and difficulties of the early days are faced and discussed with care. Once these were overcome, the College continued to grow steadily year by year.

The story opens with an eyewitness account of the first day and a special mention of the seven pioneer students, who had the courage and confidence to trust the new foundation. An interesting verbal picture is given of the development of the campus grounds, of the story behind the acquisition of each of the three estates, and of the history of the ownership back to the days of the American Revolution. The development of the city of White Plains, as the birth place of the State of New York from a small hamlet of colonial days to its present day status as the County seat of Westchester, is outlined.

The chronicles in the archives of the Sisters of the Divine Compassion were consulted for the years 1924-1932, giving an interesting account of the day by day life in the College. Special attention is paid to the erection of each building, giving the significance of the name assigned to each. The great events of the Sisters of the Divine Compassion and the College are interwoven: The Golden Jubilee of the Religious of the Divine Compassion in 1936, the Silver Jubilee of the College in 1948, the Diamond Jubilee of the Religious of the Divine Compassion in 1961, and the Golden Jubilee of the College in 1973.

The Presidents and the Deans of the College are given special mention and the contributions of each to the growth of the College are recorded.

Presidents

Mother Mary Aloysia Kelly 1923-1948
Mother Mary Dolores Hayes 1948-1970
Charles E. Ford 1970-1972
Katherine Restaino 1973-1975

Deans

An interesting section of the history is devoted to the special friends of the College. Their outstanding contributions are gratefully remembered and recorded. The rich traditions, which bound the students together in bonds of love, devotion and loyalty, are outlined. A sampling of impressions and memories of students from the early days, the mid years and later years, gives a personal picture of the devotion of the "Good Counsel Girl" to her Alma Mater.

Topics of special interest relating to the College, such as the chapters about the library, the statue of Our Lady of the Thruway and the introduction of the Journalism major are given consideration. The growth of the College Library from the original one room to the beautiful, well-equipped Hayes Library of today is a fascinating story. The statue of Our Lady of the Thruway, a gift of the Knights of Columbus, stood for 17 years overlooking the Cross Westchester Expressway. In 1959 it attracted national attention to Good Counsel College and brought a telegram of congratulations from President Richard Nixon. The first collegiate department of Journalism in Westchester County was introduced in 1964 by Mother Mary Dolores Hayes, President of the College, and became a popular choice as a major course for many future journalists.

Appendix 3 gives some very interesting statistics which, if studied carefully, give the story of the growth and development of the College of Good Counsel.

Sister Mary Basil Hayes, R.D.C.

Table of Contents

Table of Illustrations

Following page 159:   Mother Mary Aloysia, R.D.C.
First President of Good Counsel College

Mother Mary Dolores, R.D.C.
Second President of Good Counsel College

Dr. Charles E. Ford, Third President of
Good Counsel, with Sr. M. Teresa Brady;
Sr. M. Charles Moran, Dean; Sr. M. Basil
Hayes; Terence Cardinal Cooke

Dr. Katherine Restaino
Fourth President of Good Counsel College

Sr. Mary Carmelita; Rev. Thomas P. Cahill;
Mother Mary Compassio; Msgr. Joseph
Breslin; Sr. Mary Ligouri; Bishop James
Kearney; Mrs. Helen Gerety; Mother M.
Aloysia; Sr. Mary Cyril, Dean; Msgr. Joseph
Clune; Dr. Leo I. Kearney

Sr. Mary Basil; Sr. Mary Trinitas; Sr. James
Marie (Ellen McGrath); Sr. Mary Alice;
Sr. Mary Ligouri; Mother Mary Ethelburge;
Sr. Mary Teresa; Msgr. Charles McManus;
Mother Mary Dolores; Sr. Mary Leona;
Sr. Mary Charles (Miriam Moran); Sr. Mary
Dolorita (Rita Dougherty)

Bishop James E. Kearney

Dr. Leo I. Kearney, Grand Marshall,
Commencement Day

Mr. John J. Gerety; Mrs. Helen Gerety;
Professor Iole Gardella; Professor Elena
Chavez

Sr. Mary Basil, Grand Marshall,
Commencement Day 1975

CHAPTER ONE

THE BEGINNING

A year to remember, 1923! On a beautiful day in September, Good Counsel College opened its doors to the first freshman class, seven bright eager young ladies from the Academy of Our Lady of Good Counsel. In any history of the College these seven should receive special mention for their courage and trust. Each one felt the glory of the pioneers. With great confidence in the wisdom of the undertaking, they were willing to begin their studies in a college in its infancy.

At 9:00 a.m., on September 19th, the Seven assembled in the reading room of the library, where in the presence of members of the faculty and administration, a very convincing talk was given by Father R. Rush Rankin, S.J., stressing the advantages of a small college and a Catholic College, but more especially the privilege of beginning their college days with the Sisters they knew so well and who were so interested in their own girls.

After the talk the students were shown into Room 101 for their first class taught by Sister Mary Liguori -- Latin 10 covering Virgil's works. Then followed History, English and Biology, Mathematics and French.

Who were these courageous young women who with confidence and trust made possible the beginning of the infant institute Good Counsel College?

With pride we record their names:

Carol C. Carmody, Brooklyn, New York
Evelyn C. Dolan, Jersey City, New Jersey
Marguerite C. Dolan, Jersey City, New Jersey
Wanda J. Graboski, Port Richmond, Staten Island, New York
Anna E. O'Reilly, Brooklyn, New York
Annette C. Perron, Montreal, Canada
Margaret F. Reynolds, White Plains, New York

The Seven Pioneers

Carol C. Carmody, B.A. English cum laude.

Carol was the first student to receive her degree from Good Counsel College, and was known for her exceptional devotion to her Alma Mater. After graduation, Carol spent the summer traveling in Europe. In the fall of 1927 she registered at Smith College and was awarded her M.A. in English in 1929. In 1933 she married a graduate of the University of Copenhagen, Mr. Schach Von Steenburg.

Evelyn C. Dolan, B.A., Mathematics.

Evelyn, a Good Counsel girl since 1917, was noted for her enthusiastic spirit of loyalty. She filled with dignity the office of President of the Sodality of the Blessed Virgin Mary. After graduation, Evelyn took many courses in Education toward her M.A. degree at Fordham University from 1928 to 1930; she also studied at City College in 1929. Evelyn married Mr. William J. Kehoe who died in May 1949. Their daughter Betty Ann attended Good Counsel College for a short time in 1951. Evelyn was very active in both civic and parish affairs.

Marguerite C. Dolan, B.A., Latin.

Marguerite was chosen first President of the Student Government when it was introduced in February 1927. All her actions while a student were influenced by her high ideals, and her loyalty to Good Counsel. When the Alumnae Association was organized in 1927, Marguerite was chosen as its first President. After graduation she engaged in teaching. She married Mr. Andrew Sapienza.

Wanda J. Graboski, B.A., Mathematics.

As a student Wanda was cheerful, fun-loving and at times serious. She was Art Editor of the Vestigia and active in other college organizations. Wanda married Mr. Edward Kuberski, who died in 1942.

Anna E. O'Reilly, B.A., Latin.

Anna, who came to Good Counsel with her sister Perry in 1918, was one of the most active and prominent members of her class. She was chosen President of the Student Body in 1926 and was the first Editor-in-Chief of The Prestonian. Anna was an excellent student and a brilliant social figure, always in demand for her conversational powers. After graduation Anna studied Sociology at New York University where she obtained her M.A. degree in 1930. She taught in the New York City public schools for a number of years. Later she was Supervisor of the day classes for adults in English and citizenship. Anna married Mr. Raymond Kniphuisen. Her two daughters attended Good Counsel College, Avalon for a short period and Anne Wilma to graduate in 1962, after entering the community of the Sisters of the Divine Compassion. Mrs. Kniphuisen returned to Good Counsel in 1957 where she filled the position of Supervisor of Student Teachers and taught several courses in Education until 1959.

Annette C. Perron, B.A., Mathematics, cum laude.

Annette came to Good Counsel from Montreal, Canada, in 1917. Reliability, punctuality and accuracy were prominent traits of her character. She was President of her class in the senior year and held many other offices during her college career. After graduation Annette had a very successful business career. She now resides in Ottowa, Canada.

Margaret F. Reynolds, B.A., English.

Serious, sincere, she possessed a wealth of common sense and good humor. Margaret was Vice President of the Alumnae Association. After graduation she taught school in Brooklyn while continuing her studies at Fordham University in applied sociology and literature of England and Ireland. Later Margaret prepared herself for work in personnel and guidance and filled with great success the position of Senior Employment Counselor for the United States Employment Service. Margaret married Mr. George D. Devlin.

During the first year no attempt was made to secure students from other sources. The enrollment was limited to girls from the Academy of Our Lady of Good Counsel who had expressed such a strong desire to remain and continue their education on the college level.

In the fall of 1924, after a restful summer, the original seven pioneers returned to begin their second year as sophomores. Five more students joined the ranks of the original seven pioneers, bringing the number of the first class to graduate in 1927 up to twelve.

Grace A. Dodworth, B.A., Mathematics.

In the fall of 1924, Grace joined the class for her sophomore year. She transferred from St. Joseph's College in Brooklyn. She soon became one of the most popular students. Grace was Associate Editor of The Prestonian and Editor-in-Chief of Vestigia. After graduation, she entered the teaching field. Grace married Mr. William Canfield. She showed her esteem and love for her Alma Mater by sending her daughter Anne Grace Canfield to Good Counsel in September 1960. Anne, in her turn, was a devoted and active member of her Class of 1964.

Margaret M. Wall, B.A., Mathematics.

Margaret joined the ranks of the original seven in the Spring of 1925, a transfer student from Georgian Court College in New Jersey. Margaret was a bright, witty young lady full of fun and good humor. After graduation she followed a teaching career. She married Mr. Douglas Ashe.

Mary R. Corley, B.A., Latin, cum laude.

Mary came to Good Counsel in 1920. She graduated from Good Counsel Academy in 1924 and received a gold medal for excellence in Latin. She enrolled at Good Counsel College and joined the original group in 1925. Having accelerated her course, she completed the requirements for the degree in three years and graduated first in the class, cum laude. She was awarded the Mary Caroline Dannat Starr medal for excellence. Mary was outstanding as a Latin scholar and as a debater. She took an active and convincing part in the yearly debates and was chosen President of the Preston Debating Society. After graduation Mary continued her studies at Fordham University where she obtained her Master's degree. She taught in the New York City Public Schools for 34 years. Mary married Mr. Edward Taylor and is the mother of four children, Christopher, Mary, Edward and Conrad.

Among the twelve graduates who received their degrees at the first commencement were two Religious of the Divine Compassion, Sister Mary Liguori Mistretta and Sister Mary Basil Hayes.

What Went Before

When a number of graduates of the Academy of Our Lady of Good Counsel requested a college, Mother Mary Aloysia began to consider whether it would be possible to provide a college for these eager young girls who wished to remain and continue their education on the college level. She began discussing the subject with Father R. Rush Rankin, S.J.; Father Robert Johnson, S.J.; and Father Arthur Scanlan. Encouraged by their interest and sound advice, she next placed the matter before the Archbishop of New York, Patrick J. Hayes. He approved wholeheartedly of the idea and suggested that she submit a complete report of the proposal to the Diocesan Council for consideration. At the meeting held on January 3, 1923, the Council unanimously approved the petition for the establishment of a college at White Plains. Great was the joy experienced by Mother Mary Aloysia and the community when on January 4th she received the following letter from Father Joseph P. Dineen, Secretary of the Diocesan Council:

January 4, 1923

Dear Mother,

You will be pleased to learn that the Diocesan Council yesterday approved unanimously of your petition for the establishment of a college at White Plains, so that you are now free to take the requisite steps for the realization of this project.

With a blessing,
I am Sincerely yours in Christ
Jos. P. Dineen, Secretary of the Council

Immediately steps were taken to contact the Regents of the University of the State of New York. Father Joseph Dunning, Superintendent of the Schools of the Albany Diocese, went to see Augustus Downing, Assistant Commissioner of Education on February 21, 1923, bringing with him the papers for the new college. Unfortunately, Dr. Downing had been called to San Francisco on account of the illness of his son George who was the victim of a mine disaster which resulted in his death.

Again on March 26, 1923, Father Dunning presented the reports to the Commissioner for Higher Education in the hopes that the Regents would be able to take up the matter at its next meeting to be held in April. As a result, Good Counsel College was registered by the University of the State of New York.

On June 26, 1923, His Grace, the Most Reverend Patrick Hayes, Archbishop of New York, came to Good Counsel to bless the three new wings of the Convent and to preside at the commencement of the Academy of Our Lady of Good Counsel. In the course of his address to the graduates he announced that the Sisters were to open a college in the fall. Overjoyed, seven of the graduates immediately registered for the new college before departing for the summer vacation, happy with the thought that they could return to Good Counsel in September as the first freshman class.

Before the Archbishop left that day, he appointed Mother Mary Aloysia President of the College and the Reverend Patrick N. Breslin Honorary President. Monsignor Breslin had become the Ecclesiastical Superior of the Community upon the death of Monsignor John Edwards.

While the students rested for the summer, there was no rest for Mother Mary Aloysia. She gave first consideration to the faculty and staff. Sister Mary Edmund was appointed Dean; Sister Mary Cyril, Assistant Dean; Sister Mary Ambrose, Registrar; Sister Mary deSales,

Librarian. Next she turned her attention to the buildings and rooms to be used by the college. Saint Joseph's House and Saint Ann's cottage would serve as residences for the boarding students. The college proper would be located in the east and south wings of the new building. This structure, 160 by 140 feet, contained the library, reception and lecture rooms, art room and science laboratories for biology, chemistry and physics. A cozy Club Room was also made ready.

Then the curriculum of studies had to be drawn up and teachers assigned. Latin was to be taught by Sister Mary Liguori and Sister Mary Hyacinth, English by Sister Mary Edmund, French by Sister Mary Fidelis, Biology by Sister Mary Carmelita, Mathematics and Physics by Sister Mary Cyril, and History by Sister Mary Cecilia. Sister Mary Joseph would be available if anyone wished to study German, and Sister Mary Liguori for Spanish, Sister Mary deSales for Italian.

During the first year the faculty was composed of Sisters only. In 1924, Father Rankin, Father John X. Pyne, Father Aloysius Weber and Sister Mary dePazzi joined the faculty. In the following years new names were added, including lay men and women: Father Robert H. Johnson, Hannah M. Egan, Grace Gallagher, Walter Hynes, Leo I. Kearney, Theodore Maynard, Maurice Rogalin, Mrs. J.K. Summers, Sister Mary Augustine, Sister Mary Basil, Sister Marie Therese, and Sister Mary Berchmans (Byrne).

In 1928 Father James E. Kearney joined the faculty to teach Religion, after the death of Father Aloysius Weber. Thus began Father Kearney's lifelong service and devotion to the college first as a young priest and later as beloved Bishop.

Once the first year had been completed, the next step was to obtain a Charter. The application for incorporation of Good Counsel College was forwarded to the Board of Regents for consideration at the meeting to be held on May 29, 1924.

The Provisional Charter was granted on May 29, 1924. The first Board of Trustees of Good Counsel College consisted of seven members, all Religious of the Divine Compassion:

Mother Mary Aloysia (Catherine A. Kelly), Sister Mary Joseph (Frances J. Scheuer), Sister Mary Ignatius (Sarah I. Butler), Sister Mary Hilda (Anna M. Zeigelmeyer), Sister Mary Fidelis (Georgiana E. Mead), Sister Mary Compassio (Ethel M. Harris), Sister Mary Reparata (Agnes E. McGuire).

The success of this undertaking was due in great measure to the assistance and professional advice of Dr. Augustus S. Downing, a true and proven friend, who was to remain so over the years until his death in 1936.

Mother Mary Aloysia invited Dr. Downing to be present at the second commencement of the College which was to be held on June 11, 1928. During the course of the exercises, in the presence of Cardinal Hayes, the faculty, friends and relatives of the graduates, he announced the good news that Good Counsel College had been granted an Absolute Charter by the University of the State of New York, with power to confer degrees. The Charter arrived at the college on July 6th. It is dated May 17, 1928, recorded number 3773 and signed by Ernest E. Cole, Acting President of the University.

Year by year the enrollment grew slowly but steadily. An increasing number of students asked to be admitted, coming not only from surrounding areas, but from Long Island, upstate Buffalo, out of State, New Jersey, Massachusetts, even Illinois and Panama City.

The first college students resided in St. Joseph's Hall, and St. Ann's Cottage. As the number increased, it was found necessary to find other quarters. There was great rejoicing when it was announced that an additional piece of property of almost 12 acres, including a new dwelling for the students, was to be added to the existing 28 acres.

The College continued to grow and by the academic year 1927-28 had a total enrollment of 89 students, 27 freshmen, 30 sophomores, 20 juniors and 12 seniors. Twelve students had graduated in June 1927, including the seven pioneers. The faculty numbered 21, both religious and lay, eleven of whom possessed doctoral degrees. Forty applicants were accepted as freshmen for the fall of 1928, bringing the total enrollment up to 115 for year 1928-29.

The following expenses were listed in the first catalogue issued by the College for the year 1924-25:

RESIDENT STUDENTS
Tuition and Board
    for the year - $400.00
Library Fee - $5.00
Laboratory Fee - $10.00

DAY STUDENTS
Tuition a year - $120.00
Luncheon - $80.00

Later additional charges were made for resident students for the use of rooms for the year ranging from $50.00 up to $300.00, depending upon the residence hall occupied:

Preston Hall	$100.00 - 300.00
St. Joseph's Hall	$50.00 - 150.00
St. Ann's Cottage	$50.00 - 100.00
Faculty Hall	$50.00 - 100.00

Over the years there was a gradual increase in the tuition and board so that by the year 1975 it reached $3700.00.

Student Life in the Early Days of the College

The students were expected to act with womanly dignity and decorum both on and off the campus and to be earnest and scholarly in their work. A simple uniform, consisting of a dark blue dress, with matching sash and white collar and cuffs, was prescribed to be worn by the students at class recitations and other scholastic exercises. The cap and gown was donned for the weekly assembly and more formal occasions. The young ladies were allowed as much liberty as was deemed conducive to the development of individual character. However, certain regulations were imposed for the smooth running of college life. Students were expected to report upon leaving campus by signing their names, with destination, in the Campus Book. No student was permitted to leave the campus after 6:00 p.m. without the express permission of the Dean.

The school day began with roll call. Sister Mary Ambrose, the Registrar, went from room to room noting the presence or absence of students. This practice soon had to be abandoned when the schedule became more complex and the students more numerous. The checking of attendance was then carried on by each individual professor and reports handed in to the Registrar.

Physical education was a "must" for all students. The first gym suit consisted of bloomers and middy blouse. This was soon replaced by a simple gym suit. Numerous athletic activities were pursued by the students during the year and culminated in a great show of skill on Field Day held in the late spring.

Sister Mary deLourdes Muench, a native of Friendship, New York, was a Good Counsel girl in the twenties. She summed up her remembrances of college life as follows:

"The Good Counsel College girl in the '20s was protected, supervised and happy. We were happy. I was a small town girl who had never been away from home before, but Good Counsel quickly became home to me, and many of the friendships formed then have remained to the present day. Perhaps my picture of the G.C.C. girl of those years does not reflect a 'liberated' woman, but I saw a great deal of initiative shown by my creative classmates, and the discipline we experienced taught us the self-discipline which I am sure resulted in the formation of Good Counsel Alumnae who are in 1980 predominantly mature, Christian women."

Class Day 1927

Class Day 1933

Class Day 1942

Class Day 1956

Class Day 1960's

Class Day 1970's

Student Organizations and Activities

The student body, though small in number, was large in ambition. A number of organizations came into being, providing a wide range of activities for various interests. Prominent among them were the League of the Sacred Heart, the Sodality of the Blessed Virgin, the Glee Club, the Preston Debating Society organized in 1923, the Catholic Students Foreign Mission League, the Athletic Association with basketball, tennis and archery teams. There was also a club for those wishing to improve their fluency in the French language, known as Le Cercle Francais.

The young ladies of the college were expected to engage in one or more of these activities. The record shows that they took advantage, according to their interests, of the many opportunities offered.

Student Publications

The Prestonian

The first issue of The Prestonian, the college newspaper, appeared in October 1924. At that time the entire student body consisted of only twenty students, nine sophomores and eleven freshmen. The task of producing a newspaper seemed superhuman, but the strong desire of the seven pioneers and the eager enthusiasm of the other students soon overcame all obstacles.

With the aid of the Dean, Sister Mary Edmund, and the sound advice of Father R. Rush Rankin, S.J., who suggested the name, what seemed impossible soon became a reality.

The first Prestonian staff, the result of the elections held in October, consisted of the following members:

Anna E. O'Reilly '27, Editor-in-Chief; Mary Corley '28, Assistant Editor; Ethel McGuirk '28, Assistant Editor; Marguerite C. Dolan '27, Business Manager; Muriel D. Tichenor '28, Assistant Business Manager; Elizabeth Chrystal '28, Assistant Business Manager; Evelyn Dolan '27, News Editor; Carol Carmody '27, Social Editor; Wanda Graboski '27, Athletic Editor; Margaret F. Reynolds '27, Mirth Editor; Annette Perron '27, Verse Editor; Grace Dodworth '27, Prose Editor.

After much deliberation and discussion, the students decided to take Father Rankin's suggestion to name the paper The Prestonian, in honor of Monsignor Thomas S. Preston the learned and saintly founder of the Sisters of the Divine Compassion who were instrumental in bringing the college into existence in 1923.

In the November 1924 issue of <u>The Prestonian</u>, an editorial appeared explaining the reason for the choice of name and giving a brief sketch of the life and works of Monsignor Preston taken from a eulogy delivered by Reverend Henry A. Brann, D.D. in 1891:

The Right Reverend Thomas S. Preston D.D. was born at Hartford, Connecticut in July 1824. He completed his classical studies in Trinity College of that city in 1843. He had been an Episcopalian, and being pious and zealous, he determined to become a clergyman, and for this purpose he entered the Episcopalian General Theological Seminary in New York City, and after finishing his theological course there he was ordained a minister in 1846.

Mr. Preston became a Catholic in 1849, and after a short course in theology in the Catholic Seminary at Fordham, he was ordained a priest in 1850.

Father Preston was an ardent champion of Christian education. He is the author of several well known works. Among his controversial works may be singled out: <u>God and Reason</u>, <u>Reason and Revelation</u>, <u>The Vicar of Christ</u>, and among his ascetical works are conspicuous <u>The Divine Paraclete</u> and <u>The Divine Sanctuary</u>.

He had all the priestly virtues. He was pious and prayerful and a skillful spiritual guide. The polar star of his asceticism was obedience. He was much sought after as a confessor of intelligent Catholics who strove to make spiritual progress and walk in the thorny path of perfection. He had the care of many pious souls, and notably of the religious community which he founded and to which he gave the name of Sisters of the Divine Compassion. In the history of the Church of New York, his will always be an illustrious name.

As the years passed, the appearance of <u>The Prestonian</u> became more professional and merited the praise of several Press Associations. In 1945-46, the paper was given an Honor Rating by the Catholic School Press Association. The survey conducted by the CSPA centered at Marquette University, Milwaukee, Wisconsin, gave <u>The Prestonian</u> the highest rating "all Catholic". It also received a rating of First Class, Excellent by the Associated Collegiate Press with headquarters in Minnesota.

<u>Vestigia</u>

The college year book, <u>Vestigia</u>, was made possible by the interest and hard work of the senior class, and the generous contributions of the patrons, friends and advertisers. The book has appeared each year beginning with that of the first class of 1927.

Vox Studentium

1937 marked the inauguration of a student literary quarterly -- Vox Studentium. Through the efforts of Dr. Anna Mary Keenan, Professor of English, and the Creative Writing Class, an Editorial Board and Literary Staff was organized, consisting of at least two members from each class. Dr. Keenan served as the Moderator. The first issue appeared in May 1937.

EDITORIAL BOARD
    Editor-in-Chief: Eileen Joan Touhey '39
    Assistant Editor: Kathryn Lyons '38
    Business Manager: Elizabeth Hanley '38

LITERARY STAFF
    Elizabeth Drury '37   Mary Gousalves '39
    Madeline Neumann '37   Catherine Barclay '40
    Eileen Sexton '38   Grace Harvey '40
    Maureen Colgan '39

The main purpose of the quarterly was to stimulate the art of writing either as a vocation or for sheer pleasure; the secondary purpose was to provide the students with an instrument for the publication of poems, essays, and short stories. All classes were invited to submit articles, though the quarterly was to be published by the Literary Club and edited by the Sophomore class. It was supported by subscriptions and patrons. The first issue, which was released in May 1937, listed nearly one hundred Patrons.

Student Government Association

On January 14, 1927, Dorothy Ridder Naumann, a graduate of Trinity College in Washington, D.C., visited the College to talk to the students about self-government. The girls met in the west library and listened with interest as Miss Naumann outlined the procedures to be followed in an organization of student government. Its powers, duties and responsibilities were discussed. The governing board known as the Student Council was to be made up of nine members with at least two representatives from each class. Its members were to be chosen from the students whose scholastic standing placed them on the eligibility list.

With approval of the Administration, when a sufficient number of students made the plan feasible, the Student Government Association was introduced in February 1927.

THE FIRST OFFICERS

President:	Marguerite C. Dolan '27
Vice President:	Grace A. Dodworth '27
Secretary:	M. Elizabeth Wilson '28
Treasurer:	Anna Osterman '29
Senior Representative:	Carol C. Carmody '27
Junior Representative:	Mary Fideles Fearon '28
Sophomore Representative:	Helen F. Keenan '29
Freshman Representatives:	Donata A. Lombardi '30
	Dorothy G. McKneally '30

STUDENT COUNCIL PRESIDENTS

1926	Anna E. O'Reilly	1954	Audrey J. Shiebler
1927	Marguerite C. Dolan	1955	Irma Patricia Ryan
1928	Elizabeth Wilson	1956	Helen Patricia Halloran
1929	Helen F. Keenan	1957	Margaret P. Varlotta
1930	Regina C. Spelman	1958	Eleanor E. Gilbertie
1931	Una Falls	1959	Carol Ann Landers
1932	Mary Cohane	1960	Loretta J. Longo
1933	Frances W. Bingham	1961	Lucille Massi
1934	Rita Cashin	1962	Patricia C. Wortmann
1935	Winifred Fisher	1963	Judith E. Paladino
1936	Doris Dowd	1964	Mary P. Cichetti
1937	Anne Powers	1965	Janet E. O'Shaughnessy
1938	Rose May McCabe	1966	Catherine G. Thompson
1939	Claire Patricia Kelley	1967	Marguerite Shea
1940	Doris Marie Hayes	1968	Lynn Waldmann
1941	Lorraine R. Gaffney	1969	Kathryn Waters
1942	Virginia Schoman	1970	Ann Mullen
1943	Louise Cutler	1971	Maryellen Noonan
1944	Dorothy McCabe	1972	Elizabeth Forester
1945	Anne B. Woods	1973	Shaileen Shanley
1946	Kathleen A. McCarron	1974	Dorothy Ward
1947	Maria F. Stack	1975	Nancy Louden
1948	Dolores E. Trumpler	1976	Claire Brown
1949	Mary T. Morris	1977	Deborah Pullan
1950	Patricia J. McOwen	1978	Susanne M. Quinlivan
1951	Mary T. Anderson	1979	Terry Brookins
1952	Joan F. Bailey	1980	Frank Sabia
1953	Alice K. Conrad	1981	Carlos Gutierrez

Traditions

College traditions, the bonds of unity -- accepted, loved, cherished and passed on from one class to another. Good Counsel College was rich in traditions, customs and ceremonies. These formed the sweetest and lasting memories of college days -- the ties which bound the students forever in love and gratitude to Good Counsel College.

Harvest Campfire Festival

One of the first events of the year, one which made the new students really feel at home at Good Counsel, was the Harvest Festival. Under a clear moonlit sky the students gathered at the old rock for an evening of fun and getting acquainted. A fire was kindled on a large rock foundation at the northeast end of the campus. A picnic supper was served. All classes participated in the fun and games and the singing of old and new songs. As the blazing fire died down, marshmallows were toasted in the glowing embers. Tired and happy, all returned to their rooms for a good night's sleep.

This event, repeated year after year, became a tradition at Good Counsel. It was one of the first social functions of the year and succeeded greatly in making the freshmen feel right at home and off to a happy start for the school year.

Investiture

One of the most impressive, solemn, and dignified ceremonies of the year was that of Investiture, when the freshmen received the cap and gown of the College and were admitted to full membership in the college.

The ceremony began in a very simple way when on Thursday, October 16, 1924, 12 freshmen received the cap and gown at a rather informal exercise held in the college library. As the girls entered the room, each one received the cap and gown from the hands of Father R. Rush Rankin, S.J., of the Graduate School of Fordham University, assisted by Father Aloysius Weber, the Chaplain of the College.

Then in the presence of Mother Mary Aloysia, the faculty and the entire student body, totaling 20 students, Father Rankin delivered a very interesting and instructive talk on the meaning of the cap and gown -- the dress of the scholar. He urged the little group to apply themselves to study but emphasized the importance of character formation while in college. The ceremony ended with the singing of the hymn to Our Lady of Good Counsel, after which all went to the Chapel for Benediction of the Most Blessed Sacrament. Thus ended the first Investiture ceremony at Good Counsel College.

As the years went by this exercise took on a formal splendor that was most impressive. It was always presided over by a very special person, a good friend of the College, in the early days by Father R. Rush Rankin, S.J., and then for 36 years by His Excellency Bishop James E. Kearney who made his visit to Good Counsel for Investiture a part of his very busy schedule.

As the program of Investiture took shape, it followed a familiar pattern. The ceremony took place in the auditorium in the presence of the entire student body, faculty, special guests, parents and friends. After the processional and the singing of The Star Spangled Banner, the President of the Student Council would address the freshmen. This was followed by an address of welcome delivered by the Honorary President of the College; then followed the blessing of the caps and gowns and the presentation of the candidates, each by name.

The highlight of the program was the address given by Bishop Kearney. He always inspired this audience by his fatherly words of sound advice and never failed to tell the students to develop devotion to Our Lady of Good Counsel who would always listen to them and tell them what to do.

Throughout the program the Glee Club rendered several selections, the last number before the recessional always being the Hymn to Our Lady of Good Counsel.

From time to time other features were introduced and made part of the exercise, among them the Turning of the Tassels and the Induction of the members of the Student Council. The Turning of the Tassel indicated that the student had advanced another year in wisdom and knowledge. The President and the Vice President of the Student Council had their tassels turned by Bishop Kearney. These two officers then turned the tassels of the seniors, juniors, and sophomores as they filed up to the stage.

The Ring Ceremony

One of the happiest occasions in the student's life at Good Counsel came in the Junior year with the reception of the college ring. This ceremony, like so many others, began in a very simple way, but as the years passed it developed into a ceremony rich in symbolism. The time chosen for this happy event to take place was during the month of December. It often formed part of the program on Founders Day, December 21.

The ring is the outward symbol of all that the student has learned to cherish during her days at Good Counsel. The cross is a reminder of the value of her Catholic Faith. The seal is there, too, marking her as a graduate and alumna of Good Counsel College. The lamp of learning tells her she must ever keep it burning by continually increasing her knowledge after her text books are closed and lectures forgotten. The ring is the external sign of the lasting bond that unites the graduate to her Alma Mater -- a symbol of the union of beliefs, ideals and hopes.

The President of the College always presided at the Ring Ceremony. The Juniors, attired in cap and gown, assembled at a convenient location. After an inspiring and intimate talk to the girls on the meaning and symbolism of the ring, the President would place on the finger of each one the long-awaited treasure.

The college ring was one of the most cherished possessions of the student. Yet one member of each of the first ten classes was willing to make the sacrifice of this treasure by donating it for use in the Ostensorium which was presented to the Sisters of the Divine Compassion on the occasion of the Golden Jubilee of the Community in 1936.

Carol Night

One of the earliest, most colorful and best-loved of all the traditions, Carol Night, began in a very simple way, on December 22, 1924, when the girls from Saint Joseph's Hall and Saint Ann's Cottage got together and began singing Christmas carols, moving around the campus, stopping at each building to hang a holly wreath on the door. The first building visited was the convent, where they were greeted by the Sisters who were surprised and delighted by this action initiated by the students. At this time the entire college enrollment of freshmen and sophomores numbered only 20 students.

The following year on Tuesday, December 22, 1925, the ceremony was repeated at the request of the students who wished this custom to become standard practice. The College enrollment had more than doubled, now consisting of 44 students, freshmen, sophomores and juniors.

In 1926 several new features were added. The day chosen for the singing of the carols was December 21, the feast of Saint Thomas the Apostle. The day was designated as Founder's Day in honor of Monsignor Thomas S. Preston, the co-founder of the Sisters of the Divine Compassion.

Carol Night of 1927 saw the introduction of the use of costumes. A new thrill of excitement took hold of the students as they donned the dress of gallant knights and fair ladies, kings, pages, shepherds and town folk. To add to the beauty of the scene, living trees at selected spots near St. Ann's Cottage, the Convent and the Church, were decorated with colored lights.

By 1931 the Carol Night ceremony had reached a full splendor of development into a rich Christmas pageant. For the first time the procession started from Preston Hall, the new building opened in the fall of that year. The events of the day fell into a familiar pattern, beginning with a Mass in the morning, followed by entertainment in the afternoon. A formal dinner, given by the faculty, was served in the evening followed by the singing of the carols. Arrayed in medieval costumes the carollers moved around the campus, stopping at each building, where the President of the Student Council assisted by her attendants would hang a holly wreath on the door. The procession ended in the Church where the Sisters, friends and guests awaited. The organ now took up the strains and all joined in the singing of the carols. The Church, beautifully decorated with evergreen trees, garlands and brilliant red poinsettias, made a fitting setting for the Stable of Bethlehem set up in the sanctuary. The beauty of the scene was enhanced by the presence of Angels standing around the crib; the privilege of impersonating Angels was reserved for senior students. The student president, arrayed in a gold cap and gown, carried a bundle of straw representing the acts of kindness and self-denial performed by the students during the Advent season. The straw was placed at the feet of the Infant Jesus in the crib. The ceremony was brought to a close with a sermon and Benediction of the Blessed Sacrament.

Whenever possible, Bishop James E. Kearney tried to be at Good Counsel for Carol Night, much to the delight of the students. Year after year, with few exceptions, we were able to greet our steadfast friend and to be inspired by his words of wisdom and counsel.

Twelfth Night

Twelfth Night, the evening of January 6th, the feast of the Epiphany, marked the concluding period of the Christmas festivities. The students made use of this opportunity for another delightful ceremony. On a convenient day within the octave of the Epiphany, the old evergreen trees and wreaths which had adorned the chapel and other buildings were gathered up and taken to the great rock at the northeast end of the campus to be burned. The students assembled around the rock and the fire was lighted giving welcome heat to the cold night air. Joyful singing of old and new Christmas songs filled the air with music. With the strains of the Alma Mater, students pledged anew their love and loyalty for Good Counsel. The singing continued until the fire was reduced to red glowing embers and finally extinguished. All then returned to Preston Hall for refreshments.

One Hundred Nights

In the early 1950's a new custom was introduced and as the years passed it became traditional. One hundred days before graduation the seniors got together at a local restaurant for a gala dinner which came to be known as "One Hundred Nights". Among the many events that marked the senior year at Good Counsel, the Hundred Nights dinner served as a reminder that not many days were left before graduation. The banquet, while joyful, was tinged with a touch of sadness. It was the beginning of the end of four years of college activities: hard study, exams, term papers, mixers, socials, late hours, lights out, snow holidays and vacations. The carefree life of the student was soon to be changed for the sterner realities of life in the adult world.

Field Day

In a lighter vein, a Spring afternoon was chosen for the exploits of our athletes. All classes competed in the varied contests of skill on the great athletic field at the southeast corner of the campus. The field was alive with color and action as games of basketball, soccer, baseball, volley ball, hockey, archery and tennis tested the ability of the players.

One especially colorful field day took place in May 1937 under the expert direction of Elizabeth Callahan, instructor of physical education. Along with the games of skill, much fun and amusement was provided by the relay races, obstacle races and a hoop race, the hoops being decorated with bright streamers. The cheerleaders and the spectators added much to the mirth by their cheers and applause.

Birthday Party

Another delightful tradition enjoyed by the resident students each year was the general Birthday Party. This custom was introduced by the Administration in 1943.

The students, appearing in lovely pastel-colored formal evening gowns, attended a dinner in Preston Hall. Groups were arranged at the tables by classes; each class had its own birthday cake. This was a real happy celebration for everyone's birthday, which took place on a lovely spring day in April or May, and was thoroughly enjoyed by all. Often a surprise gift was waiting for the students. In April 1961, Mother Mary Dolores, President of the College, presented the students with a birthday gift of a television set.

After the dinner all assembled in the reception room for entertainment. On several occasions a movie was provided as a special treat.

The May Candlelight Procession

The flicker of hundreds of candles illuminated the darkness of the night sky on a lovely evening in the month of May when, each year, the whole Good Counsel community came out to honor Our Lady. The students of the College and the Academy, the members of the Fathers' Club and the Mothers' Guild, friends of the College and the Sisters, all joined together in tribute to Our Lady in the annual May Candlelight procession. The group assembled in front of the Church.

The officers of the Sodality, carrying the banner, led the procession followed by the college girls in cap and gown and wearing the medal of Our Lady; then came the other pilgrims each holding a lighted candle. The long line proceeded from shrine to shrine around the campus grounds, reciting the fifteen mysteries of the Rosary and singing the traditional Marian hymns.

The procession ended at the temporary altar which had been set up on the outdoor pavilion near the church. When all were in place, the crowning of the statue of Our Blessed Mother took place. This was performed by the prefect of the College Sodality, and assisted by the prefect of the Academy Sodality. A number of little children in white dresses and gold capes formed a guard of honor around the altar of Our Lady.

After the crowning of the Blessed Virgin a sermon was delivered, followed by Benediction of the Most Blessed Sacrament which concluded the service. Members of the Fathers' Club carrying lighted torches accompanied the priest with the Blessed Sacrament from and back to the church.

All hearts were uplifted by this thrilling experience of sight and sound. As the music died away and the crowd dispersed a feeling of calm, peace and joy settled over the campus at Good Counsel.

Commencement Week

College traditions at Good Counsel reached their peak during the events of Commencement Week -- a week of social affairs, traditional ceremonies and religious services -- a happy blending of the spiritual, intellectual, physical, social and emotional aspects in the life of the student.

The first event of the week was usually the Baccalaureate address delivered by a prominent member of the clergy and followed by solemn Benediction of the Blessed Sacrament. This exercise was held in the College Chapel in the presence of the entire student body and faculty along with the friends and relatives of the graduates.

During the week a special solemn high Mass was celebrated for the seniors by the Honorary President of the College and when possible by His Excellency Bishop James E. Kearney, who wished to pay this last tribute to the graduating class. The Mass was followed by a Communion Breakfast, introduced in 1948 as the President's gift to the seniors.

Day of Recollection

In the excitement of the many activities of the week, a pause was made for a day of recollection when the seniors spent time in quiet prayer and reflection. The day began with the Holy Sacrifice of the Mass in the morning, included several conferences during the day and ended in the evening with Benediction of the Blessed Sacrament.

Junior-Senior Banquet

Each year the juniors invited the seniors to a formal banquet. Arrayed in lovely bright colored gowns, they met in the tastefully decorated dining room to enjoy one of the last evening meals together. Members of the faculty and special guests were invited to attend.

With the opening of Preston Hall in 1931 this new tradition was introduced. The broad main stairway was reserved for senior use only; now this privilege was handed over to the juniors. The seniors in their lovely gowns, each carrying a rose, descended the stairs and offered the rose to a junior as a symbol that they now have the honor of using the stairway.

After the dinner the most loved of all the old traditions began, the Pine Walk Ceremony.

Pine Walk

After the banquet and the rendering of the Senior stairs, the seniors and juniors, wearing the black academic robe over their evening gowns, and each carrying a candle, the seniors' lighted, the others' unlighted, marched in procession to the Pine Walk, one of the most beautiful spots on the campus. On this lovely tree-lined path, known as the Senior Walk, an impressive and inspiring ceremony was enacted. On this night the graduates surrendered the walk to the prospective seniors. During the singing of the song "Our Senior Walk Farewell" the junior candles were lighted from the flame of the seniors' -- thus signifying the transfer of the walk.

The glow of the lighted tapers in the darkness and the echoes of the farewell song which rose through the still night air, all carved an indelible impression which will remain in the memories of the graduates.

With a final farewell, the graduates left the Pine Walk and carried their now extinguished candles to the shrine of Our Lady of Good Counsel and placed them here to be burned out during the remaining days of the week. Singing the hymn to Our Lady of Good Counsel, the seniors gathered for the last time as a class at this beloved and hallowed shrine.

Through the decades, the stately evergreen trees on the pine walks grew old, many of them toppled by wind storms. In January 1947, it was decided to remove the old historical trees and to plant a new crop in the spring. The trees were felled one by one. Our neighbors on North Broadway felt a pang of sorrow as the trees disappeared. On a bright day in Spring, April 14, sturdy young trees were planted and a new walk was laid. The famous old walk leading to the chapel was once more enhanced in beauty by a double row of evergreens which still flourish on the Senior Walk.

Class Day

Class Day is rich in color and traditions. The entire campus was filled with life and gaiety on this memorable day held each year at Good Counsel. The entire student body, clad in full-length afternoon dresses, were present for the exercise. They all met in front of the old gray mansion at the southwest end of the campus where the lines formed.

The seniors carrying old fashioned bouquets, the gift of their freshman sisters, were accompanied by the sophomores bearing the ivy chain, which they had prepared the day before. The other classes followed in line and marched across the campus singing "As We Gaze Down The Passage Of The Years". The procession ended at the outdoor pavilion where the exercises took place. When they reached the spot the sophomores presented the ivy chain, the symbol of friendship, to the seniors who took their place on the platform. The ivy chain remained around the seniors until the end of the program when they carried it to the shrine of Our Lady of Good Counsel and placed it at her feet.

The program that followed consisted of several speeches, the two most important being the Salutatory and the Valedictory, assigned to the two top-ranking members of the class. Awards were presented by the President of the College, to individuals for outstanding achievement in the activities of the various clubs and organizations.

Presentation of the College Shield

An important part of the afternoon's ceremony was the presentation of the College Shield, the symbol of authority of the Office of the Student Council, to the new President by the outgoing President. In accepting the Shield, the new President promised to carry out her duties to the best of her ability with the help of God and under the direction of Our Lady of Good Counsel.

Planting of the Tree

Scattered around the campus are a number of trees, each one representing a given class of graduates. The tree was planted as a sign of esteem, gratitude and love for Good Counsel College. Accompanying the planting of the tree was the Tree Oration in which was expressed the sentiments of the class. Here are the excerpts from several orations:

"May this grow strong and extend ever upwards as a symbol of the hope which is in our hearts today -- that we, too, may extend our thoughts, actions and desires ever upward, that our eyes may always be upon Heaven as the goal of our lives and that we may never die in the sight of God, but may grow strong in His wisdom and love. As this tree lives serving God to the fullness of its capacity, may we too make our lives one of service to Our Lord and His Blessed Mother, Our Lady of Good Counsel."   Nan Cuddy, B.S. Cum Laude, Class of 1949

"With this small flowering dogwood the graduating class places its faith in Good Counsel. We leave it as a token of our love and esteem for our Alma Mater.

May our tree be nourished and grow till it reaches its greatest beauty, just as we have been nourished and strengthened. It will stand as a symbol of our youth as we entered these hallowed portals. Each year will add to it the grace and serenity we hope we have developed through these past four very short years."   Marie Spletzer, B.S., Class of 1954

"The campus has been an essential part of our lives these past four years, and we have grown and thrived both spiritually and intellectually. We hope that this tree will grow from this same ground spreading its branches and standing as a symbol of our class."   Lavelle Dwyer, B.S., Class of 1963

After the planting of the tree the procession formed again. Led by the new student president, bearing the College Shield, followed by the graduates carrying the ivy chain, all made their way to the shrine of Our Lady of Good Counsel. The shield was placed at the shrine and the ivy chain laid at the feet of Our Lady. Class Day ended with the singing of the favorite hymn to Our Lady of Good Counsel.

The custom of planting class trees dates back to 1944. Before that time, ivy was planted by each class to cling to the walls of the newly constructed convent building and Preston Hall. The Class of 1969 was the last to plant a tree on the campus of Good Counsel College.

The Class Day program underwent a change in 1969. Known as The Awards Convocation, it was greatly simplified, the main emphasis being on the awards. The program consisted of the Salutatory, the presentation of the awards by the President of the College and the Valedictory, followed by a reception and tea in Preston Hall for the graduates and their parents and friends.

Commencement Day

The crowning event of the week came on Commencement Day, the day so long awaited when the degrees are conferred on the graduates by the Cardinal.

His Eminence Patrick Cardinal Hayes conferred the degrees on the first graduates in 1927. He returned every year to honor Good Counsel with his presence at Commencement until the year of his death in 1938. The first twelve classes had the privilege of receiving their degrees from his hands.

Francis Cardinal Spellman, his successor, did the same, gracing Good Counsel College Commencement with his presence twenty-two times during his busy lifetime.

Terence Cardinal Cooke continued the practice of coming to Good Counsel to preside at Commencement or to give the final blessing until the College consolidated with Pace University in 1975.

Anne Gallagher Curley, B.A., Class of 1931, remembers well the scene on the campus on Commencement Day. The entire college assembled in their places under the trees facing the platform on which were seated the cardinal, other dignitaries and members of the faculty. She recalls that it never rained, but that their chief worry was concerning the pigeons flying overhead and leaving their "calling card".

The Alumnae Reception for the Graduates

At a convenient time during Commencement week, the graduates were feted by the Alumnae and formally accepted into the Association. In the early days this ceremony took place on the evening of commencement day and was a fitting culmination of all the activities of the week. At other times the reception of the graduates into the Alumnae Association followed the exercises of Baccalaureate Day, at a Tea held in their honor.

Enjoying the Lake 1939

Field Day 1939

Athletic Association 1930's

Mission Unit 1939

Carol Night 1938

Carol Night 1950's

Glee Club Officers - honoring Mr. Joslyn

Children's Day - Bishop Kearney

Reflections by Good Counsel Alumnae

Memories of a College Freshman of the Early Days -- Julia M. O'Reilly, Class of 1930

When I entered Good Counsel College in September of 1926, it was the first year the College could boast of having the four levels: freshmen, sophomores, juniors and seniors.

The "pioneer" group of seven girls and two religious had added to their ranks three more students. By June of 1927 the College Directory showed a total of 76 students. This modest number of students had many advantages. The older girls roomed with the younger ones, thus dispelling loneliness. Many lifelong friendships were formed. In fact those who lived at a distance were frequent guests at their roommate's homes. More than one marriage resulted. My own sister, Anna O'Reilly, Class of 1927, met her future husband, Raymond Kniphuisen, through her roommate, Elizabeth Kennedy, Class of 1929.

St. Joseph's House was the main dormitory. Here, on the first floor, all resident students took their meals. To the left of the dining area was our social room, then called the parlor. But it is the dining room that holds the most nostalgic memories for me. It was here during our meals that we conversed and "digested" the news of the day. I can still recall vividly the morning we learned that Charles A. Lindbergh had made the first solo nonstop flight from New York to Paris. The news electrified us. The "Lone Eagle" had conquered, not only the sky, but also our hearts as well.

In the early days of the College, the students were required to "sign out" in the campus record book, and "sign in" on their return. The large book lay on a table outside the Dean's office. It was then unheard of to be out as late as eight p.m. on a school day. How times have changed!

One day in May, when a holiday fell in the middle of the week, my sister and I decided to celebrate. Rosemary had won the magnificent sum of $5.00, put on chances for the missions. With this, together with a few more dollars, we went to the city. In New York we stopped at Alice Foote McDongall's, a well-known restaurant. For the then princely sum of $2.50 we were served a seven-course luncheon. We followed this by going to a "movie". Our spirit of adventure then led us to still another theater. Our fun day was more than satisfying until we discovered the time. Alas! We had missed our train. Although darkness had not yet fallen, we had to report to the Dean, Sister Mary Edmund. She received our apologies graciously. However, her quiet demeanor reproached us more than any harsh words could have done.

One particular Field Day, probably in June 1928, an incident occurred which comes to mind now. In the morning time hung heavy on our hands. The morning was dragging on. What could we do to relieve our boredom? Light dawned! We decided to pool our slim resources and hire a car. The agent gave us a car -- very likely of the 1920 "vintage". Our one question was "will it go"? It did, but for awhile only! Suddenly our jalopy began to cut up. We had difficulty in both starting and stopping it. Oh, for some timely help! With the motor chugging away, we maneuvered our burden into a nearby garage. The diagnosis was "Your motor is corroded and full of rust". Our car medic then moved around and cleaned some ancient wires. Action thus became possible and we were off again in our rust-filled buggy. We felt we had a good cause to ignore red lights. Such was our thinking. (The reasoning of young people defies logic at times.) As we drove toward Rye, we waved and smiled at passing motorists -- calling out, "We can't stop, our engine is corroded." How we got home to White Plains unscathed that day was truly a miraculous feat.

Among the members of our class was a girl from North Bergen, New Jersey. Clementine was well-liked by both faculty and students. Every year Clem's invitation to attend a festive dinner at her home was eagerly anticipated. Her parents and her older sister, Tillie, welcomed us warmly. You can imagine how we enjoyed the ten- course Italian banquet.

On Graduation Day of June 1930, I said, "Au Revoir" to my classmate Clem. Fifty years were to pass before we would meet again at my Golden Jubilee in June 1980. What a delight it was for us to reminisce about our college days!

I should not end these memoirs without a word about the girls who formed the first graduation class. They were the foundation stones of the college. These students gave evidence of fine leadership and earned the respect of their younger sisters.

What shall I say of our professors, both religious and lay instructors? They held aloft the "Torch of Learning" to be passed on to future generations.

My last thoughts are with the many deceased classmates. Numbered among them is my sister Rosemary. No longer need they pursue their quest for knowledge. At this moment they quench their thirst at the fountain of the Eternal Godhead!

(Julia Margaret O'Reilly, familiarly known as "Perry", graduated from Good Counsel College on June 5, 1930. After three years she returned to Good Counsel on February 2, 1933 to enter the community of the Sisters of the Divine Compassion -- in religion she is known as Sister Mary Josepha.)

Reminiscences of the Old Days -- Maria Stack Kinsella, Class of 1947

(At the annual Alumni Reunion held on March 23, 1980, Maria Stack Kinsella, M.D., a magna cum laude graduate of Good Counsel College of the Class of 1947, was presented with the Outstanding Alumna of the Year Award. The following are some of her remarks on this occasion.)

Coming Home is "one of my favorite things". It is seeing many familiar faces and being enveloped in the warm glow of bygone friendships once again. Returning to the College of White Plains of Pace University -- after thirty-three years -- is truly Coming Home!

My mind is filled with pleasant and lasting memories and my heart is overflowing with gratitude and love. I am most grateful to you all for your warm and heartfelt welcome.

Today, "Flash Backs" are the featured attractions. Memories of praying in the chapel; pageantry on Carol Night; excitement of Military Balls and Junior Proms; parties at the rock; classroom stories; Preston Hall and Dannat Hall escapades; radio waves after 10 p.m., much to Sr. M. Therese's dismay; senior staircase, ring and investiture ceremonies; ivy chain; Class Day and Graduation. All hold their own secret enchantment and could engender conversation for days. One story would lead to another and we, who lived and loved it all for four years, would enjoy those special moments again. These were years, giftwrapped, tied together and preciously kept forever in memory. I am most grateful for all the friendships I was privileged to make here and will look forward to renewing them again -- anytime and anywhere. It is wonderful to be with you all to share another day together and to add a new dimension to my souvenirs.

Looking back at the ideals and loves of my college life, I have echoed my gratitude down through the years that I was privileged to attend this Catholic institution. The precious legacy of achievement, both scholastic and moral, was given by Good Counsel to each and every one of her graduates. One was taught a way of life here -- the right way of life -- through Thomistic philosophy and religion. Though, under vicious and vigorous attacks in our lifetime, these religious beliefs can be stood up for and lived by, because of our college teachings. Ideals of family life, the ethics of everyday living, love for husband, children, and life itself were all spelled out so clearly here that little doubt remained. The basic truths remain unchanged. Our allegiance to them must be steadfast also. Abiding by these standards, the assaults can and will be withstood. Appropriately, the college shield encompasses these thoughts succinctly. Emblazoned thereon -

- a cross -- to show that for which a Catholic college student should be thankful.
- a spear -- to show the courage with which one must face the world.
- a hyacinth -- to show the purity for which one must strive.
- a nail and thorn -- to show the suffering which all will encounter and which all must endure.
- a ladder -- to show the way to Our Lord's Sacred Heart.

A constant remembrance of these symbols gives one the needed strength to conquer. They have served as a guide, an incentive, an inspiration and refuge to me and for that I am truly and deeply grateful. I am grateful too, to Bishop Kearney, a dear family friend, who first encouraged me to attend this college.

Impression and Memories of a Boarder, 1952-1956 -- Marie A. Bradshaw, Class of 1956

While life was more carefree then in many ways, students bore a lot of responsibility, especially Student Government members. Our job was to enforce quiet during study hours at night, enforce lights out at 10:00 p.m., get students up for breakfast in the morning, enforce quiet in the classroom corridors, take attendance at compulsory functions, such as Assembly and Choral Class, and assign punishments for infractions of various rules. It was quite a challenge to be a good officer and at the same time not lose all your friends.

Homesickness persisted through the first semester of freshman year. Then I gave up going home on weekends for Lent. After that I felt at home on the campus.

My roommate and I became the best of friends and we stayed together for the four years, sharing many a laugh and many a trial.

The Smoker was always the hub of great activity -- homework, term papers, debates, plans for the next social event, card games, problem solving -- all made for a lively exchange of thought.

It was a delight to have meals in the Preston dining room, -- white table cloths and napkins, three well balanced meals a day, served while the Student Government officers presided on the dais.

We enjoyed the luxury of using the large parlor in Preston on special occasions and had fun dressing up for formal tea served in the dining room.

Off campus hours were rather restricted -- 6:00 p.m. on weekdays and 9 or 10 o'clock on weekends. "Campusing" was the penalty for lateness, so rather than have to miss going out altogether, most people managed to keep the curfew. In those days when we signed out, our destination always was "the Village".

Classes were held in the convent building, so there was always the temptation to wander into places that were off-limits.

(Marie Adele Bradshaw of Wildwood, New Jersey came to Good Counsel College in the fall of 1952 at the early age of 17 years. An excellent student, she majored in French with a minor in music and graduated on June 6, 1956, B.A. Cum Laude. She was admitted to Kappa Gamma Pi, the national scholastic and activity Honor Society of Catholic Women's Colleges.

Marie Bradshaw returned to Good Counsel on February 4, 1957, this time to enter the Community of the Sisters of the Divine Compassion. She received the habit on August 15, 1957 and a new name -- Sister Mary Madonna, a fitting reward for her great devotion and love of Our Blessed Mother.

Marie Bradshaw, Professor of French and former Chairman of the Department of Modern Languages, has been teaching in the College since 1964.)

Reminiscences of a Good Counsel Student, 1957-60 -- Katherine M. Restaino, Class of 1960

I remember arriving at Good Counsel College in September, 1957, as a transfer student. My schedule was rather full because I had to make up various courses for which I had not taken an exact equivalent at my previous college. As a result, I took freshman and sophomore English, freshman and sophomore Philosophy courses, freshman and sophomore Theology courses, in addition to everything I needed for my major in one year.

I remember you scolding me because in my first semester in Good Counsel I had a 4.0 average until Mrs. Curry sent in my grade for speech. She thought I was a C student. Junior year was the best year because I really began to feel at home at Good Counsel. The highlights of that year are those rich in the old traditions -- the Junior-Senior Banquet, Pine Walk, and an unusually exciting Saint Patrick's Day. The best moment for me in Senior year was delivering the Salutatory address at the Commencement.

I certainly remember such things as being fined $.50 for wearing knee-socks without stockings, walking on the lawn, and going off campus for lunch on Friday afternoon with Arline Harney, one of my classmates. Dr. Leo Kearney spoke to me many times about my poor penmanship and tried to get me to write my f's more clearly. Today, my secretary complains about a's and o's, but she thinks my f's are perfect!

As a faculty member, I remember returning to a college which seemed to have some real problems with enrollment and student morale. As I look back on the academic year 1970-71, I realize that students and faculty were caught in the transition between the tradition of Good Counsel College and the pressure of an institution trying to meet new challenges. My first year of teaching at Good Counsel was an extremely rewarding one for me because I thoroughly enjoyed the courses, and I was so pleased to be working with Sr. Teresa to whom I give full credit for my professional career.

It was a real thrill for me to teach English Literature in the very same classroom where I had been a student 10 years before. In that same year my class had its 10th anniversary reunion one year late.

(Katherine M. Restaino was President of the College of White Plains from January 1973 to June 1975. At the present time, Dr. Restaino is Dean at Saint Peter's College, Englewood Cliffs, New Jersey.)

Chronicle

In order to give a more realistic picture of the life and activities of the college girls during the early days, the following entries were taken from a chronicle, covering the years 1924 to 1932. Here and there some explanatory notes are added.

September 20, 1924

Father Ignatius Cox, S.J. visited the college. He suggested changing the name of the college from Good Counsel to Preston College in honor of Monsignor Preston. (The suggestion to change the name of the college was made in good faith; nevertheless Mother Mary Aloysia, President and Founder of the College wished to retain the name Good Counsel College in honor of Our Lady of Good Counsel who had already obtained many favors for the infant institution.)

December 22, 1924

The college girls went around the grounds singing Christmas Carols. They stopped at each building and hung a wreath on the main door. (This exercise, which came to be known later as "Carol Night", was initiated by the students themselves. At this time there were 20 college girls, freshmen and sophomores only.)

February 23, 1925

Monday. College Debate. Resolved that the United States should join the League of Nations. The auditorium was filled with guests. The judges for the debate were Mayor Frederick E. Weeks and Carl Whitney. The girls were praised for an excellent performance.

February 24, 1925

Fordham University Glee Club recital followed by a dance and supper. (The recital and dance took place in the auditorium. The supper was held in St. Joseph's House.)

March 26, 1925

Euchre held in St. Joseph's House. Many prominent people of White Plains were present, thanks to Mrs. Robert L. Crawford who sponsored the affair.

May 1, 1925

College girls held their prom in the auditorium. Fordham boys were invited to attend. Supper was served by Mazzetti in St. Joseph's House.

May 21, 1925

Ascension Day. College girls went to Bronx Park accompanied by Reverend Mother and several sisters.

June 4, 1925

The Literary Club conducted by Sister Mary Edmund gave an entertainment in the auditorium, "The French Maid and the Phonograph". It was very funny and well performed. Reverend Mother and all the sisters attended.

September 21, 1925

Monday. Mass of the Holy Ghost offered by Father Weber to welcome students to Good Counsel. (The total student body reached the number of 44. 24 new students joined the ranks as freshmen.)

December 21, 1925

Founders Day. Feast of Saint Thomas the Apostle. High Mass in the morning and Solemn Benediction in the evening at 8:30 -- attended by the High School juniors and seniors in white cap and gown -- the college girls in black cap and gown. The college girls walked around the grounds singing Christmas carols and hanging wreaths on the doors. A very holy and wonderful day.

December 22, 1925

College girls leave for Christmas vacation. Before going home they were allowed to visit Sister Mary Hyacinth, their Latin teacher, who had been very ill. The visit took place in one of the lecture rooms.

January 23, 1926

A few of the college girls went to St. Agnes' Hospital to give a violin and piano recital for the crippled children. Sister Mary Compassio and Sister Mary Regina accompanied the group.

February 2, 1926

Children of Mary had a party in St. Joseph's House. In the evening a concert was held in the Sisters' parlor given by three singers from the Metropolitan Opera House and attended by the college girls, children of Mary and other guests from St. Joseph's House.

February 10, 1926

The college girls gave the play "Agamemnon" using the vestibule of the convent for a stage. Party followed the play. Deep snow on the ground.

May 12, 1926

Theodore Maynard gave a lecture to the college girls on the subject "Catholic Propaganda". (Theodore Maynard, Litt.D., a noted author, was Professor of English at the college from 1926 to 1929.)

May 30, 1926

May Procession and crowning of the Blessed Virgin by Anna O'Reilly.

August 11, 1926

Miss Egan and Dr. Rogalin came to Good Counsel to make arrangements for the coming school year 1926-27. (Hannah M. Egan, Ph.D., Professor of Education. She also taught Logic. Maurice E. Rogalin, Ph.D., Professor of Education at Good Counsel from 1926-1940. He continued as a visiting lecturer until 1943. His two daughters attended the college and graduated, Irene in 1932, and Ruthanne in 1934.)

December 21, 1926

Founders Day in the College. High Mass in the church celebrated by Monsignor Patrick N. Breslin assisted by his brother Monsignor Joseph Breslin who had just returned from Rome. Monsignor Joseph gave a talk to the college students. Dinner in the evening in honor of Monsignor Joseph Breslin. College girls toured the campus singing Christmas carols and hanging wreaths on the doors. This year Mrs. Wheeler's house at 50 North Broadway was included.

The sign of Christmas at Good Counsel was the lighting of a real live evergreen tree growing on the campus.

January 14, 1927

Dorothy R. Naumann came to Good Counsel to talk to the college girls on self-government. (Dorothy Ridder Naumann, a graduate of Trinity College in Washington, D.C. is a sister of Sister Mary Clement. Dorothy later entered the cloistered division of the Maryknoll sisters, as Sister Mary Christopher, MM.)

March 27, 1927

An excellent concert was given by the Glee Club under the direction of Mr. W. Kenneth Bailey. Mayor Frederick C. McLaughlin and his wife were present along with many people from White Plains.

June 6, 1927

Freshmen gave a luncheon to the seniors. Field day and sports in the afternoon. Mother Mary Aloysia presented the juniors with their class rings, explaining the meaning of the seal. Today, Gladys Muench made application to enter the convent -- the first fruit from the college. Gladys Muench, a native of Friendship, upper New York State, entered the community of the Sisters of the Divine Compassion on February 2, 1928 while in her sophomore year. She is now known as Sister Mary deLourdes. This was the first of many vocations from Good Counsel College.

June 8, 1927

First college graduation. His Eminence Patrick Cardinal Hayes, Archbishop of New York, presiding. Address to the graduates was given by Honorable Humphrey J. Lynch. Father R. Rush Rankin presented the candidates for degrees. For Bachelor of Arts: Carol C. Carmody, Mary R. Corley, Grace A. Dodworth, Evelyn C. Dolan, Marguerite C. Dolan, Wanda J. Graboski, Anna E. O'Reilly, Annette C. Perron, Margaret F. Reynolds, Margaret M. Wall, Sister Mary Basil Hayes R.D.C. and Sister Mary Liguori Mistretta R.D.C. The commencement exercise was held in the auditorium.

October 10, 1927
   Mr. Wetmore gave a lecture to the college girls on the subject "Catholic Woman".

February 17, 1928
   College Prom. Supper was served in the new Club Room. Mr. and Mrs. J.J. O'Shaughnessey and Mr. and Mrs. J.J. O'Reilly acted as chairpersons.

February 22, 1928
   College Debate. Monsignor Breslin and several priests attended. The medal for Debate was awarded to Marguerite Kinsley.

May 21, 1928
   Names on the entrance gates to be changed to Good Counsel College. Received word today that we are to get an Absolute Charter. (The Absolute Charter was granted on May 17, 1928 by the Regents of the University of the State of New York executed under their seal and recorded in their office. Number 3773. Signed by Ernest E. Cole, President of the University.)

August 14, 1928
   Mr. and Mrs. Danahy, their daughter Julia, with her friends Eileen Feniwick, Kathryn McDonald and Mary Pyne, came from Buffalo to remain overnight as Julia Danahy is to enter the convent tomorrow.

August 15, 1928
   Four Postulants entered the Community today. Among them Julia Danahy, the second student to come from the college and the first graduate from Good Counsel College. (Julia Danahy received the religious name of Sister Mary Juliana.)

November 19, 1928
   College girls in cap and gown went to St. John's Church to a funeral Mass for the mother of Gertrude Duffy.

December 6, 1928
   College girls losing many things. Reverend Mother hired a private detective. Found out the girl who was doing the stealing. She was dismissed from the college.

January 13, 1929

Sister Mary Berchmans died today. (Sister Mary Berchmans (Mary Josephine Byrne) M.A., Professor of History, taught in the college from 1928 until her death on January 13, 1929.)

February 12, 1929

Mary Rita Flannery, a college Freshman, died very suddenly from spinal meningitis.

February 13, 1929

Ash Wednesday. Mass for Mary Rita Flannery in Our Lady of Mercy Church, Bronx. College students and several sisters attended.

February 17, 1929

Alumnae held a meeting today. (College Alumnae at this time consisted of 24 members.)

March 19, 1929

Feast of St. Joseph. College girls had an entertainment for Monsignor Patrick N. Breslin's Feast Day. They read papers on the History of Ireland and sang songs. Monsignor was very pleased.

May 9, 1929

Ascension Day. Senior Class started on their trip to Washington, D.C. Mrs. O'Shaughnessy, Miss Grace Gallagher and Miss Mary England were the chaperones. Sister Mary Cecilia held a dance and a sale in the Club Room -- proceeds for the Missions. (Miss Grace Gallagher, LLB, Ph.D., was Professor of English, Economics and Sociology from 1926 to 1932. Dr. Gallagher died on November 10, 1932.)

June 3, 1929

Mass in the Church at 8:00 a.m. for the college girls. Reverend Arthur Scanlan was the celebrant. The girls gave a beautiful presentation of the Gregorian Chant; it even pleased the taste of Professor Bogatto who had trained the girls.

June 4, 1929

In the afternoon the college girls presented a three-act play "Womanhood" by Thomas B. Chetwood, S.J. The play was performed at the south entrance of the main building, the stone loggia with steps on either side making an admirable setting for the dialogue, action and costumes.

June 6, 1929
College graduation held outdoors for the first time, on the lawn, north side of the Church. The Alumnae gave a banquet to the seniors held in the library in the convent.

February 22, 1930
Annual Debate. An excellent presentation. Fine crowd present. Una Falls won the medal for an outstanding performance.

November 17, 1930
Good Counsel College placed on the approved list of the Association of Colleges and Secondary Schools of the Middle States and Maryland College.

November 20, 1930
Rev. Hubbard, S.J., a famous scientist and explorer in Alaska gave a lecture on the glaciers and volcanoes of Alaska -- moving pictures.

January 17, 1931
Letters and posters in the mail announcing Good Counsel College as the Westchester Center of Fordham University courses to be given in History and Philosophy.

January 28, 1931
Lecture given by Rev. Ignatius Cox, S.J., on Modern Civilization.

January 29, 1931
Father Bull's lecture will be attended by fourteen people who registered for the course.

May 26, 1931
Laying of the Cornerstone of Preston Hall by Monsignor Patrick N. Breslin. Many friends present including Father James Kearney and Leo I. Kearney.

March 14, 1932
Debate between Good Counsel College and New Rochelle College. Good Counsel College won.

March 20, 1932
College girls gave the play "The Upper Room" for the Missions.

August 15, 1932

Feast of the Assumption. Three young ladies from the College entered the community of the Sisters of the Divine Compassion, Mary Hanley, Alodie Barry and Alice Doyle. Mary Hanley graduated in June, 1932. (They became, respectively, Sister Mary Vincentia, Sister Mary Alberta and Sister Mary Modesta. Sister M. Modesta died on January 2, 1972; Sister M. Vincentia on June 15, 1988.)

October 28, 1932

Consecration of Bishop Kearney in St. Patrick's Cathedral, New York City. Sisters and college girls attended.

CHAPTER TWO

THE GROUND ON WHICH WE STAND

The land now occupied by the College was once upon a time the home of the American Indians. The western part of the White Plains belonged to the Weckquaskech Tribe, a portion of the great Mohican nation. The eastern section was in the possession of the Siwanoys. Several other tribes lived in different parts of the County but they belonged to the original stock, the Algonquins, and all were subject to the powerful Iroquois who dominated the Federation known as The Six Nations.

The Indians of Westchester were peaceful and industrious. They lived by fishing, hunting and farming. The well-watered country, rich soil, numerous lakes and streams stocked with plenty of fish, deer and other game provided an ample supply of food. They cultivated the land raising crops of maize or Indian corn, sieva beans and pumpkins in the fertile Westchester soil. They were skilled workmen, as can be testified by the remains which have been unearthed.

From an historic document, the "deed of sale" dated November 22, 1683, we learn that the inhabitants of Rye bought from the Indians a tract of land which extended northward including what the English called "the white plains" and the Indians called "the white marshes" or in their language Quarroppas. A prior claim had been made to the same land by Mr. John Richbell, who asserted that he bought the land from the Indians in 1660.

In 1701 the Honorable Caleb Heathcote, the grantee of the Richbell title, obtained a confirmation of his rights to the Richbell estate, which included White Plains. The dispute over the ownership remained unsettled for a good number of years. Finally on March 13, 1721, a royal patent was granted to Joseph Budd and his associates, giving them the parcel of land lying in Westchester County and commonly known by the name of White Plains.

How White Plains Got Its Name

There are several interesting accounts of how White Plains got its name. Some historians seem to think that the name was suggested by the presence of the many white balsam shrubs. However, at the time when the Indians sold this section of land in 1683, there were few, if any, of these shrubs in the vicinity.

Another possibility for the name of White Plains was the profusion of white daisies. The field and meadows in the early days known as The Commons, where herds of cattle grazed, were covered with white daisies. But again, we are forced to abandon this fanciful theory, since botanists of renown tell us that the daisy was not native to this country, but was imported from Holland to England and then brought into this country by the settlers.

Probably the most satisfactory explanation of the origin of the name comes from the Indians. They called this section of land the white marshes or in their language Quarroppas. This name appeared in the deed of sale of November 22, 1683. The name was suggested by the presence of a heavy white mist which arose from the marshy ground covering a part of this section of land. From the top of Chatterton Hill looking eastward across the valley were fields and meadows. Much of the low lying land was a boggy swamp from which a white mist arose. We have an eye witness account given by Mr. John Rosch who came to White Plains in 1874. He states, "I have seen the mist and fog rising from the swampland in enveloping clouds that remained suspended in mid-air for days at a time. From a distance it suggested a great, grey-white inland sea." General Heath, in command of Hatfield Hill in 1776, speaks of this unusual sight which made it impossible for him to catch sight of the enemy.

Thus it seems that the most trustworthy origin of the name comes from the Indians who called this land "The White Marshes".

The Development of the City of White Plains

In colonial days, White Plains was a small hamlet originally settled by residents of Rye. The County Court House was moved from the village of Westchester to White Plains in 1759, resulting in the growth of the life of the hamlet. Small dwellings, shops and taverns grew up along its main street with the Court House as the center. The peaceful life of the inhabitants was soon disturbed by the War for Independence, in which many of its citizens played an important role. It was here that the Battle of White Plains took place on October 28, 1776, one of the most decisive in our War for Independence.

After the defeat of the American forces in the Battle of Long Island, Washington withdrew his army from Manhattan and marched northward to White Plains where he arrived on October 21, 1776, and rested on the hilly grounds. His lines extended from Chatterton Hill, over the Bronx River to Purdy Hill (now called Dusenberry), across Broadway and eastward to Hatfield and Merritt Hills. On the following day three lines of breastworks were thrown up on the hillside getting ready for battle; these lines extended over the grounds now occupied by the College.

On the 28th of October the battle raged. The American forces on Chatterton Hill were overpowered and forced to retire, leaving General William Howe of the British Army occupying Chatterton Hill and later Purdy Hill, just to the west of the present Good Counsel property. General Heath of the American forces was situated on Hatfield Hill to the east, with Colonel Malcolm on Merritt Hill.

In order to attack the American forces, Howe's army crossed Broadway with the intention of engaging in battle with General Heath on Hatfield Hill. His soldiers, therefore, crossed the present campus of the College heading east, but were hindered by the nature of the land (the ground from Broadway was all downhill to a deep ravine and brook) from attaining their goal. Finding it impossible to pass over the deep water in the pond, they returned again across the campus and marched up North Broadway, where the forces were engaged in battle on Mount Misery to the north.

While the battle ended with a victory for the British forces, it was in many ways a move in favor of the Americans. General Howe of the British Army had laid his plans for what he believed would be a final engagement that would crush the rebel army and end the rebellion. But as it drew toward the close of the day, no action was taken. Washington took advantage of the darkness of the night to strengthen his forces with additional works and thus occupy a stronger position. The next day it rained. Howe still procrastinated. Finding it impossible to oust Washington from his strong posts on the hills, General Howe withdrew his forces from White Plains on November 4, 1776. After the Battle of White Plains on November 4, 1776, the Court House was burned to the ground by the Americans under the command of Major General Israel Putnam in order to prevent it from falling into the hands of the British. The homes and shops of the settlers along the Main Street (now Broadway) shared the same fate.

A short distance from the most northern boundary of White Plains, in the town of North Castle, stands a national shrine, Washington's

Headquarters. It was the home of Elijah Miller and his wife Ann, located on Virginia Road between the railroad and Miller Hill. In this house, it is believed, Washington spent some time while in White Plains. A bronze tablet near the entrance reads:

> *"General George Washington occupied this house as head-quarters from October 23rd to November 10th, 1776. This tablet is dedicated to his memory -- May 11, 1918 by the White Plains Chapter, Daughters of the American Revolution."*

White Plains, the Birthplace of New York State

On the fourth of July, 1776, the Continental Congress met at Philadelphia and adopted the Declaration of Independence. On July 6th, John Hancock, President of the Continental Congress, sent a copy of the Declaration of Independence to White Plains with a letter requesting that the Document be promulgated in such a way that all the people of the Colony be informed.

The Provincial Congress of the Colony of New York met in session on July 9, 1776, at the old Court House which was situated on the spot of the present State Armory on Broadway and Mitchell Place. After grave deliberation and discussion, the Congress solemnly approved and ratified the Declaration of Independence. All allegiance to Great Britain was forever renounced, and a resolution was passed changing its name from the Provincial Congress of the Colony of New York to the Convention of the Representatives of the State of New York. The next day the Declaration of Independence was read and proclaimed for the first time by John Thomas, from the Court House to the assembled people of Westchester County. The historic site thus became the birthplace of the State of New York.

In 1910, the White Plains Chapter of the Daughters of the American Revolution erected a monument on the spot to commemorate the great event. It reads:

> *Site of the County Court House where on July 10, 1776 the Provincial Congress proclaimed the passing of the Dependent Colony and the Birth of the Independent State of New York, 1910.*

After the American Revolution, the town sprang up again along this pleasant site. The Court House was rebuilt on the same foundation, life was carried on during more peaceful times, and the population continued to grow.

By an act of the Legislature in 1788, under George Clinton, the first Governor of the State of New York, White Plains was created a Town.

The Harlem Railroad came to White Plains in 1844, resulting in a shift of the business life from Broadway to Railroad Avenue (the present Main Street). The Town continued to grow in wealth and population so that by 1866 another change was made in its status. By an act of the State Legislature, Reuben E. Fenton being Governor, passed April 3, 1866 and amended April 22, 1867, declared White Plains to be a Village. And a village it remained for the next fifty years.

Then by an act of the Legislature of the State of New York and signed by Governor Charles S. Whitman on May 3, 1915, White Plains was created a City, to become effective as of January 1, 1916. The White Plains Battle Flag design was adopted as the official seal of the City of White Plains by the Common Council on January 1, 1916.

White Plains has continued to grow and prosper. Today its 47,000 inhabitants enjoy a well planned city. The old colonial Main Street has become Broadway -- a lovely park-lined thoroughfare, with flowers, shrubs, well-cared-for trees and fountains. The beauty of this street with its bordering park owes its present loveliness to the untiring efforts, interest and support of Mr. Charles H. Tibbits, for whom the park is named.

Good Counsel College, now the College of White Plains of Pace University, occupies a place on North Broadway. The wide lawns and many trees on the campus enhance the beauty of this section of the city.

Picture of The Times

What was the world like in the early twenties when Good Counsel College came into existence? The world was in a state of confusion and unrest after World War I (1914-1918). The unsettled times gave rise to a great desire to get back to normal. The world was out of balance -- it lacked equilibrium. There was a yearning for peace, serenity, for something of permanence and stability.

The altered conditions after the Great War gave rise to new standards or theories of government, Communism in Russia, Fascism in Italy 1922, and ten years later Nazism in Germany 1932. Old standards of morality were shattered.

Another factor that made for a new and different world was the number of scientific and mechanical inventions. Electric power, with electric light, replaced the use of oil and gas. The telephone, invented by Alexander Graham Bell in 1876, was now in common use. Radio, invented by Guglielmo Marconi in 1895, by 1921 became a practical instrument for communication. Motion pictures, developed by Thomas A. Edison in 1893, became a means of popular entertainment. The first picture with synchronized musical score, "Don Juan", appeared in 1926. The first motion picture with spoken dialogue, "The Jazz Singer", came a year later in 1927. Both of these were produced by Warner Brothers. The automobile and airplane, as rapid means of travel, replaced the slow moving horse and buggy.

The effects of these material innovations were many, but the one of greatest importance was the rapidity of communication. Peoples and nations were brought closer together. The world was made smaller.

Two amendments to the Constitution, one a mistake, the other a citizen's right, came into focus at this time. The 18th amendment, the Volstead act or Prohibition, had been passed by Congress in 1919, but was vetoed by President Wilson. Repassed over his veto, it went into effect at midnight, January 16, 1920. The law continued to be defied. Enforcement of the law was generally inefficient and undignified -- sometimes violent and corrupt. Many crimes were committed. Even people, who at first, favored the 18th Amendment, began to see its folly. Prohibition finally ended with its repeal in 1933, December 5.

The 19th Amendment stated the "right of citizens to vote shall not be denied because of sex." Woman suffrage had first been granted in the United States back in 1869 by Wyoming Territory. Now the Law, which became effective August 26, 1920, extended to every state in the Union. Woman suffrage placed an added responsibility upon the schools and colleges to prepare women to become intelligent voters.

The decade of the twenties was one of freshness, daring and realism, a down-to-earthiness that shocked members of the older and more sedate generation. On the college campus, all over the land, students vied with one another to dress in nondescript fashions. Their manners, attitude toward life, and especially their clothes, served as a record of the earthiness of the times. This unkemptness in dress in the colleges of both men and women contrasted sharply with the neat, tasteful and simple uniform worn by the girls at Good Counsel College.

In December, 1925, Bryn Mawr, one of the leading American Colleges for women, revoked a 28 year old rule against smoking by students within the confines of the College. At Good Counsel College the rule against smoking was rigidly adhered to. Infractions of this rule led to expulsion. A case in point came up in February, 1929, when two girls were dismissed from the college for breaking this rule. The ban against smoking within the College confines was not lifted until 1959. Then smoking was permitted in the student lounge only and strictly forbidden in any other building on the campus.

In the Twenties you could mail a letter for two cents and a postcard for one cent. There were two deliveries a day and excellent service. One could take a trip from White Plains to New York City on the Boston-Westchester railroad for 35 cents and then continue on your way on the subway for 5 cents.

Among the fads that captured the imagination of the students in the twenties may be mentioned cross-word puzzles, marathon dancing and Couéism. Émile Coué arrived in New York in January, 1923, with his theory of healing by auto-suggestion -- a system for curing mental and physical disorders by repeating over and over -- "Every day, in every way, I am getting better and better."

Among some of the best motion pictures which appeared in 1923, may be listed "Covered Wagon", "Robin Hood", "Green Goddess", "Hunchback of Notre Dame", "Scaramouche", "Down To The Sea in Ships". In 1924, came "Thief of Baghdad", "Beau Brummel", "Ten Commandments", "America", "Girl Shy", "Abraham Lincoln". In 1925, "Gold Rush", "Merry Widow", "Phantom of the Opera", "The Freshman", "Big Parade".

A controversy which was to hold the attention of the country and indeed of the whole civilized world, for years, was that over evolution. In January 1923, a group of ministers at St. Paul, Minnesota, encouraged by William Jennings Bryan, denounced the theory of evolution as a "program of infidelity masquerading under the name of science." Those who agreed with these ministers were called Fundamentalists; those who opposed this view were known as Modernists.

The State of Tennessee had enacted a law prohibiting the teaching of evolution in State-supported schools. In July, 1925, John Thomas Scopes, a young high school teacher, was accused and found guilty of teaching the theory of evolution in the Dayton, Tennessee, High School. The trial lasted for twelve days during one of the most intense heat waves. The chief prosecutor, William Jennings Bryan, was opposed by Clarence Darrow, as defense counsel. The heated debate between the two giants went on for days and finally ended with Scopes losing.

A sad aftermath of the trial was the death of William Jennings Bryan before the month of July ended. The strain and fatigue of defending his religious beliefs, no doubt, was the cause of his death on July 26, 1925.

Another trial which drew considerable attention and interest was that which took place about a year before, in September 1924. Clarence Darrow, criminal lawyer, had defended the case of the two young men Leopold and Loeb, and saved them from the gallows. Nathan Leopold Jr., and Richard Loeb confessed to kidnapping and killing Bobby Franks, a fourteen-year-old boy, just for the "thrill of it". They were sentenced to life imprisonment. Loeb was killed by a fellow convict on January 28, 1936. Leopold was paroled February 20, 1958.

An event which took the world by surprise for its daring and courage occurred in May, 1927, when Charles Augustus Lindbergh made his solo flight across the Atlantic in his monoplane the "Spirit of St. Louis". Returning to New York, he was greeted by a ticker-tape parade on Broadway. Lindbergh paid a high price for his popularity when on March 1, 1932, his baby son was kidnapped, held for ransom and finally found slain on May 12, 1932.

Before the "Roaring Twenties" ended a great tragedy struck the nation. On October 24, 1929, the worst stock market crash on Wall Street ushered in the Great Depression. The College felt its impact, yet it continued to grow slowly but steadily each year. Board and Tuition was kept at a minimum of $500.00 over the years 1929 to 1938, thus making it possible for well qualified students, lacking an abundance of means, to attend the College. It was not uncommon at Good Counsel for a student, feeling the effects of the Depression, to have her bills remitted or payment deferred to a future date. Many a grateful student was thus able to complete her education and obtain her degree at a time when, more than ever, it was a necessary step to earning a living wage.

An event which had a profound effect on the Catholic World and caused great rejoicing at Good Counsel was the momentous settlement of the Roman Question of February 11, 1929.

Briefly the story may be summed up as follows: During the reign of Pope Pius IX on that fateful day, September 20, 1870, Victor Emmanuel's troops overran Rome with pillage, sacrilege and bloodshed. In protest, Pius IX made himself a prisoner of the Vatican, letting it be known that henceforth he would never again leave the Vatican until there was some return to reason and justice.

Symbolically, the great bronze doors of the apostolic palaces were closed and the Holy Father ceased to appear above St. Peter's entrance to give his traditional blessing to the City and the world. Thus conditions remained during the Pontificates of Leo XIII, Pius X and Benedict XV. Pius XI, however, immediately after his election, went to the balcony and gave his blessing urbi et orbi.

Finally, after long and secret negotiations the Lateran Treaty was signed on February 11, 1929, by Cardinal Gasparri and Benito Mussolini. After 59 years of bitterness, there was to be at least a measure of understanding. Pope Pius XI would henceforth be known as the Pontiff of Reconciliation.

Another epoch-making event which occurred during the reign of the same Pontiff Pius XI was the first radio address from the Vatican on February 12, 1931. Guglielmo Marconi, the inventor of wireless telegraphy, had presented the Holy Father with a fully equipped radio-transmitter station. While the Holy See paid for the installation, Marconi received public recognition as the donor of this marvelous instrument. Now, for the first time in history, the Holy Father could speak directly to his children all over the world at the same time.

The formal opening of the Vatican radio station came on February 12, 1931. It was awaited everywhere with more than ordinary interest. Broadcasting systems in practically every country stood by and canceled their usual programs to get the speech in full which lasted one half hour.

The following description of the event is taken from The Cardinal Spellman Story, by Robert I. Gannon, page 72. The circumstances made it an unusually important statement and the text was worthy of the occasion. It rose to a universality that belonged not the Bishop of Rome or to the Patriarch of the West, but to the Vicar of Christ on earth. He began with great solemnity:

"To all Creation: Having in God's mysterious designs become the successor of the Prince of the Apostles -- those Apostles whose doctrine and preaching were by Divine Command destined for all nations and for every creature -- being the first Pope to make use of this truly wonderful Marconian invention, we, in the first place, turn to all things and to all men, and we say to them:

Hear, O ye heavens, the things I speak. Let the earth give ear to the words of my mouth. Hear these things, all ye nations; give ear, all ye inhabitants of the world, both rich and poor together. Give ear, ye islands, and hearken, ye people from afar."

Then, after a prayer to God, he turned successively, with appropriate exhortations, to Catholics, to the hierarchy, to the religious, to missionaries, to all the faithful, to unbelievers and to those outside the fold, to leaders of peoples, to subjects, to the rich, to the poor, to laborers and employers, to the afflicted, ending with the simple words:

"It remains for us to import to the city and to the world and to all who dwell therein Our Apostolic Blessing. This we do in the Name of the Father and of the Son and of the Holy Ghost."

The Holy Father delivered the address in Latin. At the suggestion of Cardinal Pacelli, Secretary of State, Monsignor Francis Spellman prepared an English translation of the text and delivered a digest of the speech after the Pope had finished. His father and mother, seated by the radio at home in Whitman, Massachusetts, had the unique experience of hearing their son, the future Cardinal Archbishop of New York, broadcast a translation of the address of Pius XI, on February 12, 1931.

The Prestonian for February, 1931, carried the following article on the front page:

Students Hear First Radio Address from Vatican. His Holiness Speaks to all Peoples.

February 12th, 1931 was a memorable day at the college. From all directions we eagerly thronged to the Assembly room long before the hour set for the event which will go down through the ages, an event which concerned not a country nor a nation, but the entire world. We waited in breathless suspense for the voice of the Vicar of Christ, and when that voice, vigorous, clear, and resonant, delivered in the language of the Universal Church, his message of peace and fatherly love, a thrill of awe swept over the reverent audience.

"Glory to God and Peace on earth" was the message of the Holy Father to all the world. No words could express the joy of the Catholic world who heard simultaneously for the first time the voice of the Vicar of Christ. The Gift of Tongues enabled a few thousands to hear and understand the voice of the apostles, but the world-wide broadcast enabled many millions to hear the message of the present successor of Saint Peter. Apart, too, from the exultation of the Catholic world, there was the interest manifested by those outside the fold -- all giving proof that the event is regarded as an epoch-making one by the entire world.

Headline History of Important Events

1933, January 30, Hitler made Chancellor of Germany by Hindenburg.

1933, December 5, Prohibition ended in the United States.

1941, December 7, Japan attacks Pearl Harbor, forcing the United States into war on December 8.

1944, June 6, D-Day. Allies launch the invasion at Normandy.

1945, February 11, Yalta agreement signed by President Franklin D. Roosevelt, Churchill and Stalin.

1945, April 12, Death of President Franklin D. Roosevelt. Harry S. Truman becomes President of the United States.

1945, August 6, A-bomb blasts Hiroshima.

1945, August 9, Nagasaki hit by A-bomb.

1945, August 14, Japan surrenders.

1945, October 24, U.N. officially established.

1958, October 9, Death of Pope Pius XII.

1958, October 28, Angelo Roncalli elected Pope. He took the name of John XXIII.

1960, November 8, John Fitzgerald Kennedy elected as President of the United States.

1961, March 1, President Kennedy sets up U.S. Peace Corps: Young people to aid underdeveloped countries.

1961, March 5, first U.S. spaceman, Navy Commander Alan B. Shepard Jr., rockets 116.5 miles up in 302-mile trip.

1962, February 20, Lt. Colonel John H. Glenn Jr., is the first American to orbit the earth 3 times in 4 hours and 50 minutes.

1962, October 11, Pope John XXIII opens the Second Vatican Ecumenical Council.

1963, April 10, Pope John XXIII issues an encyclical Pacem in Terris (Peace on Earth) proposing world political community to insure peace.

1963, June 3, Death of Pope John XXIII.

1963, June 21, Cardinal Giovanni Battista Montini was elected Pope taking the name of Paul VI.

1963, November 22, President John F. Kennedy was shot and killed by a sniper in Dallas, Texas. Lyndon Baines Johnson took the oath of office in the presidential jet plane on the Dallas airfield.

1964, August 10, Pope Paul VI issues encyclical <u>Ecclesiam Suam</u> (His Church) in which he proclaims his readiness to intervene for peace between nations.

1965, January 20, President Johnson and Vice President Humphrey inaugurated.

1965, March 31, Pope Paul VI revises Holy Week prayers to eliminate degrading references to Jews and atheists.

1965, April 30, Pope Paul VI issues second encyclical <u>Mense Maio</u> (In the month of May) appealing for prayers and conciliatory action by world leaders to hasten world peace.

1965, October 4, Pope Paul VI historic visit to New York City -- the first Pope to set foot in the New World . He celebrated Mass in the Yankee Stadium on a chilly cold day. Pope Paul VI brings his peace pilgrimage to the U.N. telling the delegates, "No more war, war never again." He confers with President Johnson. Millions see him driving through New York City, at St. Patrick's Cathedral and at the Vatican Pavilion of the World's Fair.

1965, November 2, John V. Lindsay, Republican Liberal, elected Mayor of New York City.

1967, December 2, Death of Francis Cardinal Spellman, Archbishop of New York.

Marietta Hall

St. Joseph House

Leeney Estate - Preston Hall - Dannat

Pine Walk

Garden - Rose Arbor

Lawn - Relaxing between Classes

Chapel of the Divine Compassion

Chapel of the Divine Compassion

Library 1938

Library 1965

Preston Hall

Aloysia Hall

Leo J. Kearney Sports Building

CHAPTER THREE

THE DEVELOPMENT OF THE CAMPUS

The Tilford Estate

In the Spring of 1890, the Sisters of the Divine Compassion came to White Plains to the Tilford estate which had been purchased for them by Monsignor Preston. The history of the twelve acres of land, lying east of North Broadway and stretching eastward to Kensico Avenue, can be traced back many years. The original owner was one Daniel Horton, Jr., born in White Plains on September 13, 1744. His father had been given one of the first royal patents by King George I for his land in White Plains. Daniel Horton was a soldier in the War for Independence. Being strongly patriotic and devoted to the cause of freedom, he was chosen by General Washington to store and guard essential military supplies. However, the watchful British soon discovered the whereabouts of the material hidden away in Horton's house and set fire to his home and other buildings, thereby destroying the much needed military supplies. Horton, his wife Rhoda and family were able to escape to Bedford.

Through the years the ownership of the land has changed many times since the days of Daniel Horton. In 1805 it was in the possession of Obidiah Bostwick and his sons William and Charles Bostwick. Other names appearing in the list of owners include Elijah Hebard (1826), Francis Seney (1833), William Sneffin (1848), John Fisher (1848), Randle McDonald (1853).

Randle McDonald sold the property (1855) to Eugene T. Preudhomme, the owner of the White Plains Gas Company. It was he who built the stately house in 1856, and enriched the property with many beautiful trees and shrubs. He remained the owner of the land for twenty-five years. In 1880, he sold the mansion with its twelve acres of land to John M. Tilford, a member of the well-known Park and Tilford Company in New York City.

Mr. Tilford was born in Washington County, New York, on March 16, 1815. He left his farm in his native county and came to New York City in 1835. He was married to Jennie White in 1840 and had two sons, Charles E. and Frank. In New York City he was employed in the grocery store of Benjamin Albro where he met his future partner, Mr.

49

Park; together they formed the prosperous Park and Tilford Company. Mr. Tilford purchased land in Westchester County in Harrison and White Plains. In 1880 he moved to White Plains to occupy the handsome residence set back about 75 feet from North Broadway. A double row of evergreen trees bordered the path leading up to the entrance of his beautiful home. After residing here for ten years, he sold the property to Caroline M. Boyce, who in turn sold it to the Sisters of Divine Compassion in May 1890.

The original Motherhouse of the Sisters of the Divine Compassion was located in New York City, on Second Avenue at number 132. For a long time both Monsignor Preston and Mother Mary Veronica had been desirous of obtaining a place in the country where the growing community and the girls might spend a few months for rest in the summer.

In April 1890, Monsignor Preston engaged Father John Edwards and Mr. O'Connor to find a suitable place in Westchester County. A fine piece of property, belonging to a Mr. Ryan, was discovered. Mother Mary Veronica visited the place and thought it seemed very desirable for a convent, except for one factor -- it was too far from the Parish Church of St. John where the Sisters were to have daily Mass. Nor was it possible for Father William Dunphy, the Pastor of St. John, to have Mass offered in the house, as he did not have an assistant.

Again, on April 23rd, Father Edwards and Mr. O'Connor visited White Plains to take a second look at the Ryan property. On the way they stopped to visit another place which was for sale and situated on North Broadway. This beautiful 12 acres of land and stately mansion of 20 rooms set in a surrounding of trees and orchards seemed just perfect for the needs of the Sisters. They did not continue on their way to the Ryan property. but returned to the city to inform Monsignor Preston and Mother Mary Veronica of their find. They were so enthusiastic in their report and gave such a glowing picture of the place that Monsignor Preston authorized Father Edwards to enter into negotiations to buy the place for the Sisters. Arrangements were concluded on April 26, 1890, the feast of Our Lady of Good Counsel. Thus it was decided to name the place in honor of Our Lady.

It was not until the end of May that Mother Mary Veronica had a chance to visit the newly acquired property. She was delighted with all she saw and described the place in her report "A Brief Review of Seven Years":

> *"Our Father had asked Monsignor Edwards to find a suitable country place for us and he discovered this. The estimated value of the property was $50,000. That sum had been offered to the*

owner and refused. However, the result of Monsignor Edward's negotiations was that it was bought for $25,000. The purchase consisted of twelve acres of land, a dwelling-house, partly furnished, a carriage house and stables, a small out-building in the rear of the dwelling, and certain farm implements. A kitchen garden, large enough to supply a private family, was stocked with fruits and vegetables. There was a fine lawn with magnificent trees in front and an apple orchard with pear, cherry and peach trees in the rear. All the rest of the land was unused and uncultivated. It was a pretty private residence. Ten thousand dollars was paid in cash and the balance remained on bond and mortgage."

The down payment of $10,000 for the house, land and brook came from the offerings made to Monsignor Preston on the occasion of the 40th Anniversary of his ordination to the priesthood.

The Sisters took possession on June 7, 1890. During the first season, the house was used as a restful haven during the summer months.

On April 15, 1892, the novitiate was removed from the city to Good Counsel, which from that date became the Motherhouse and the first convent of the Sisters of the Divine Compassion in White Plains.

The original Tilford House is pictured in Scharf's History of Westchester. It shows a two story house with an attic and cupola, and a long veranda stretching along the front from end to end. During the winter of 1891, Mother Mary Veronica made several alterations in the house. She had built two new wings on the second floor, one on the south side over Monsignor Preston's quarters, to serve him as additional space for his work when he was able to come to White Plains, and another on the north side, making a long dormitory. She also had the veranda built on the second story to correspond with the one on the first floor. To the cupola she added a belfry tower, in which was placed a bell.

The room to the right of the front entrance was used as a chapel. It was here that Monsignor Preston said the first Mass ever offered on these grounds. Here, too, he blessed the bell named Our Lady of Good Counsel, which was hung in the belfry and rang out to call the Sisters to their prayers and other community exercises. The south wing adjacent to the Chapel was reserved for Monsignor Preston. Later these rooms were set aside for the Chaplain. The rooms on the left side of the entrance were set up as a parlor and a refectory. Mother Mary Veronica's office was on the second floor in front, over the Chapel. To the rear of it was the wardrobe. On the left side of the hall were located the Community Room and the infirmary. The dormitories were on the third floor.

The Hand Estate

When the Sisters of the Divine Compassion bought the Tilford property, some of the inhabitants of the town were quite disturbed that the place had come into the possession of Catholics. However, their next door neighbors, the elderly Protestant couple, Nathan Hand and his wife, did not share this sentiment. They were quite content to have the Sisters as neighbors. As the years went by, the Sisters and their good neighbors to the south became very friendly.

Nathan H. Hand was born in Placham, Vermont, on March 11, 1819. He grew up in New England. As a young man he was a manufacturer of palm-leaf hats in Massachusetts. Later he bought a marble quarry in Vermont known as the Hand's Pittsford, Vermont Quarry, which supplied marble for many a structure in Boston and New York. After the Civil War, Hand's interests turned to gold mining. He went to Georgia where he organized Hall's Gold Mining Company, of which he became President. He accumulated a large fortune, which enabled him to purchase the beautiful estate on North Broadway in White Plains, known as "Mapleton" because of the numerous maple trees surrounding the house.

The one idea cherished by Mother Mary Veronica was to build a Chapel. For this she would need more land. On one of her many visits to the Hands, she approached them on the subject of selling their property. By this time the Hands were retired. Sister Mary Fidelis accompanied Mother Mary Veronica on this occasion. She vividly remembered the incident and records the reaction: "*Mr. Hand's astonishment was great. He said the idea was simply preposterous, unthinkable, and not to be harbored for an instant.*" Wisely, Mother Mary Veronica did not press the subject. On leaving the house she buried a little metal case containing a statue of Saint Joseph, with the simple prayer, "*Get this house for us dear Saint, and we will name it St. Joseph's House.*"

Mother Mary Veronica and the Sisters continued to be on friendly terms and made calls on Mrs. Hand every three or four weeks. This amicable relationship continued and grew stronger, so that by the summer of 1893 they invited the children to come over to their orchards and play every afternoon.

Then, on the Feast of St. Mary Magdalene, July 23, 1983, the anniversary of Monsignor Preston's birthday, Mr. Hand rang the doorbell of the Convent and asked to see Mother Mary Veronica. He greeted her with the words, "*Good morning, Mother, I don't know why I am doing it, I do not want to, but I will sell you the place.*"

For the present he wished to retain the house with about three acres, but the remaining 12½ acres could be sold. He even pointed out that the abundance of fieldstone scattered all over the place could be used for building the Church.

On August 12, 1893, Mother Mary Veronica wrote to Archbishop Corrigan informing him of the situation:

> "I mentioned our good Protestant neighbors, Mr. and Mrs. Hand. The friendship has grown apace and a few days ago they offered to sell us twelve and one half acres of their land adjoining ours. There is nothing more valuable in White Plains. It is bounded on two sides at the further end by two avenues, lately laid out where building lots are in great demand. It will give us a very beautiful site for the Chapel and a Convent, pasturage for cows, and land for cultivation and thus enable us to supply our New York house with milk, butter and vegetables. Mrs. Hand has been frequently importuned by speculators to sell this part of their property, but Mr. Hand wishes us to have the opportunity to buy it, if we want to. The price is $30,000. They will take a mortgage for $25,000 and give us eighteen months in which to pay the remaining $5,000..."

The Archbishop was greatly interested in the project and wished to see the property. However, he was not able to come to White Plains for several months. In the meantime, two events took place that changed the situation regarding the purchase. Mr. Hand decided to move to New York City and, therefore, was willing to sell the house and its three acres along with the original offer. And on the death of her mother, Susan J. Dannat, Mother Mary Veronica came into her inheritance of over $200,000 from her uncle David Jones, along with a legacy from her mother of $10,000. One third of this fortune was set aside for the Sisters of the Divine Compassion and the remainder made it possible for her to buy the property to build the Church.

Late in January 1894, Archbishop Corrigan found time to visit White Plains. Together with Mother Mary Veronica he explored the adjoining property. He thought it an excellent buy and authorized her to enter into negotiations for the purchase of the house and lands now consisting of 15 acres. The price asked was $55,000. On May 5, 1894, Nathan H. Hand sold his estate to the Sisters of the Divine Compassion.

The Hand estate, formerly called "Mapleton", has a fascinating history of its own. This land with its lovely dwelling, one of the oldest and most picturesque structures on the White Plains campus, clearly visible from North Broadway but set back about 75 feet amidst a bower of trees, has a long history of ownership dating back to the year 1794.

Just 100 years later it became the property of the Sisters of the Divine Compassion.

The 15-acre parcel of land belonged to Daniel Hatfield and was part of a 150-acre farm. The Hatfield family was one of the earliest to settle in White Plains. On a map of 1776, the Hatfield name is clearly marked. Hatfield Hill, west of Silver Lake, played an important role in the American Revolution. After the war the ownership of the land passed through several hands. When Daniel Hatfield died on August 17, 1830, the property went to his daughter, Anna, and her husband, James S. Fisher. It remained in the Fisher family for a good number of years. Through the years, several parcels of the original 150 acre estate were sold to various individuals. Some of the names mentioned in the list of owners include Abraham Horton (1836), Allan McDonald (1843), Guillanme Preaut (1849), Henry Preaut (1864). In 1865 the property became the possession of William Franklin Dusenberry, a carriage manufacturer. It was he who had the house erected shortly after the Civil War, about 1867. The mansion and lovely grounds remained in his possession until 1884 when he sold it to Nathan H. Hand. Ten years later, in 1894, the house and 15 acres were sold to the Sisters of the Divine Compassion. The property lies just south of the Tilford estate. To this day the line of demarcation between the two estates can be seen, a long line of evergreen trees extending from the end of the southwest wing of the Convent to North Broadway.

Shortly after the settlement, in 1894, Mr. Hand fell ill and was hospitalized to undergo a serious operation. Mrs. Hand sent for Mother Mary Veronica and told her that the doctors informed her that he would not recover. Since they had made no plans to move to a new place, they continued to dwell in their old home although it now belonged to the Sisters. Mother Mary Veronica, in all charity and compassion, permitted this to remain so, not wishing to disturb them at this critical time.

Mr. Hand returned from the hospital to convalesce at his old home. Despite the doctor's prediction, he continued to improve during the summer. In the fall, he informed Mother that they would be able to move out of the house in November and that the Sisters could begin plans to take possession. By the end of November the Hands were gone, leaving the keys with Mother Mary Veronica. She now went over to inspect the house of 22 rooms. A few repairs and some painting had to be done, but the Sisters could make preparation to move in around Christmas time. A few days after the Hands had settled in a hotel in New York, Mother Mary Veronica got the sad news that Mr. Hand had died quite suddenly.

The Sisters packed their few belongings and prepared to move across the lawn into their new convent, named St. Joseph's House in honor of the Saint who had so speedily obtained the place for them. This became the second convent of the Sisters of the Divine Compassion in White Plains. Moving operations began on December 26th, Wednesday, St. Joseph's Day. A heavy snow storm prevented further moving for a few days. On December 28, 1894, Father Joseph Maréchaux blessed the house, and the Sisters had supper and slept there for the first time. Next the chapel furniture was moved in readiness for Mass and exposition of the Blessed Sacrament on the First Friday of January in the new year 1895.

St. Joseph's House was to remain the convent for the Sisters of the Divine Compassion for the next ten years. It was in this house that Mother Mary Veronica died on August 9, 1904. Her room was on the second floor at the northwest corner of the building.

Dr. Marilyn E. Weigold, Associate Professor of History at the College of White Plains, wrote an article, "The Mapleton", the official name of the Nathan H. Hand estate. The article appeared in the Winter 1975 issue of The Westchester Historian, the quarterly of the Westchester County Historical Society. Dr. Weigold also prepared the documentation required for the registration of Mapleton as a landmark to be entered on the National Register of Historical Places on September 28, 1976. This honor was conferred upon the house after a complete study and careful review of the structure, the tower, bay windows, pavilions and other details popular at the time of its construction in 1867.

For 86 years this house has been serving the Community and the College in many and diverse capacities:
- A Convent from 1895 to 1905.
- A Guest House from 1905 to 1934.
- Student dormitory from 1923 to 1931.
- Music Department for the College from 1934 to 1937.
- Library from 1938 to 1965.
- Offices for faculty, student publications, student organizations and alumnae from 1966 to 1970.

Today it houses offices for the faculty of the College of White Plains of Pace University.

St. Stanislaus House
Oblate Fathers of St. Francis deSales

Having established the convent in St. Joseph's House, the second step toward building the Chapel was to move the former convent to a new location, from its site on North Broadway, back 700 feet to the east. Many lovely trees had to be felled in the passage way as the house moved slowly over the ground to its new location. The operation took three months to accomplish.

The old Tilford house now received a new name, St. Stanislaus, in honor of Monsignor Preston's baptismal patron. Over the years this house has served in many and various capacities. From 1895 to 1900 St. Stanislaus House served as a school for very young boys, eight years old and younger. The school was under the direction of the Oblate Fathers of St. Francis deSales, who also used the house as their Convent and Novitiate until 1897 when they found a house of their own and formed a Community. Father Joseph Maréchaux and Father Charles Fromentin also served as Spiritual Directors and Chaplains at Good Counsel. The Oblates discontinued their work for boys in September 1898, having been recalled by their Superior to engage in other missions in South Africa. The Sisters continued the work for boys for awhile, but, since the Sisters of the Divine Compassion were committed by Rule to the training of young girls, Mother Mary Veronica asked and received permission of the Archbishop to transfer the boys to other Catholic institutions dedicated to this work.

Catholic Girls Club

In 1901, Mother Mary Veronica began another work which she felt was important for the honor and glory of God and in keeping with the spirit of the Divine Compassion. It was the establishment of the Working Girls Club. The house at 134 Second Avenue in New York City was made ready for their use. It was formally blessed by Archbishop Corrigar. on October 28, 1901, and named the House of Our Lady of the Wayside. Later the headquarters of the Club moved uptown to 126 Street, where two lovely brown-stone houses, No. 52 and 54, were renovated with provisions for a chapel and a gymnasium. This came to be known as Our Lady's House.

When the Club was a year old, the name Working Girls Club was changed to the Catholic Girls Club. It prospered greatly and began to spread its influence for good. Mother Mary Veronica felt that these girls, working and living in the city, needed something more, a summer vacation house in the country. Therefore, she had St. Stanislaus renovated for the purpose. The House was ready and opened on June 14, 1902. Summer after summer, the members of the Catholic Girls Club came to White Plains for a restful vacation. In 1904, when St. Stanislaus House again became the Convent, the Club girls were welcomed to stay in St. Joseph's House along with the other guests.

Academy and College

When the Academy of Our Lady of Good Counsel was established by Mother Mary Aloysia in 1910, St. Stanislaus House served as a residence for the boarding students. In 1918, the lower veranda was bricked in, thus extending the front rooms on the first floor. Later these rooms were converted into classrooms for the high school department of the Academy of Our Lady of Good Counsel.

By 1946, the college enrollment had increased so rapidly that more classroom space was needed. To meet this demand, the College took over St. Stanislaus House. Mother Mary Aloysia changed the name of the building to Marietta Hall in honor of Dr. Marietta Riley of Fordham University, who had done so much in connection with the education of the Sisters in the early days before the establishment of the College. The lower story was used for business education, the upper story for the Art Department and other lecture rooms.

The College continued to use this house for the next 12 years. With the erection of Aloysia Hall in 1958, the College withdrew from Marietta Hall and it was again turned over for use by the Academy. Today it serves as classrooms for the elementary department of the Academy of Our Lady of Good Counsel.

The appearance of the house has lost a little of its old charm. In 1979, a leaking roof necessitated the removal of the belfry and cupola. However, it still stands as a monument to the gracious living of the past.

Building Good Counsel Convent

By the turn of the century, the crowded conditions of the convent in Saint Joseph's House made it imperative to begin to think of finding a more suitable place where community life, according to rule, might be lived. No room in Saint Joseph's House was large enough to serve as a community room or refectory.

Mother Mary Veronica approached Archbishop Corrigan with her problem. He advised her to draw up plans as a preliminary step and then to wait for the actual building of the convent when sufficient funds became available.

Mother Veronica worked closely with the architects and together they completed drawings for a Spanish-Mission style structure built around an open court. Work stopped here as there were no more funds. "We wait now," said Mother Mary Veronica, "for light to take the next step."

By April 1902 she informed the Archbishop that she had sufficient funds on hand to start the foundation of the convent, but nothing else. Archbishop Corrigan gave permission to start the excavation.

On Sunday, April 27, 1902, the day after the Feast of Our Lady of Good Counsel, a simple ceremony of groundbreaking took place. The Sisters and children went in procession to the spot chosen -- to the right of the Church and a little to the rear. A small altar was set up upon which was placed a picture of Our Lady of Good Counsel. Father Fromentin blessed the ground, consecrating it to Our Lady of Good Counsel, for whom the new convent was to be named. He then turned up a sod while the Sisters and children sang the Litany of Our Blessed Mother. The simple ceremony ended, they returned to the Church singing the hymn to Our Lady of Good Counsel. Father Fromentin then gave Benediction of the Blessed Sacrament.

Although permission had already been given by Archbishop Corrigan, upon his death in 1902, Mother Mary Veronica had to seek the approbation of his successor Archbishop John Farley for the project. The Archbishop referred the matter to Monsignor John Edwards whom he had appointed Ecclesiastical Superior of the Community. At the end of October 1903, Mother Mary Veronica announced to the community the happy news that work on the convent could begin. Mother Mary Veronica wrote to the Sisters at Good Counsel from New York:

"I got permission yesterday to begin the convent! On the twenty-eighth of October, mind you, the feast of hopeless cases. I didn't get the money to begin, but we are going to do it, if only by setting our own men to digging. Of course, I had permission from our dear late Archbishop, but the permission had to be obtained again."

The sale of two pieces of property in New York City brought in $52,500. The proceeds of this sale enabled Mother Mary Veronica to begin work in earnest -- or so she thought. Though she had received permission back in October 1903 to begin the building, Monsignor

Edwards would not allow her to proceed. She wrote of the situation in her notes:

> "*All winter, Monsignor Edwards had put us off from signing the first contract for the convent on the score of strikes. The strike being over on the ninth of May 1904, I broached the subject again. It was a shock to hear him say, 'Well I don't think you have money enough'.*"

But he advised her to put in writing what she wanted. This she did and in a letter to him she explained that they had $25,000 on hand and wished at this time to sign the contract for the foundation only. A few days later she received a telephone message from Monsignor Edwards, "*Tell Mother to go on at once. It's all right.*"

Mother Mary Veronica wrote in her notes: "That evening we telephoned for the contractor to call. We found the prices of last winter still hold. We have only money enough to build to the water table, but thank God if He allows me to see that much done. May He Himself finish it in His own good time."

On May 23, 1904 she signed the contract and on June 6th the work began. Mother Mary Veronica died on August 9, 1904. While she had planned and designed the whole structure with love and concern for the Sisters' needs and comfort, she did not live to see it become a reality.

The election for a superior took place a few weeks after the death of Mother Mary Veronica. Archbishop Farley presided at the Chapter and confirmed the Sisters' choice of Sister Mary Clair (Emma Carter) for their new Superior General.

One of the first works undertaken by Mother Mary Clair was to continue the work already begun on the new convent. Severely harassed by financial problems, Mother Mary Clair went forward with courage to try to build the cherished dream of Mother Mary Veronica. In order to secure funds for the building project, Mother Mary Clair removed the Sisters from St. Joseph's House. For the second time the Sisters took up residence in the Tilford house, now named St. Stanislaus House.

To ease the financial situation she rented out Saint Joseph's House to select boarders and placed Sister Simplicien in charge, thus assuring the community a steady, although small, income. She also encouraged Sister Mary Hilda, in charge of Our Lady's House, to take in as many young business women, as possible, as boarders, in the two houses situated on 126th Street in New York City.

However, even these funds were not sufficient to carry on the building project. Mother Mary Clair had to alter the original plan for the convent and to undertake the construction of only one wing. The north wing was completed in 1908 and dedicated on June 3rd. The ground floor contained the kitchen, refectory and study room. On the first floor were the chapel, community room, parlors and offices for Administration. The second floor was devoted to the Novitiate. Here were located a large community room, two dormitories, a wardrobe and bathrooms. A bright sunny corridor ran the length of the building on the south side. The cells for the professed Sisters were on the third floor with accommodations for twenty-seven Sisters.

As soon as the north wing was completed in the summer of 1908, the Sisters moved from Saint Stanislaus House to their spacious new quarters. There was no more make-shift crowding into rooms: each professed Sister had her own individual cell, simply furnished with bed, bureau, washstand and wardrobe. The booming bell of the Church tower clock adjacent to the convent, striking the hours, kept them awake for many a night, but they soon got used to it and were able to sleep soundly.

The cells on the north side faced the Church and the apple orchard. Those on the south side overlooked the foundation of the other three wings yet unbuilt. Trees and shrubs soon sprang up in the open courts. Thus things remained for a good number of years.

The Second Wing of the Convent
Auxiliary of Our Lady of Good Counsel

In 1910, Mother Mary Aloysia (Kelly) came to office as General Superior. Her one great dream and ambition was to complete the building of the convent as envisioned by Mother Mary Veronica. Money was needed -- but prayer, she felt, could do wonders. In 1912, she had the men who worked on the grounds erect a grotto facing the unfinished wings. In the grotto she placed a statue of Our Lady of Good Counsel, charging her to obtain the money needed to build her convent. Toward the same end, in 1913, she organized the Auxiliary of Our Lady of Good Counsel, composed of ladies interested in the community and its works. Monsignor Patrick Breslin served the group as Chaplain, and Sister Mary Philomena was appointed Moderator.

The prayers of the Sisters and monetary aid of the Auxiliary and other friends of the community began to bear fruit. By 1922, sufficient funds were accumulated. Mother Mary Aloysia asked permission to resume the building of the unfinished wings of the convent. Permission was received in the mail on Easter Monday morning, April 17, 1922. The letter was dated April 15, which was Holy Saturday. The Sisters at once began a novena to Our Lady of Good Counsel which ended on her feast day. Work began again in earnest. The original masonry of the foundation walls was found to be in excellent condition so the structure could be raised without delay.

The Sisters watched the daily progress of the building. The first hollow tile block for the walls was laid on June 20, 1922. By July 26th, the Feast of Saint Ann, the walls were sufficiently high to block out the view of the shrine of Our Lady of Good Counsel from the windows on the south side of the north wing. Work continued without interruption during the Summer, Fall and Winter. In the Spring of 1923, things looked so good that Mother Mary Aloysia asked Archbishop Hayes to bless the completed structure. Here is her letter of February 12, 1923, addressed to Right Reverend Monsignor Joseph P. Dineen, 452 Madison Avenue, New York City:

Right Reverend dear Monsignor,

Several months ago I asked His Grace to do us the honor of blessing our new convent when completed. He very graciously promised to grant us this great favor and told me to mention it to you when asking for the appointment.

The building will be finished and in readiness about the middle of June. I beg you, dear Monsignor, to do me the favor of reserving a day in June for His Grace to confer this honor upon us.

This will be a memorable event in the history of our Order and our happiness on this occasion will be complete in having our beloved Archbishop present in person to bless the future home for which we have waited and labored so many years.

Thank you most cordially for your kindness, and begging a blessing for the community and myself, I am

Your servant in Christ
Mother Mary Aloysia

On Tuesday, June 26, 1923, His Grace the Most Reverend Patrick J. Hayes, Archbishop of New York, came to Good Counsel for a two-fold purpose, to bless the three wings of the completed convent and to preside at the commencement exercises of the Academy of Our Lady of Good Counsel.

The Leeney Estate

In the fall of 1925 Good Counsel College was entering upon its third year and already beginning to feel the pinch of overcrowding. The increasing number of resident students soon exhausted the available facilities.

An opportunity was presented to purchase an adjoining piece of property to the north of the campus, the lovely estate of William L. Leeney at 78 North Broadway. Mr. Leeney was a partner in the firm of Genung, McArdle and Leeney, holding the positions of secretary and treasurer.

Mother Mary Aloysia began negotiations to secure the Leeney estate, writing to Cardinal Hayes on November 30, 1925, for permission to make the purchase, pointing out the desirability of adding this choice piece of land to the college campus. The Cardinal answered promptly on December 2, giving his approval for the purchase.

Frederick E. Weeks, Attorney at Law and former Mayor of White Plains, was engaged to take care of all the transactions in connection with the purchase of the estate. The price asked for the land of nearly 12 acres (11.346 acres) with the house and barn was $150,000. A deposit of $500.00 was made on December 4th. Then on December 11, 1925 the contract was signed and an additional payment of $14,500 given. The final payment was made on February 15, 1926 and the Sisters of the Divine Compassion took possession.

The Leeney parcel of 11.346 acres has the same origin as the Tilford estate, going back to the days of the American Revolution when it was owned by Daniel Horton, Jr., and was part of a vast farm land covering many acres. It passed through several hands down through the years. In 1846 Leonard Miller became the owner. Upon his death on May 31, 1884 he left his estate to his three sons, Elijah Miller, George Miller and Frank M. Miller. The property remained in the Miller family until 1922, when Esther A. Miller, widow of George L. Miller, sold it to William L. Leeney on December 15, 1922. He in turn sold it to the Sisters of Divine Compassion on February 15, 1926 for $150,000.

The lovely English style country house facing North Broadway with a frontage of 220 feet became a residence for the senior students. As the express wish of Mother Mary Aloysia, it was named Preston Hall in honor of Monsignor Thomas S. Preston, co-founder of the Sisters of the Divine Compassion.

The students greeted, with joy, the news of the purchase of the Leeney estate and watched every move made on the new addition to the campus. There was great excitement when the fence separating the properties was torn down and the long row of privet hedges removed, giving ready access to the new territory.

Mother Mary Aloysia and Sister Mary Philomena inspected the lovely two-story stucco house which had been recently remodeled. The grounds too had been improved. After a few alterations made during the summer, the first Preston Hall was furnished and made ready for the seniors to take possession in September 1926. For five years the college seniors enjoyed residing in this homelike dwelling.

With the completion of the new Preston Hall in 1931, the Leeney House, then renamed Dannat Hall, was no longer needed as a student residence. In 1933 it was equipped for the Art Department. Later Business Education was accommodated on the first floor.

In 1946 a housing shortage again hit Good Counsel, and the new Preston Hall was filled to capacity. The seniors were delighted to take up residence in Dannat Hall, and the Art and the Commercial Departments were moved over to Marietta Hall. This condition lasted for several years.

When the new six-story residence was completed in 1968, Mother Mary Dolores wished it to be named Dannat Hall as a more lasting memorial to Mother Mary Veronica Dannat Starr. Again the old Leeney house had to renounce its name, and it became known as St. Edmund's Hall in honor of Sister Mary Edmund, the first Dean of Good Counsel College. Today it houses the Education Department and the Reading Center, and is often referred to as Education House.

When Mother Mary Aloysia purchased the Leeney estate did she visualize that it would become the main campus of the college upon which, one day would arise a lovely building (Aloysia Hall) dedicated in her honor, as well as two student dormitories, a dining room, ball courts and other student facilities?

Preston Hall

By the late 1920's, the increasing number of students coming from upstate and out-of-state, wishing to enroll in the college, soon exhausted the available facilities. The resident students were scattered over the campus, some in St. Joseph's House, others in St. Ann's Cottage, the seniors in Preston Hall (the Leeney House) at the northwest end of the campus. It was even found necessary to devote the west wing of the convent known as Faculty Hall to student use. A more ample dormitory building now became essential. The project was given priority by Mother Mary Aloysia, in all the discussions for the development of the College.

At the suggestion of good friend Father R. Rush Rankin, Mr. Emile Perrot was engaged as the architect. By October 5, 1929, Mr. Perrot was able to submit blueprints for the proposed building. Then on December 4, 1929 the contract was signed. Negotiations continued over the next few months, with Mr. Frederick E. Weeks, the former mayor of White Plains, handling all the legal affairs. The City of White Plains granted permission to erect the new building on February 26, 1930.

After this matters began to move more rapidly. On April 26, 1930, the feast of Our Lady of Good Counsel, the bids for the building were opened, and the following contracts were awarded: Builder - John J. McMahon, Plumbing - Frank Martin, Steam Fitting - Thomas Callahan, and Lighting - Walter Whiffin. A few days later, on April 29, 1930, the contracts were signed.

First, the old Preston Hall (the former Leeney house), standing on the site intended for the new dormitory, on North Broadway, had to be removed. The move was accomplished in the spring and summer of 1930. Resting on its new position, overlooking the hills at the northeast end of the campus -- the house now received its new name, Dannat Hall, in honor of Mother Mary Veronica's family name. The title Preston Hall was to be bestowed on the new dormitory.

The ceremony of Groundbreaking took place on May 20, 1930. Monsignor Patrick N. Breslin officiated, assisted by Father James E. Kearney. In the presence of Mother Mary Aloysia, President of the College, the faculty, and students arrayed in cap and gown, the ground was blessed, and the sod overturned. Monsignor planted a medal of the Little Flower and prayed for God's blessing on the project. The College girls then sang the hymn to Our Lady of Good Counsel as they moved away from the site. After the little ceremony was completed, the workmen were there with the bulldozer and dug up the ground in earnest, tons at a time.

Day by day the Sisters and the students watched the progress of the building with keen interest. On the evening of July 16, 1930, the feast of Our Lady of Mount Carmel, Reverend Mother and the Sisters visited the site of the new building. Holy pictures and medals were placed in the foundation. The Rosary was recited and special prayers were offered for the safety of all the men working on the building.

The work advanced steadily over the summer and through the winter. On Easter Sunday, April 5, 1931, the Sisters made a tour of the new building and were delighted at what they saw. The new Preston Hall is of Tudor Gothic style. Entering by the front door into the foyer, they were faced by a monumental stairway in the center of the building running to the second floor only, with a beautiful stained glass bay window picturing Our Lady of Good Counsel, on the landing. On the first floor to the right were found a spacious reception room and parlors, to the left a large handsome dining room. Kitchen, storerooms, cafeteria, lavatories and locker rooms were located in the basement. The three upper floors were given over to private single and double rooms for the resident students. Several of the rooms had private baths, all were equipped with hot and cold water. Ample bathing and shower facilities were found on each floor. The south end of each corridor featured a small but pleasant sitting-room. The whole structure, modern, substantial, artistic and fire-proof, had a capacity for two hundred students. The cost of the building ranged around $364,000.

A drive was set in motion to secure funds to pay for the new building. The Alumnae, consisting at that time of 70 members, contributed $500. The college students, numbering 130, were able to give $1,300. Larger donations came from friends and well wishers of the community. Those contributing $1,000 and more were honored with the title of Founder; to the amount of $500 or more, Benefactor; those who donated $200 or more received the title of Donor.

The laying of the cornerstone for Preston Hall took place on a beautiful afternoon, May 26, 1931 at 3:00 p.m. The ceremony was simple but impressive, with no eulogy nor long speeches, only the prescribed ritual conducted by Monsignor Patrick N. Breslin, Honorary President of the College. An improvised platform covered with a red carpet was erected to the right of the main entrance. The cornerstone bearing the inscription AD 1931 was set in place. The trowel used in the ceremony was the same used by Archbishop Corrigan 36 years before for the laying of the cornerstone of the Chapel of The Divine Compassion in 1895 on June 25. Assisting Monsignor Breslin were Father James E. Kearney of St. Francis Xavier Church in the Bronx, Father Vincent DiMichele, O.P. of Valhalla, Father John B. Murphy, Pastor of St. Bernard's Church, White Plains, and his assistant, Father John J. Corrigan, and Father James Hackett, Elmsford. The architect, Emile Perrot, and the builder, John J. McMahon, were also present for the occasion, along with Mr. Leo I. Kearney.

The procession to Preston Hall was formed in the Administration building. Led by three acolytes from St. Bernard's Church, carrying the crucifix and tall lighted candles, they moved in solemn order across the lawn to the site. First came the girls from the Academy of Our Lady of Good Counsel in uniform, the seniors in white cap and gown, then followed the College students in academic attire; next came the faculty and Sisters and many friends and finally the priests with Monsignor Patrick N. Breslin. At the conclusion of the ceremony, the recessional began, led by the College students, to the Chapel of the Divine Compassion where Monsignor officiated at Benediction.

A few weeks later, on June 4, 1931, His Eminence Patrick Cardinal Hayes officiated at the blessing and dedication of Preston Hall. The ceremony was performed in the presence of the faculty, students and a vast crowd of parents, friends and well wishers.

Following the Dedication Ceremony, degrees were conferred upon the Class of 1931, bringing the total number of the alumnae up to 92.

Before going home for the summer vacation, the students packed all their belongings in readiness for the move into Preston Hall. St. Joseph's House and the other cottages were vacated by the College girls and put to other uses. All eagerly awaited their return in September 1931 to take up residence in the new and beautiful dormitory.

Preston Hall became the center for all the important events taking place in the college for the years to come. Special dinners, dances, the annual bazaar, all found ample accommodations in the spacious rooms and gracious setting. The first formal reception held in the new Preston Hall on October 6, 1931 was given to honor Monsignor Arthur J. Scanlan, a steadfast friend of the college.

In a letter dated November 30, 1931, Mother Mary Aloysia expressed her appreciation to Emile Perrot, the architect, for the splendid work accomplished. She said in part -- *"The completion of the new Preston Hall at Good Counsel College provides me with a very special occasion for performing a pleasurable duty, namely, that of expressing my deep feelings of gratitude and joy for the splendid work which you, as the architect, have accomplished.*

Beautifully situated and artistically designed, Preston Hall is a worthy structure about which future developments will blend harmoniously and find their model for a unified effect of chaste dignity and classic beauty."

The construction of this first college building set the standard of excellence for the many other structures that were to follow in the years ahead.

The joy experienced at the successful completion of Preston Hall was soon dampened when it was discovered that certain defects resulting in damage to the structure necessitated extensive repairs on the roof and walls both outside and inside. After a long law suit, a settlement of $15,000 was granted to repair the damage.

Year after year Preston Hall welcomed an ever increasing number of students who made this their home for four years. The girls came to love and cherish this dwelling with all its memories. Their appreciation was well stated by one of its later occupants.

Mary Elizabeth Conway, a chemistry major who graduated cum laude with the Class of 1950, expressed it well when she wrote the poem "Preston Hall" which appeared in The Prestonian, May 1949:

Preston Hall

Rising from the trees and shrubs
    and towering over all,
Tall and graceful, there it stands,
    Our pride, our Preston Hall.
Monument to one long dead
    It proudly stands, and ever seems
To realize its high intent
    A symbol of his dreams.
A home, away from home, for us
    We've grown to love it well,
And could a building only speak,
    What stories it could tell.
We may know its halls and rooms
    And stairs and every nook
But hasn't it had longer time
    Within our lives to look?
How many girls have called it home!
    How many has it seen
Come bring their youth and happiness
    To the college of their Queen!
And when four years have sped away
    The girls, each one and all
Bid sad farewell to rooms that were
    Their homes in Preston Hall.

By Mary Elizabeth Conway, Class of 1950

Williams Property

As early as January 1947, Mother Mary Aloysia began to think about purchasing the Williams property adjoining the College campus at the northwest end. She asked Mr. Gerety to look into the matter, but the land was not for sale at this time. The enrollment in the College continued to increase and the curriculum to expand, and by 1946 a peak enrollment necessitated looking for more classroom space. Since the time was not yet ripe for building, new quarters had to be found. The most feasible plan seemed to be to discontinue the resident students in the Academy and to take over St. Stanislaus House, which had been serving as their dormitory.

The house was completely renovated and equipped to accommodate the commercial and art departments of the College. Classroom space, so sorely needed was now provided until a more substantial classroom facility could be built.

Mother Mary Aloysia announced that the name of the building was to be changed from St. Stanislaus House to Marietta Hall, in memory of Dr. Marietta Riley, a professor of Fordham University, who spent herself in preparing the Sisters for their degrees in the early days before the establishment of the College.

However, a few years later, on November 18, 1949, the owner, Mr. David L. Williams informed Mother Mary Aloysia that the property was now being offered for sale for the price of $50,000. Mr. Gerety felt that we could get a better price for this two-acre piece of land.

Mother Mary Aloysia consulted the Archdiocese, explaining the desirability of having this property for the future expansion of the College. On Christmas Day 1949, Mother Mary Aloysia announced the good news that we had received permission to purchase the Williams property. The contract was signed on December 27, 1949. Mr. Williams agreed to sell his premises for $45,000. A first payment of $10,000 was made for the convenience of the owner, the balance to be paid over a period of five years. The final papers for the transfer of the Williams property were signed on February 16, 1950, and the Sisters of the Divine Compassion took possession.

When Reverend Mother went over to inspect the house and land, she found ten rooms in the house all in good condition, and a five room apartment over the garage. The grounds were also in good order.

At this time the Sisters of the Divine Compassion also owned a lovely piece of property at 148 North Broadway, which covered about 1.87 acres with a house and garage, a gift of benefactor Frank L. Lambrecht, who died on November 5, 1935. The Sisters took possession of the house and land on August 19, 1936. It was used for several years as a vacation house for the Sisters.

In order to obtain funds with which to purchase the Williams and Winterroth lands adjacent to the College, it was unanimously agreed by the Board of Trustees of the Sisters of the Divine Compassion to sell the Lambrecht property.

In July 1952, the Community was offered $20,000 for the estate. The Chancery Office, however, informed us that the property at 148 North Broadway was worth much more and to hold on to it for the present. Then on January 17, 1953, the Lambrecht estate was sold for $28,000 to the Archdiocese of New York.

Due to the foresight of Mother Mary Aloysia, Good Counsel College obtained its first opening on Crane Avenue with the purchase of a vacant lot adjacent to the Williams property. This plot had been sold to Anna B. Winterroth on July 5, 1923 by Julia C. Mullen, who was in possession of the land on the corners of North Broadway and Crane Avenue since 1907. With Mr. John B. J. Gerety's assistance, on June 29, 1951, Anna B. Winterroth sold her land with 100 feet frontage on Crane Avenue and 50 feet deep to the Sisters of Divine Compassion for the sum of $2,200.

The opening up of Crane Avenue for public use goes back to the year 1905, when Laura C. Crane and Elijah E. Miller each owned tracts of land facing North Broadway; a foot path between the two properties was known as Miller Place. They agreed to lay out a street along the boundary line between their two plots, running easterly from North Broadway. Each contributed 25 feet of land to make a road 50 feet wide, which was named Crane Avenue. The extensive farm lands of the adjacent estates, having been divided into building lots, were sold, and lovely new homes began to appear on Crane Avenue.

The Williams and Winterroth lands both have the same history as the Tilford and Leeney estates, being formerly the property of Daniel Horton. When in 1846 Leonard Miller became the owner of a 30-acre farm, extending a good distance up North Broadway to what is now the Red Cross Station at 106 North Broadway, and back to the east to the present Cross Westchester Parkway, he added two wings to the original Colonial house which had been built around 1800. The Miller family lived in this old historic homestead for many years. On the death of Leonard Miller, on May 31, 1884, the large farm was divided among his three sons. Elijah retained the old homestead and the barns, George Miller taking the southern part of the farm, where he built his house at 78 North Broadway (this later became the Leeney property). Frank M. Miller was allotted the vacant farmland to the north of what is now Crane Avenue.

Frank Miller and Col. Alexander B. Crane opened up Crane Avenue, when Frank Miller decided to break up his farm into building lots.

Elijah Miller then sold the old historic mansion to Alice B. Williams in April 1901. David L. Williams came into its possession on May 17, 1927. Here he lived on this old historic site with his growing family for many years. The Williams family traditions were Southern. He lived in great elegance in his home at 80 North Broadway. At one time there were five house servants as well as a gardener and a coachman. He owned fine horses and shining buggies which were sheltered in the great barns at the back. At the time of the sale of his property in 1950 to the Sisters of the Divine Compassion, Mr. Williams was a retired magazine publisher.

One of the first acts of Mother Mary Dolores was the opening of the kindergarten in September 1951, which she placed in the charge of Margaret O'Brien, a Good Counsel alumna of the class of 1943. Margaret O'Brien had received special training in the education of young children at Columbia University.

The lovely colonial house with its many rooms and wide veranda made an ideal setting for the education of young children. Four-year-old Victoria Ann Fechtman, daughter of Mr. and Mrs. Louis Fechtman and niece of Sister Mary Leona Fechtman has the distinction of being the first child to register for the new kindergarten.

Under the direction of Mother Mary Dolores renovation began on the great barn and garage. The reconstruction was in the hands of John Jensen. All the work was completed in the spring of 1956 and ready for the blessing which took place on June 4 by Bishop James E. Kearney who installed the crucifix in the entrance, the gift of Leo I. Kearney.

The Biology department moved into the new two story structure in September 1956. An attractive foyer was added to the first floor containing the general biology lab, a combination bacteriology and genetics lab, along with rooms for storage of animals and equipment. The second floor housed the histology and comparative anatomy labs, and a dark room for photography. A department library and offices were also included in the facilities.

Friends of the college and alumnae contributed generously in response to an appeal for funds to help cover the cost of the renovation. Among the outstanding gifts may be mentioned that of Elizabeth Kennedy, who gave the comparative anatomy lab and that of Lorraine Cullo Marra, who supplied the furnishings for the foyer. The list of other donors is long and contains the names of alumnae, students, and friends, who will always be held in grateful remembrance.

When all was settled and the deal closed, Mother Mary Aloysia expressed her appreciation for the splendid work accomplished by Mr. John B. J. Gerety who labored so diligently to secure the Williams property for the College. In a letter dated February 18, 1950, she wrote:

"I file this report with great pleasure and I want to assure you how happy we are, that, after waiting for so many years to possess this property (so much needed for the expansion of the college in the future), the matter is at last closed, and that you, our trusted, legal advisor and sincere personal friend, were the one to bring about the final settlement, -- and untold happiness to the Community!"

Today, on this old farmland, now stand two very imposing buildings -- the beautiful Hayes Library, completed in 1965, and a student dormitory. The old Colonial homestead was demolished in 1967 to make way for the new six story residence to be called Dannat Hall -- a fitting and more lasting memorial to Mother Mary Veronica Dannat Starr, completed in 1968.

CHAPTER FOUR

DEVELOPMENT OF THE CAMPUS CONTINUED

Aloysia Hall

The next project to be undertaken was a lecture hall to accommodate the growing student body. The rooms in Good Counsel Convent, occupied by the college since its foundation in 1923, had to be reclaimed by the Community to provide space for the increasing number of vocations.

Prior to the fund-raising campaign, Community Counseling Services conducted a survey to determine the College's building needs and the possible sources for obtaining funds, with campaign headquarters in Marietta Hall under Edwin F. Oswald as Director. The results of the survey showed a fruitful source for income among the alumnae, Fathers' Club, Ladies Guild, friends and relatives of the Sisters, and the schools conducted by the Religious of the Divine Compassion, and the Building Campaign was set in motion.

In order to defray the cost of the new venture, a gigantic Building Fund Campaign was launched in 1957 with an appeal to alumnae and friends of the College and Community. His Eminence Francis Cardinal Spellman agreed to lead the campaign as Honorary Chairman. Mother Mary Dolores served as Campaign Moderator. A minimum goal of $225,000 was set to help defray the cost of erecting a $700,000 college classroom building, and for extensive renovation at the Motherhouse. The new college building was to be named Aloysia Hall in memory of Mother Mary Aloysia R.D.C., founder and first President of Good Counsel College, who had died on December 29, 1953.

The week of October 21, 1957 marked the official opening of the alumnae drive. Karolyn Melchinger Robinson '41 was named General Chairman with Virginia T. Hyland '29 and Lorraine Cullo Marra '39 as her associates. Members of the Fathers Club, Leo Carey, Raymond Kniphuisen, Martin M. Moran and Stanley Sicinski also assisted as workers. The Guild of Our Lady of Good Counsel and parents of the College and Academy students cooperated as volunteer workers.

By November 1957, a total of $135,075 was realized. By December, the figure rose to $292,000 and continued mounting up to $339,000, then to $350,000. Work on the construction of Aloysia Hall was ready to begin. The site chosen for the new building was set back to the east of Preston Hall, on the ground occupied by the tennis and basketball courts. Soundings had been made for rock early in November, with satisfactory results.

All was ready for the ceremony of ground-breaking which took place on Sunday, January 19, 1958, a sunny but icy windy afternoon. From a temporary platform erected for the occasion, Bishop Edward V. Dargin spoke to the assembled crowd of faculty, students and friends of the College and Community, emphasizing the importance of the expansion program of the Sisters to meet the demands made upon them by the fast-growing community of Westchester County. After the site was blessed, the sod was turned over in succession by His Excellency, Bishop V. Dargin; Mother Mary Ethelburge, Superior General; Mother Mary Dolores, President of the College; Dr. Leo I. Kearney, K.M., representing the faculty; Madeline Dinger Schaeffer, President of the Alumnae; Karolyn Melchinger Robinson, Chairman of the Drive; and Eleanor Gilbertie, President of the Student Council, representing the students.

Father Thomas P. Cahill gave the main address. He said in part:

"This is indeed an historic occasion -- the breaking of the ground to make way for the foundation that will support the structure of the future Aloysia Hall. Today is historic because today the vision of a dream takes on the realization of reality. The hoped-for becomes the actual and symbolism invades the real order. For the scar which we inflict upon this good earth, in the ground-breaking ceremony, recalls the work, the labor and the sacrifices that have led up to this happy moment. -- Today we are laying the foundation of a noble building dedicated to the pursuit of Christian learning. ---

The name of the building to take shape here and indeed the inspiration of this moment is that of a great and sainted lady, Mother Mary Aloysia, who is now enjoying the merited reward of an inspired and dedicated life. -- Her persevering vision and her undaunted courage set the scene for what is transpiring here. -- She planned and prayed and planted and now others must reap the harvest. Mother Ethelburge, Superior of the Sisters of the Divine Compassion and Mother Dolores, the President of Good Counsel College, hold the sacred charge to bring to fulfillment the dream of this pioneer; to meet effectively the challenge of present circumstances. -- The road ahead may be strewn with difficulties but of the outcome there can be no doubt; Our Lady shall lead the way and that way leads to success."

Present on the platform with Bishop Edward V. Dargin and the speaker were a number of priests interested in the progress and advancement of the College, among them were Father Joseph Clune of Hawthorne; Father Charles Deane, S.J., Fordham University; Father Leonard DiFalco of Harrison; Monsignor Joseph Krug of St. Bernard's in White Plains; and Father William Ludessi, C.P.S. of Mount Carmel in White Plains.

One week after the official ground-breaking, the work of construction began on Aloysia Hall. The project was in the hands of George Hils Ferrenz, architect of the firm of Ferrenz and Taylor, who designed the building, and William A. Berbusse Jr., General Contractor, in charge of construction. John B. Foster took care of the plumbing.

With the coming of the pleasant spring weather, the work began in earnest and progressed rapidly. By the end of the summer the exterior of the building was completed.

Tuesday, October 7, 1958, the feast of the Holy Rosary, was the day chosen for the laying of the cornerstone of the nearly completed building. The day began with a High Mass celebrated by Monsignor John J. Hartigan in honor of the feast day of Mother Mary Dolores, President of the College. Following the Missa Cantata sung by the students, all went in procession to Aloysia Hall. Here in the presence of trustees, faculty, students in academic attire, alumnae, religious and friends, Monsignor Hartigan, assisted by Father Cahill, blessed the limestone slab inscribed 1958, and placed it in the southwest corner of the building beneath the eight-foot stone statue of Our Lady of Good Counsel.

The silver trowel used in the ceremony was the same used on several former occasions, the first being June 25, 1895 when Archbishop Michael Augustine Corrigan laid the cornerstone for the Chapel of the Divine Compassion, the other May 26, 1931, as Monsignor Patrick N. Breslin placed the cornerstone for Preston Hall. Various documents in a metal box were inserted in the cornerstone, including medals and pictures of Our Lady of Good Counsel, photographs of Pope Pius XII, Cardinal Spellman, the Founders Monsignor Thomas S. Preston, Mother Mary Veronica and Mother Mary Aloysia, along with the names of the trustees of the College, the Board of Advisors, and a list of the names of all those who had contributed to the development fund.

Among the clergy present at the ceremony with Monsignor Hartigan were Monsignor Joseph Krug, Monsignor John T. Halpin, Father Thomas Cahill and Father William Ludessi, C.P.S. Happy to witness the results of their labors, the architect George H. Ferrenz, William A. Berbusse, the builder, and John B. Foster were also present for the occasion.

At the close of the ceremony, a luncheon was served in the Administration Building for the clergy and special guests, and a tea in Preston Hall for the students and friends.

A few days after the joy and jubilation of the ceremony, all were saddened by the news of the death of Our Holy Father, Pope Pius XII, who went to his reward on October 9, 1958.

Work continued on the building through the fall so that by Thanksgiving all was ready for occupancy. Before leaving for the holiday, the students were given a preview of the building. Since the furniture had not yet arrived, each one was asked to carry a chair across the campus so that the rooms would be ready for classes on December 3rd when faculty and students would take possession of Aloysia Hall. Anxious to get a look at the new building, the students readily complied with the request. Passersby could see a long line of girls, stretching across the campus, each carrying a chair, with sparkling eyes and happy hearts as they moved into the new and spacious Aloysia Hall.

All were delighted with what they saw in the four-story brick and stone structure: eighteen classrooms, administration offices, faculty rooms, audio-visual theater, language laboratory, with a cafeteria, locker room and book store located on the ground floor.

To commemorate the event, a special issue of The Prestonian was prepared, outlining the story of Aloysia Hall, and listing the names of the alumnae and friends who so generously supported the Building Fund Campaign.

The following letter was sent to the alumnae:

November 1958

Dear Alumna:

The Thanksgiving season is a most appropriate time for us to express again our gratitude to you for the sacrifice you have made to make Aloysia Hall a reality. The building, dedicated to the memory of Mother Mary Aloysia, foundress and first president of the college, will always stand as a tribute to the loyalty, devotion and generosity of her daughters to their Alma Mater.

Knowing your great interest in all that has been done, we have prepared this special issue of The Prestonian and have recorded the highlights in the story of Aloysia Hall for you. We are moving into the building during the Thanksgiving holidays and shall have an alumnae open house in the near future.

Your enthusiastic participation in the project has been a source of joy and consolation to us, revealing as it did the wonderful spirit which animates the alumnae.

May Our Lady of Good Counsel, whose spirit has bound you to each other and to Alma Mater, bless and protect you always.

Gratefully in Our Lady
Mother M. Dolores

The opening of Aloysia Hall was a great satisfaction and joy to all, especially to those who were to use it. Mother Mary Dolores received many expressions of appreciation; among them we mention a few:

"Aloysia Hall is a gem on Good Counsel grounds. It is a splendid and worthy memorial to our dear Mother M. Aloysia. To you belongs the glory of having it executed. May you enjoy it all your days." ...Sister Mary de Sales

"Although we all realize that Aloysia Hall memorializes that grand Lady, the Foundress of Good Counsel College. However -- I think it is also a great memorial to your wisdom, taste and planning ability.

Congratulations on your achievement!" ...Leo I. Kearney

On December 8, 1958, Mr. John B. Gerety sent the following letter:
"My dear Mother Dolores:

I am sorry I did not see you last Wednesday to extend to you personally my congratulations on the opening of Aloysia Hall. We, of the college, know that you are entitled to all the credit for its planning and construction and we are extremely happy and proud of the results of your labors.

I do not think that any college has a better conceived building for the purposes for which it is meant to serve. No detail for usefulness, convenience and comfort has been overlooked and the decorations, furnishings and equipment are beautiful.

All the members of the faculty are inspired by have such a fine place in which to put forth their efforts.

Now that the building has been completed, I hope that you will have been relieved from some of the pressure under which you have been working for many months. ---

Sincerely,
(signed) John B.J. Gerety

The sisters also had their turn to visit the new building. During the Christmas holidays all were invited to an Open House on Monday, December 29, 1958. Bishop James E. Kearney was present for the occasion and offered Mass at 10:00 a.m. in the audio-visual room, in memory of Mother Mary Aloysia.

The promised open-house for the alumnae took place on Sunday, February 22, 1959. A large number attended with representatives from the five regional chapters. Bishop Kearney, who had been present at the Home Coming Report on November 19, 1957, when the alumnae surpassed their goal of $225,000, came to congratulate the alumnae again on their achievement.

The formal dedication of Aloysia Hall took place on Sunday, April 26, 1959, the feast of Our Lady of Good Counsel. The day dawned with lowering skies and a threat of rain; however by 3:30 p.m., the sun broke through the clouds with the promise of a pleasant afternoon for the large crowd that had gathered to witness the ceremony of the dedication of Aloysia Hall "*to the glory of God and the education of women*".

The Catholic News, on Saturday, May 9, 1959, carried the following story written by J.E. Pridday, who noted in part:

"His Eminence Francis Cardinal Spellman, Archbishop of New York, presided at a Solemn Blessing and Dedication of Aloysia Hall, the new administration building at Good Counsel College in White Plains, on Sunday, April 26, in ceremonies which were attended by more than 3,500 students, faculty, members of the community, alumnae, parents, friends, local civic leaders, priests and Sisters. Aloysia Hall was erected in the memory of Mother Mary Aloysia, founder and president of the college for 25 years, which is staffed by the Sisters of the Divine Compassion.

The Rt. Rev. Msgr. John J. Voight, Ed.D., secretary for education for the Archdiocese of New York, was the principal speaker at the dedication.

His Eminence was greeted by Mother Mary Dolores, president of the college, Rev. Mother Mary Ethelburge, Superior General of the Sisters of the Divine Compassion of the Motherhouse and Convent in White Plains, and the Rt. Rev. Msgr. John J. Hartigan, honorary president of the College of Good Counsel and pastor of St. John the Evangelist Church of White Plains. Before bestowing his blessing upon the exterior of the new hall, Cardinal Spellman invoked the special blessings and guidance of the Holy Spirit upon the teachers and students who would give and receive learning in the new building. He then blessed the exterior facade. His Eminence reentered Aloysia Hall and blessed each room and office before blessing and erecting the dedicatory cross in the main lobby.

His Eminence was assisted by Rt. Rev. Msgr. Thomas A. Donnellan, J.C.D., Chancellor of the Archdiocese and the Rt. Rev. Msgr. John T. Halpin, Professor of Philosophy at Good Counsel College and paster of St. Frances De Chantal Church in the Bronx. Rt. Rev. Msgr. John J. Hartigan was the assistant priest in the ceremony.

Speaking for the student body of the college, Carol Landers, President of the Student Council, thanked His Eminence for

honoring the occasion with his presence. She then presented the
spiritual bouquet and a bouquet of roses from the students.

    The Glee Club of Good Counsel College under the direction
of Frederic Joslyn presented selections during the dedications and
during the ceremonies in the auditorium. Ellen Greene, pianist,
and Charles Touchette, organist, were the accompanists during the
ceremonies.

    The guests were invited to attend a buffet supper served in
Preston Hall."

During the ceremonies, a temporary public address system was set up. The College Glee Club, conducted by Frederic Joslyn, sang the responses to the Cardinal's invocations and other selected hymns, heard across the campus. Among the guests of honor present for the occasion were Dr. Carroll Johnson, Superintendent of Schools in White Plains, Everett Penny of the State Board of Regents and William A. Berbusse, Builder.

Following the exercise, supper was served in the administration building for the clergy and special guests, in Preston Hall for faculty and friends. The students presided over an open house tea in the new cafeteria in Aloysia Hall.

Aloysia Hall stands today a constant reminder of her who gave it inspiration, and to all who so generously contributed to make the building possible, a fitting memorial to her name. On the wall in the main Hall hangs a portrait of Mother Mary Aloysia, Founder and first President of Good Counsel College, 1923-1948; the oil painting is the work of Sister Mary Juliana Danahy.

Our Lady of the Thruway

    The feast of the Holy Rosary in 1959 saw the erection of the statue of Our Lady of the Thruway on a high cliff overlooking the Cross Westchester Expressway. After removing the scaffolding from the 30-foot Madonna resting on a 15-foot stone pedestal, all was in readiness for the dedication which took place on Sunday, October 11.

    A large crowd of nearly 500 people gathered for the occasion on a lovely autumn afternoon. Bishop Edward J. Dargin, Auxiliary Bishop of New York blessed the statue and paid tribute to August F. Stavarsky for his efforts on behalf of the shrine. Among those present for the ceremony were members of the Father William A. Dunphy Council of the Knights of Columbus, who donated the shrine, County Executive

Edwin Michaelian and county and local officials, along with members of the clergy, friends and Sisters of the Divine Compassion.

The ceremony held this day was the culmination of a project many months in preparation. The huge statue of Our Lady of Fatima is the work of the American artist, Lumen Martin Winter of New Rochelle. It was fashioned of the best bronze in Pistoia, a small town near Florence, Italy, where Mr. Winter has his studio. The 30-foot statue weighing 6½ tons was transported by railroad freight car to Vatican City. Because of its gigantic size, it had to be brought in through the little-used rail gate of the Holy Office. Here in the Vatican gardens it was blessed by Pope John XXIII on July 14, 1959. Among those present for the ceremony were the sculptor, Lumen Martin Winter; Bishop Albert F. Cousineau C.S.C., of Haiti, who made the presentation to the Holy Father; Very Rev. Christopher J. O'Toole C.S.C., Superior General of the Holy Cross Congregation; Brother Theophane Schmitt C.S.C.; Rev. Bede Mac-Eachen S.A., of Graymoor; and Rev. Austin McKitteridge S.A., Director of the Graymoor Press. The William A. Dunphy Council of the Knights of Columbus of Westchester County, who sponsored the project, was represented by J. Arthur McNamara, Grand Knight, and August Stavarsky, President of the Madonna of Fatima Committee of New York, the principal organizer for the shrine. Mr. Edmund Burke, attorney for the artist, was also present with his wife. Assisting the Holy Father Pope John XXIII were members of the papal court, Msgr. Nasalli Rocco, Maestro di Camera, and Msgr. Angelo Dell Acqua of the Vatican Secretariat of State.

After the blessing, the statue was removed from the Vatican gardens and made ready for shipment to the United States. It started on its long journey from Italy to White Plains where it was to rest in its place of honor on the hillside at the northeast end of the campus, overlooking the Cross Westchester Expressway. Upon its arrival at Tarrytown, it was transported by truck to White Plains. Along the way it received an accolade of a special police escort and a motorcade of Knights of Columbus. When it arrived at Good Counsel, the arch over the gateway had to be removed in order to admit the huge crate.

The then-Vice President, Richard M. Nixon, hearing of the project, sent the following telegram to Monsignor John J. Hartigan, honorary president of the College:

> *"I am proud to join with my fellow Americans in congratulating you and your associates for your devoted work in planning the erection of the holy statue of the Virgin Mary that is to overlook the Cross Westchester Expressway in White Plains. I have been told of its magnificence and splendor and I know it will be a source of*

great spiritual comfort and satisfaction to all those who shared in making it possible. With every good wish,"

Sincerely,

Richard Nixon

The estimated cost of the entire project was well over $100,000. This included the $85,000 cost of the statue, transportation, erection, landscaping, etc. The project was financed by friends of the Dunphy Council of the Knights of Columbus. Funds were raised by private subscription.

A few months after the erection of the statue, the largest Madonna in the world, marble Stations of the Cross were added to complete the shrine. The Stations, designed by Lumen Martin Winter and executed by Bernard D. Zukermann in white Ravocione marble, were set on a winding path in the foreground of the Statue. Each Station, with its almost life-size figures, was placed on a four-foot pedestal made of native Westchester granite.

For 17 years Our Lady of the Thruway kept her vigil over the rushing motorists who sped over the road far below her. But the exigencies of the times brought about a change. When Good Counsel College, then known as the College of White Plains, merged with Pace University on July 15, 1975, the secularized college no longer seemed an appropriate setting for the shrine, and since parking space was desperately needed, the Sisters looked into the possibility of transferring it to a site on their own property. Since the cost of $20,000 was prohibitive, they found a new home for her at the Marion Shrine, conducted by the Don Bosco Salesian Fathers, in West Haverstraw. On August 21, 1976, the Lady was dethroned and set on a trailer for her last journey along the highway she had watched over for 17 years. She now stands majestic, in a lovely setting overlooking the beautiful Hudson Valley of New York.

The once quiet prayerful spot at the east end of the campus is now a busy bustling parking lot.

The New Wing to the Convent

In 1959, the Sisters took another step in the continuing expansion and development at Good Counsel, the erection of a new wing for the convent. The increasing number of candidates seeking admission to the community had exhausted the available space. From 1948 and on through the fifties 126 young women joined the community; in 1959 there were 36 novices overcrowding the rooms in the novitiate.

The completion of Aloysia Hall in 1958 had restored to the community the east and south wings of the convent which had been occupied by the College since its foundation in 1923. But even this was not sufficient to meet the needs of the growing community. The chapel, refectory and sleeping quarters were no longer adequate to accommodate the large number of sisters residing at the Motherhouse. To relieve the situation, plans were drawn up for a $640,000 addition to the convent, and an application for the building permit was approved by the City of White Plains. Contracts were awarded to the William A. Berbusse Construction Company and to the architect George H. Ferrenz.

The project was designed in consultation with Mother Mary Ethelburge, Superior of the Congregation, and the Archdiocesan Building Commission. The four story new wing attached to the east side of the existing convent would contain a chapel with a capacity of 160, an infirmary, refectory, kitchen, pantry and sleeping accommodations for 61 Sisters.

The Ground-Breaking Ceremony took place on Thursday, December 3, 1959. The Most Reverend Edward V. Dargin, Auxiliary Bishop of New York presided. After he blessed the site, sod was turned over by Bishop Dargin, Monsignor John J. Hartigan, Monsignor John T. Halpin, Mother Mary Ethelburge and members of her Council, Sister Mary Gonzaga, Sister Mary Grace and Sister Mary Benedicta. Others present at the ceremony included Father William Ludessi and Father Thomas Cahill.

Work began in earnest and continued rapidly over the year. In the early spring of 1961 the building was ready for occupancy.

Prior to moving into their new home, the Sisters attended a Mass offered for the first time in the new chapel by Bishop James E. Kearney on Tuesday, March 14, 1961. In the afternoon, His Excellency, assisted by Father Thomas P. Cahill, erected the beautiful handcarved Stations, the gift of the college students.

The students also had their special day at Open House on Thursday, March 16. They freely toured the building, admiring the light pastel-painted cells, simply and tastefully furnished, the infirmary adjacent to the lovely chapel, the refectory kitchen and other appointments.

On the feast of St. Patrick, March 17, 1961, the Sisters took possession of their new and spacious quarters amid great fun and rejoicing. All were invited to an Open House that they might inspect the work to which they had so generously contributed.

The laying of the Cornerstone followed rapidly, on the feast of Our Lady of Good Counsel, April 26, 1961. Again Bishop Dargin presided at the ceremony. The day, always very special at Good Counsel, began with the celebration of a High Mass offered by Monsignor John J. Hartigan and attended by faculty, students, and friends. A very fine concert followed in the College auditorium at 1:30 p.m., featuring Stephan Hero, the internationally known violinist. The cornerstone ceremony began in the new chapel at 3:30 p.m. with the Sisters' choir singing the "Veni Creator". Then the Sisters, followed by the Bishop and priests, went in procession outside, singing the hymn to Our Lady of Good Counsel. At the site, Monsignor Halpin welcomed the Bishop, the faculty, students and friends. His Excellency Bishop Edward V. Dargin, assisted by Father William Ludessi, college chaplain, then blessed the stone before setting it in place. Both the architect George H. Ferrenz and the builder William Berbusse Jr. were present at the ceremony. The day's celebration concluded with a formal tea in Preston Hall at 4:00 p.m. for the faculty and students.

The solemn blessing and dedication of the new east wing of the convent took place on Sunday, May 21, 1961. Cardinal Spellman had been invited to officiate at the ceremony but was unable to be present as he was hospitalized at the time. Instead he sent His Excellency the Most Reverend John J. Maguire, Vicar General of the Archdiocese, to represent him. The ceremony opened with a procession to the Church for the introductory prayers. Bishop Maguire was escorted in procession by Monsignor Hartigan, Monsignor Eugene A. Murtha, and Monsignor Joseph Krug, Deacons of Honor. Monsignor John M. Brew, Secretary to His Excellency, was Master of Ceremonies. Then followed the blessing of the exterior and interior of the new wing, the main feature of which was the erection of the dedication Crucifix in the lobby. All then returned to the Church where Monsignor Hartigan gave the address of welcome. The main dedicatory address was delivered by Monsignor Thomas A. Donnellan, Chancellor of the Archdiocese, who gave a brief account of the works of the Sisters, commenting on the rapid growth of the Community which made the building of the new wing imperative. He then thanked all those who had so generously contributed funds which made the building possible.

The ceremonies ended with Solemn Benediction of the Blessed Sacrament, celebrated by Monsignor Hartigan, with Father Cahill as Deacon and Father Eugene F. Richard as Sub-deacon. The musical program during the blessing and dedication was provided by the Choir of the Sisters under the direction of Choirmaster Paul Shields. A sound system was installed for the occasion so that the music could be heard throughout the building during the ceremony. After the dedication, dinner was served to special guests in the convent dining room and living room by caterers Thomas Fox & Sons, Inc.

At the time of the dedication of the new wing, there were 219 Sisters in the Community. By 1962 the number had increased to 237 with nearly half of them residing at the Mother House at Good Counsel. Since the four floors of the new wing with accommodations for 61 Sisters were no longer adequate, work was resumed on the fifth floor to add 19 rooms, bringing the total in the new wing up to 80. The work was completed and ready for the blessing on March 25, 1963.

His Excellency the Most Reverend John J. Maguire, Vicar General of the Archdiocese of New York again presided. The ceremonies began with a procession to the convent chapel. After the prayers in the Chapel, all proceeded outdoors where Bishop Maguire, accompanied by Monsignor John M. Brew, Master of Ceremonies, blessed the Cross, newly erected on the exterior wall facing east. This outdoor Cross on the new wing is the gift of Mr. and Mrs. George Hils Ferrenz. His Excellency, followed by the procession of the clergy, then moved to the completed fifth floor to conclude the blessing.

Returning to the Church, Monsignor Thomas A. Donnellan delivered the address, explaining the significance of the ceremonies to a large audience of Sisters, students and friends of the Community. The exercises of the day ended with Solemn Benediction of the Blessed Sacrament offered by Bishop Maguire assisted by Father Thomas Cahill, Deacon, and Father Austin Vaughan, Sub-Deacon. The music was provided by the Choir, under the direction of Paul Shields.

Through the generosity of friends of the Community, including alumnae and students of the College and the Academy and relatives of the Sisters, they were in possession of their new home with a beautiful chapel, infirmary, refectory, kitchen and private rooms for 80 Sisters.

One special feature of the new wing is the Founders' Room, donated by His Excellency Bishop James E. Kearney. This room adjacent to the Chapel contains the archives and mementos of the Founders of the Community, Monsignor Thomas S. Preston and Mother Mary Veronica. Across from the Founders' Room is the Founders' Alcove, donated by Veronica and Virginia T. Hyland, which serves as a library for the many published and unpublished works of Monsignor Preston.

Crowning the building is a bright and pleasant solarium with a roof patio, with furnishings donated in memory of Mrs. William Henchey. Each room in the new wing bears a plaque on the door with the names of the donors who will always be held in prayerful and grateful remembrance.

Madonna Library and the Leo I. Kearney Sports Building

The next major additions to the Campus as a result of the Building Fund were a new library and a new sports building.

On a beautiful day in August a double ceremony was enacted on the campus of Good Counsel College. On August 6, 1963, the Feast of the Transfiguration of Our Lord, ground was broken for the two new buildings. The ceremonies began at 11:30 a.m. in the Chapel. After singing the "Veni Creator", the procession was formed and led by the clergy and the Sisters of the Divine Compassion, moved to the site chosen for the erection of the Leo I. Kearney Sports Building at the southeast end of the campus, adjoining the athletic field and overlooking the Cross-Westchester Expressway.

The Most Reverend John J. Maguire, Vicar' General of the Archdiocese of New York, blessed the ground, followed by the symbolic turning of the sod by each of the following: His Excellency Bishop Maguire; Monsignor Leonard J. Hunt, Chairman of the Archdiocesan Building Commission; Mother Mary Ethelburge, Superior General of the Sisters of the Divine Compassion; Mother Mary Dolores, President of the College; Mr. George Hils Ferrenz, Architect; Mr. Marcello Mezzullo, Builder.

The first part of the ceremony ended, the procession formed again and wended its way, singing hymns, to the site chosen for the new library at the northwest end of the campus, adjacent to Crane Avenue, on a spot between Aloysia Hall and Preston Hall. Here a similar ceremony was enacted, the blessing of the ground and the turning of the sod. The exercise ended with the hymn to Our Lady of Good Counsel.

Among those present at the groundbreaking ceremony were the Rt. Reverend Monsignor John M. Brew, Secretary to the Bishop; the Rt. Reverend Monsignor Thomas A. Donnellan, Rector of Saint Joseph's Seminary, Dunwoodie, Yonkers; the Rt. Reverend Monsignor Eugene A. Murtha, Pastor of Our Lady of Sorrows; Rt. Reverend Monsignor Daniel J. Donovan, Pastor of Notre Dame Church, New York City; Very Reverend Monsignor William J. McCormack, Assistant Director for the Society for the Propagation of the Faith; the Very Reverend Monsignor Charles J. McManus, Principal of Archbishop Stepinac High School; Reverend Leonard M. Della Badia, C.P., Pastor of Our Lady of Mount Carmel, White Plains; Reverend Vincent M. Raetz, O.P. Holy Name of Jesus, Valhalla; and the Reverend Daniel V. Flynn of St. Joseph's Seminary, Dunwoodie.

Work began at once on the two buildings and progressed rapidly over the following months at an estimated cost of $1,050,000. By the fall of 1964 all was in readiness for the laying of the cornerstones. Bishop James E. Kearney accepted the invitation to conduct the ceremony which took place on Wednesday, November 11, 1964.

Laying of the Cornerstones

The day began with the Holy Sacrifice of the Mass at 10:50 a.m., attended by faculty and students in academic attire. Following the Mass, all marched in procession to Madonna Library, singing hymns on the way. The cornerstone engraved with a monogram of Mary and the year 1963 was blessed by Bishop Kearney and set in place at the southeast corner of the building. Monsignor John J. Hartigan assisted the Bishop. All joined in the hymn to Our Lady of Good Counsel. The procession formed again and proceeded to the Leo I. Kearney Sports Building. The stone engraved with a cross and the year 1963 was blessed by Bishop James E. Kearney, who set it in place with the assistance of Monsignor Hartigan. Then, taking the trowel, Mrs. Leo I. Kearney added mortar to the stone along with several others, including Mother Mary Dolores, President of the College, and Mr. George Hils Ferrenz, the architect for the two new buildings.

In the presence of faculty, students and a large gathering of friends, Bishop Kearney gave a stirring address. All who witnessed the ceremony were deeply touched and felt honored to be present on this historic occasion which paid tribute to a beloved teacher, Professor Leo I. Kearney. Mrs. Kearney expressed her appreciation in the following words:

"Dear Mother,

It was a dignified, beautiful and heart warming tribute you so graciously arranged for Leo. I have stored every moment of it for his benefit tomorrow.

Thank you sincerely, Mona Kearney"

Blessing & Dedication

The climax came on Sunday, May 23, 1965, with the blessing and dedication of the two new buildings by His Eminence Francis Cardinal Spellman, Archbishop of New York.

The ceremony began at 3:30 p.m. on a beautiful spring day. The students in academic attire formed an honor guard on the pathway leading to Madonna Library. The Cardinal, accompanied by Monsignor John J. Hartigan, Honorary President of the College, led the procession, followed by dignitaries. Arriving at the Library, the Cardinal blessed the building and erected the dedication crucifix.

The honor guard formed again and the procession continued on its way to the Leo I. Kearney Sports Building. Here a similar ceremony took place, the blessing of the building and the erection of the dedication crucifix in the lobby. All then assembled in the auditorium of the Sports Building for the afternoon program. Monsignor Hartigan gave the address of welcome, followed by the Honorable Hugh Leslie, representing the Mayor of White Plains, Richard S. Hendey, who spoke of the civic interest in the growth and development of Good Counsel College.

The main speech of the day, the dedication address, was delivered by the Most Reverend James E. Kearney, Bishop of Rochester and brother of Leo I. Kearney, in which he defended censorship in "*The area of the soul*". During the course of the program, the Glee Club, under the direction of Dr. Edward J. Dwyer, sang several numbers.

The highlight of the afternoon was the awarding of the Mater Boni Consilii medal to Dr. Leo I. Kearney in appreciation of his many years of faithful and loving service to the College. Cardinal Spellman stepped down from the platform, approached Dr. Kearney seated in a wheel chair, surrounded by his family and many admiring friends, and presented him with the medal, the highest award of the College. All joined in singing the Alma Mater.

Janet O'Shaughnessy, President of the Student Council, then presented the Cardinal with roses and a spiritual bouquet, the gift of the students of the college. The Cardinal expressed his appreciation and before giving the blessing announced the promise of a gift of $10,000 for the purchase of "a few books" for the new library. Before the week was ended a check for the amount was received in the mail.

In appreciation, Sister Mary Alacoque Marshall, librarian, had a special book-plate made to be placed in the books purchased with the money, reminding the students that they were the gift of His Eminence Francis Cardinal Spellman. Sister Mary Immaculate of the College Art Department designed the new bookplate depicting the combined seals of the Cardinal and the College.

Both Madonna Library and the Leo I. Kearney Sports Building remained open to visitors for the rest of the day. Many volunteer students were happy to act as hostesses and guides.

After the program, refreshments were provided for the students in the cafeteria in Aloysia Hall. Dinner was served in Preston Hall for civic dignitaries, faculty administration and invited guests from area colleges and universities. The clergy were entertained at a dinner in the convent.

Among the many good friends who came to Good Counsel to honor the occasion along with Cardinal Spellman and Bishop James E. Kearney, may be mentioned just a few: Monsignor Vincent J. Kenney, Master of Ceremonies; Monsignor Thomas P. Cahill, Chairman of the Committee on arrangements; Monsignor Daniel Flynn; Monsignor John

T. Halpin, Monsignor John J. Hartigan; Monsignor Terence Cooke; Monsignor Leonard Hunt; Monsignor John Carlin; the Honorable Hugh Leslie; the Honorable Ogden Reid; the Honorable Edwin Michaelian; Dr. Carroll Johnson, Superintendent of Schools, White Plains; George Hils Ferrenz, architect; and Mr. Marcello Mezzullo and Mr. Philip Mezzullo, the builders.

Thus ended another red-letter day in the history of Good Counsel College.

Madonna Library

During 1937 and 1938 Good Counsel Library had been moved from the Administration Building to Saint Joseph's House, which from 1895 to 1905 had served as the convent for the Sisters of the Divine Compassion in the pioneer days of the Community in White Plains.

The original library on the first floor in the south wing of the Administration Building had become too small. In 1933 another room in the west wing had been added, but even this extension was not sufficient to shelve the ever-increasing number of books.

On February 20, 1937, Mother Mary Aloysia and Reverend Francis A. Mullin, Director of the library of the Catholic University of America, toured the three floors of the picturesque Victorian mansion, St. Joseph's House. Father Mullin was quick to see how the building could be used to advantage, and plans were drawn up for minor renovations. Work began at once and progressed rapidly; library equipment was purchased and installed.

The second week of February, Catholic Press Week, was chosen for the official opening and blessing, which took place on Tuesday, February 8, 1938. After an address given by Monsignor Patrick N. Breslin in the Administration Building, the students went in procession to St. Joseph's House, singing hymns to Our Lady of Good Counsel and St. Joseph. Monsignor then blessed the new library, after which all returned to the College for refreshments. To emphasize the importance of the occasion, on February 9th the Literary Club presented a Literary Pageant, depicting some of the outstanding characters and authors from ancient Biblical times to the present, and on Thursday, February 10th, Father Mullin returned to the College to give an inspiring lecture on "The Library, the Heart of an Institution".

The library, in St. Joseph's House, with its homelike atmosphere, its well-lighted and tastefully decorated rooms delighted the students, particularly the browsing room which offered a good selection of over

1,000 volumes of the world's best books, while nearly 12,000 volumes filled the general collection.

The blessing of this new library was one of the last public functions at which Monsignor Patrick N. Breslin presided. Monsignor celebrated solemn high Mass on June 6, during commencement week, and God called him to his eternal reward on June 28, 1938.

For 27 years Saint Joseph's House had served as the college library, housing an ever-growing number of volumes. While the House was cozy, home-like and picturesque, there always remained the possibility of a fire in this wooden frame structure. To remedy the situation, Mother Mary Dolores initiated the building of a safe fire-proof place for the precious collection of books.

A $10,000 gift to the college from the W.K. Kellogg Foundation, in 1962, increased the need for more room. The purpose of the grant was twofold -- first to purchase books for the library as a means of improving teacher education programs, and secondly to increase the effectiveness of the service rendered by the library.

The new Madonna Library provided a stack capacity for 100,000 volumes, with carrels for private study throughout the stacks. A spacious, well lighted reading room on the first floor contained reference and resource material for all the academic disciplines. Also on the first floor were offices for the librarians. Seminar rooms, a listening room, a rare book room, and a curriculum library for students preparing to teach, were located on the second floor. Microfilm readers and copying equipment were provided in the circulation area on the first floor. A little theater, with a seating capacity of 225, located on the ground floor, provided facilities for meetings and film viewing.

Book Exodus Day

Tuesday, April 13, 1965, was known as BE Day -- the day we moved the books from St. Joseph's House. Classes were suspended for the day. Both students and faculty took part in the moving, each carrying a load of books carefully numbered for easy location on the empty shelves of the new Madonna Library. The whole arrangement was systematically worked out by Sister Mary Alacoque.

The "big move" began at 9:00 a.m., led by Mother Mary Ethelburge, Superior of the Sisters of the Divine Compassion, who carried a copy of the Bible, and Mother Mary Dolores, President of the College, bearing copies of the Summa Theologica of St. Thomas Aquinas. The students followed carrying armloads of books. Even the tiny tots of the Mary Caroline Montessori school took part, each one happily skipping along with a book in hand.

A holiday spirit pervaded the campus all day while the students trekked back and forth -- some making as many as ten trips. The "Student Shuttle Service" was a great success. Over 60,000 volumes were moved in one day, and the new Madonna Library was opened for routine business.

The library continued to grow in the next few years. Under the College Library Resources Program of Title II of the Higher Education Oct. of 1965, the College was granted $5,000 for the purchase of library materials. Good Counsel College matched the amount of the grant, thus making it possible for the library to obtain needed reference material.

During the summer of 1966, the librarian, Sister Mary Alacoque was awarded a grant to participate in the Foreign Area Study Program, carried on cooperatively by the State Education Department and Columbia University. As a result, $600 worth of books were purchased to form a nucleus of the library's collection of material on African literature.

Two federal grants totalling more than $12,000 were received by the College in 1966, for the library and the Science Department. The College library was also awarded a grant of $5,000 from the Federal government in October 1969. To supply the students with background materials for research in special areas, the money was spent on large block purchases, rather than on single titles.

Library Staff

Sister Mary DeSales Bruno, B.A., M.L.S., was the first librarian at Good Counsel College. She served from the days of its foundation in 1923 for well over 45 years. In 1954 she was given an able assistant, Sister Mary Alacoque Marshall, B.A., M.L.S., who in 1960 succeeded her as head librarian. For 27 years Sister Mary Alacoque served the library faithfully and well until her retirement in August 1981.

The names of those who served the library over the passing years are too numerous to be recorded here. However special mention must be made of two assistant librarians who shared a large part of the activity during these very active years -- Sister Mary Charlotte Brennan, B.A., M.L.S. (1968-1970), and Sister Deborah Flaherty, B.A., M.S. in L.S. who has been serving the library since September 1970.

With the increase in the activities carried on in the library, it was found necessary to hire part-time and temporary clerical help. The best remembered and the longest to remain was Alice Pyne Hyland, a Good Counsel graduate of the class of 1931. This most loyal alumna brought her newly- acquired typing skills, her quiet charm of manner and her genuine sense of humor to enrich the library.

Just before the consolidation of the College of White Plains with Pace University in 1975, the library received a new name. The College Board of Trustees decided to change the name to the Hayes Library in honor of Mother Mary Dolores Hayes, second President of Good Counsel College, and her sister, Sister Mary Basil Hayes, a College official for many years. The change of name was officially announced at Commencement on Friday, May 23, 1975.

The consolidation of The College of White Plains and Pace University became effective July 15, 1975. Dr. Charles H. Dyson, Chairman of the Board of Trustees of the consolidated university, suggested that the pictures of Mother Mary Dolores Hayes and Sister Mary Basil Hayes be painted and hung in the newly named Hayes Library. The two portraits, showing a good likeness, were painted by Sister Mary Juliana Danahy, R.D.C. They were finished and ready for presentation in the spring of 1976.

The Advisory Board of the College of White Plains of Pace University invited all to attend the presentation of the portraits to the Hayes Library on Tuesday, April 27, 1976. The ceremony took place in the main reading room at 4:30 p.m., and was followed by a reception in Preston Hall honoring Mother Mary Dolores Hayes and Sister Mary Basil Hayes.

Dr. Edward J. Mortola, President of Pace University, presented the Dedication History, following the welcoming remarks of Dr. Edward B. Kenny, Vice-President and Dean of the College of White Plains of Pace University. The portraits were then presented to the Hayes Library by Charles H. Dyson, former Chairman of the Board of Trustees of the consolidated university. The two portraits now hang on the wall in the main reading room of the library.

During the academic year 1975-76, the Kellogg Foundation, the library's first corporate benefactor, offered to finance Hayes Library for its introduction to OCLC (Online Computer Library Center) a computerized connection to a national data-base. Hayes Library moved into a new era. Now database searching services, microfilm readers and copying equipment are available for student use. Loan arrangements with other Pace University libraries and the use of the facilities themselves, upon proper identification, provide another source of material. Hayes also enjoys interlibrary loan arrangements with libraries in the vicinity.

Today, Hayes Library, on the White Plains Campus, has a staff of 18 members, 7 professional librarians, 5 of whom are full time, 6 non-professional, 4 full time and 2 part time, along with clerical help of 5 students, all under the able direction of David T.S. Leighton, BA, MA, MSLS, Director.

Mater Dei Hall

By 1964, the increase in the enrollment of resident students crowded Preston Hall with 200 students. Rooms designed in 1931 for two had to accommodate three and sometimes four students. Since the problem needed an immediate solution, Mother Mary Dolores, as President of the College, decided to erect a new temporary dormitory until a larger and more substantial one could be built in the "distant" future.

A handsome two-story, beige brick building, was designed by the New York Architects, Samuel Shiffer Inc., and built by the Mastromarino Construction Company of Haverstraw.

Ground was broken during the late spring of 1964, and the foundation laid. Work progressed rapidly over the summer on this $200,000 dormitory with room for 56 students. Just before the Thanksgiving holiday, 28 students took possession of the new dormitory, located at the northeast end of the campus overlooking the Cross Westchester Expressway and the hills to the east, and named Mater Dei Hall.

On the first and second floors each of the rooms were provided with built-in furniture, dressers and closets and wall-to-wall carpeting. A small reception area was also located on the first floor. In the basement was a large wood-paneled lounge, with the picture windows facing east, a kitchenette, laundry and storage rooms.

Mater Dei Hall was blessed and dedicated on December 8, 1964, the feast of the Immaculate Conception, by the Most Reverend John J. Maguire, Auxiliary Bishop of New York. A solemn procession of members of the clergy, faculty, Sisters of the Divine Compassion, students in cap and gown, invited guests and friends, wended its way over snow-covered grounds down to the northeast end of the campus, where the Bishop blessed the new dormitory and erected the Dedication Crucifix.

After the Ceremony the guests returned to Preston Hall to be entertained by the College Glee Club, followed by a luncheon.

Open house was held at Mater Dei on December 13. The residents of the house played hostess to friends, relatives and members of the faculty as they toured the new dormitory and admired its facilities, home-like setting and modern conveniences.

When the new dormitory Dannat Hall was opened for use in 1969, Mater Dei served as office for the faculty, and later as a dormitory for men. It is now the Graduate Residence.

Dannat Hall

With the two new buildings completed and dedicated, Mother Mary Dolores now turned her attention to the construction of the much-needed dormitory. Preston Hall was filled to capacity; Mater Dei Hall was completely occupied. More space was urgently needed for the increasing number of resident students seeking admission. Mother Mary Dolores envisioned a building that would satisfy the needs of all, at least for the next few years. Then, too, she wanted a fitting and more lasting monument that would commemorate the name of Mother Mary Veronica, the foundress of the Community of the Divine Compassion.

In consultation with the architect, George Hils Ferrenz, plans were drawn up for a million-dollar, six-story residence hall, to be located on the front campus near North Broadway and Crane Avenue. Plans also called for an extension, at the north end of Preston Hall, for a dining room to serve 300 students. It was estimated that the two structures would cost over $1,800,000. Stewart M. Muller of White Plains was engaged as the builder.

Before construction could begin, two important obstacles had to be removed. First, funds were needed to complete this ambitious project, and second, the spot chosen for the new dormitory was already occupied by the old Williams residence, which had served as the kindergarten since 1951.

To solve the money problem it was decided to apply to the Federal Government for a loan. In the fall of 1966, a Federal Housing Loan of $1,330,000 was granted. The house occupying the site for the new dormitory was torn down in the spring, and the way was cleared for construction to begin.

The Ground Breaking ceremony for Dannat Hall took place on Tuesday, March 7, 1967, the Feast of St. Thomas Aquinas. The day began with the Holy Sacrifice of the Mass celebrated by His Excellency John J. Maguire, Coadjutor Archbishop of New York. A most impressive homily was delivered by Rt. Reverend Monsignor John A. Carlin, in which he traced the development of the College and stressed the importance of building on a strong and solid foundation. Dannat Hall, he remarked, was not just another building, but part of the complex called Good Counsel.

After the Mass, students, faculty and guests proceeded to the site, singing the hymn to Our Lady of Good Counsel. Marguerite Shea, '67, President of the Student Government, welcomed all present. The Archbishop then blessed the ground. Disregarding the snow, rain and mud, he turned over the first spade full of earth and was followed in turn by Mother Mary Ethelburge, Superior of the Sisters of the Divine Compassion; Mother Mary Dolores, President of the College; Mr. George Hils Ferrenz, the architect; Mr. Stewart Muller, the builder; and Marguerite Shea, representing the students. The ceremonies ended with the jubilant singing of the Alma Mater.

Work progressed steadily over the spring, summer and winter months. All was completed and ready for occupancy by the fall of 1968, as promised by the builders. Wednesday, October 9, 1968, was chosen for the laying of the cornerstone; the day also marked the twentieth anniversary of Mother Mary Dolores as President of the College. Archbishop John J. Maguire graciously accepted the invitation to preside at the Ceremony, which began at 11:00 a.m. on a beautiful fall day. The procession of students, faculty, religious, guests and clergy formed at Aloysia Hall and wound its way to Dannat Hall. All joined in singing the hymn "Come, Holy Ghost". Standing at the southwest corner of the building, Archbishop Maguire blessed the cornerstone and placed in it a box containing college mementos, among them pictures of administrators and a list of students presently attending the college. The stone was put in place and the Archbishop applied the cement, assisted by the following who added a share of cement to the stone: Mother Mary Ethelburge, Mother Mary Dolores, Sister Mary Charles, Mr. George Hils Ferrenz, the Architect who planned Dannat Hall, and Mr. Stewart Muller, Contractor for the building. Kathryn Waters, President of the Student Government, and Helen McCarthy, Chairman of the House Council, represented the students in applying the cement to the cornerstone.

The ceremony ended with the joyous singing of the Alma Mater and a procession to the Church for the Holy Sacrifice of the Mass celebrated by Archbishop Maguire. Lunch was served in the convent at 12:15 p.m. for the clergy and invited guests.

On Sunday, October 20, Open House was held for family and friends who were invited to tour the residence halls from 1 to 10 p.m. The students proudly exhibited their new dormitory with its tastefully decorated rooms to accommodate 192 students. Dannat Hall was also provided with lounges, reception rooms, a post office, laundry and kitchenette.

At the end of the Open House, a housewarming party was held in Dannat Hall for the resident students and the faculty. Helen McCarthy, Chairman of the House Council, made use of this opportunity to present to Mother Mary Dolores a gift in appreciation for the time, thought, and work she had put into the building of Dannat Hall and the new dining room.

The students settled down to use and enjoy their new dormitory and dining room with all its conveniences. Finally the day of dedication arrived, Saturday, April 26, 1969, the Feast of Our Lady of Good Counsel. The day was significant in the annals of Good Counsel, for on this day the newly appointed Archbishop of New York, Terence J. Cooke, made his first visit to the campus, on the eve of his departure for Rome for the Consistory naming him a Cardinal.

The dedication ceremonies began at 3 o'clock with the Cardinal-Designate blessing the new residence Dannat Hall. A choir of Sisters, under the direction of Sister Mary Celine, sang several beautiful selections while Archbishop Cooke blessed the exterior and the interior of the building and erected the dedication Crucifix in the main lobby.

At the end of the ceremonies at Dannat Hall, all repaired to the Leo I. Kearney Sports Building Auditorium for the afternoon program. Monsignor John J. Hartigan, Honorary President of the College, gave a greeting of welcome. The Honorable Carl J. Delfino, representing the Mayor of White Plains, spoke a few words expressing the interest of the civic authorities in the rapid growth and development of the College. The main speaker of the day, Father Laurence J. McGinley, gave the Dedication address, an inspiring talk on faith -- faith building a house, faith in the young, faith in the future, faith in the community. Mother Mary Dolores wrote later in thanking him, "*Your inspiring address gave us renewed confidence as we look to a troubled future for higher education.*"

The highlight of the afternoon's program was the awarding of the Mater Boni Consilii medal to George Hils Ferrenz, the architect, who had not only designed all the major buildings during the past decade, but who also had made many generous contributions to the College and became one of its most loyal and devoted friends.

The program continued with Kathryn Waters, President of the Student Government, greeting the Archbishop and presenting him with a beautiful bouquet of roses, as a gift of appreciation from the students. The program ended with the Blessing by Archbishop Cooke, Cardinal Designate, and the singing of the Alma Mater. Interspersed throughout the program, the Glee Club, under the direction of Ralph Stang, rendered several lovely selections.

After the exercises, refreshments were served in the Kearney Lounge for the students and their guests. Both Dannat Hall and the new dining room remained open to visitors for the rest of the day.

A buffet supper, catered by Liegey Food Service, Inc., was served in Preston Hall at 5:00 p.m. for delegates representing the various colleges, religious, friends and other officials and faculty and staff. Members of the clergy, Advisory Board and other special guests were served a dinner, catered by Thomas Fox & Son, Inc. at 5:00 p.m. in the Convent.

Cardinal Cooke returned each year to the College for the Commencement, and in May 1970, was awarded the first honorary degree ever offered by Good Counsel College.

CHAPTER FIVE

MAJOR EVENTS

Golden Jubilee of the Sisters of the Divine Compassion

The year 1936 marked the fiftieth anniversary of the founding of the Congregation of the Sisters of the Divine Compassion. The year was marked by several very special events. The Jubilee celebration opened on July 2, 1936, the feast of the Visitation, with a high Mass offered by Bishop James E. Kearney. Professor Serafino Bogatto, choir director and composer, presented to the Sisters of the Divine Compassion his beautiful composition "Haec Dies" which he dedicated to them on the occasion of the Golden Jubilee of the Community.

The Ostensorium

The Alumnae, now numbering 267 members, wishing to have a share in the celebration, initiated a Jubilee Fund to be used for building and college publicity. However, they wanted to make a more permanent gift, a more lasting tribute of their love, devotion and gratitude. At the suggestion of Bishop Kearney, they decided to commission a new Ostensorium, manufactured from gold and silver contributed by the alumnae, students and friends; the only precious stones would come from the class rings of the first ten classes.

On the evening of November 11, 1939, at the Alumnae Reunion supper held in Preston Hall, Marie Todd, President of the Alumnae Association, presented the beautiful gold and jewel-bedecked Ostensorium to the Sisters. The Right Reverend Monsignor Joseph Breslin, speaking in his capacity as Honorary President, accepted the gift for the college, and praised the generosity of the Alumnae.

The Pageant

In conjunction with the Golden Jubilee, the students of the College presented an historical pageant in the auditorium on the afternoon of May 24, 1937, Mother M. Aloysia's feast day. The Pageant, "Memory's Pathway Through Fifty Golden Years", was the combined work of Mother Mary Compassio Harris and Sister Mary Edmund Glynn.

The entire student body took part in the pageant depicting the founding, growth and progress of the Community. Five historians told the story of the achievement of each decade from 1886 to 1936. The Guardian Angels of Monsignor Preston, Mother Mary Veronica and Mother Mary Aloysia related in verse the accomplishments of each. The College girls took the parts of grammar school children, wearing white dresses and veils, high school graduates in white cap and gown, college students in black academic attire, and lastly college alumnae wearing Bachelor hoods.

The following students were cast in the principal roles of the pageant:

Prologue	Alice Lehmann '39
Historian 1886-1896	Harriet McDonald '38
Guardian Angel of Monsignor Preston	Ellen Gaffney '39
Historian 1896-1906	Rita Beckerle '39
Guardian Angel of Mother Mary Veronica	Rita Brainard '39
Historian 1906-1916	Margaret Higgins '37
Historian 1916-1926	Elizabeth Drury '37
Guardian Angel of Mother Mary Aloysia	Rose May McCabe '38
Historian 1926-1936	Muriel Mazac '38
Epilogue	Anne Powers '37

At the conclusion of the Pageant, Anne Powers, President of the Student Council, spoke in behalf of the students wishing Mother Mary Aloysia a happy feast day and presenting her with a purse in commemoration of the occasion, as an expression of the love and gratitude of the students enrolled in the College. Rose May McCabe, President-elect, then stepped forward with a floral offering of fifty tea roses. The program ended with the Te Deum sung by the entire audience.

The Closing of the Jubilee Year

The Jubilee Year 1936-1937 came to a close with a grand reunion of all the Sisters of the Divine Compassion held at the Mother House in White Plains on September 1, 1937.

Early in the afternoon on a bright and beautiful day, the Sisters arrived from the five branch houses, Holy Family in Throgg's Neck, New York City; Our Lady's Institute in Fordham, New York City; Saint Bernard's in White Plains; Saint Mary's in Katonah; and Saint Lawrence in Brewster. Among the Sisters who returned to Good Counsel that day was Sister Mary de Chantal, the first Sister to receive the habit of the Divine Compassion on July 2, 1886.

When all had arrived, pictures were taken of the various groups from the oldest to the youngest. At 3:30, all repaired to the convent courts for the Jubilee Banquet. Tables were set up in the two open courts which were beautifully decorated for the occasion. The senior Sisters were seated in the west court, while the novices occupied the lower east court. Mother Mary Aloysia welcomed the Sisters with a warm and loving greeting. All joined in the Magnificat in thanksgiving for the happy occasion that brought them together, then sat down to enjoy a bountiful banquet.

During the banquet, parodies of the old familiar songs were sung. When the meal was ended, all repaired to the College clubroom for entertainment. A stage was set up with a special altar for Our Blessed Mother, on each side of which were displayed large pictures of Monsignor Preston and Mother Mary Veronica.

At the end of the program, Mother Mary Compassio asked to say a few words. She expressed, beautifully, the sentiments of all present. When she finished speaking, Mother Mary Aloysia rose to thank the Sisters for their cooperation in planning and executing such a beautiful and effective program. At the conclusion of her remarks all went to Church, singing the hymn to Our Lady of Good Counsel as they entered through the Crypt. The Glorious Mysteries of the Rosary were recited and a Te Deum sung. Then the community returned to the Crypt to visit the tombs of the Founders invoking them to pray for us, protect us, and bless us.

Thus ended the eventful year of Jubilee. All returned refreshed in spirit, and renewed in vigor to the tasks at hand.

Silver Jubilee of Good Counsel

One of the first of the many events to mark the Silver Jubilee of the founding of Good Counsel College was the investiture of the Jubilee Class with the cap and gown, which took place on November 17, 1947. This was the largest freshman class in the history of the College, numbering 133 students.

Bishop James E. Kearney presided at the Ceremony. In addressing the students he took great pleasure in announcing that among their number was the great granddaughter of Mother Mary Veronica, the foundress of the Sisters of the Divine Compassion, bearing the same name as her great grandmother, Mary Caroline Dannat Starr.

Mary Caroline Dannat Starr, the daughter of Walter K. Starr and Emma MacLean Starr, was born on June 6, 1930 at Port Washington,

New York, and graduated from Orange High School, Massachusetts. She applied for admission to Good Counsel College and was accepted as a freshman in September 1947, joining the Silver Jubilee class. Mary Caroline was a young lady of superior intelligence. Unfortunately, severe headaches led her doctor to advise her to discontinue her studies for a while, forcing her to leave Good Counsel. Good Counsel was deprived of the honor of granting its degree to the great-granddaughter of the Foundress of the Community.

The many and varied activities of the year 1948 were all marked in a special way toward honoring the College in its year of Jubilee. On January 30, 1948 Good Counsel Alumnae held a Dessert Bridge and Fashion Show in Preston Hall. The Bridge was sponsored by the Westchester Chapter of the Alumnae as a part of a fund raising drive in connection with the 25th Anniversary of the College; Eileen Slater Blake of the class of 1945 featured a showing of new and original hats. All were pleased with the outcome.

Early in the year the members of the Student Council decided to issue a weekly paper The Counselor to keep before the students the ideals of the College, and to inform them of the coming events of the week. They suggested that all on campus devote the 25th day of each month to special prayers in Thanksgiving for all the blessings of the past 25 years, and in supplication for the graces needed in the future.

On April 16, 1948, the College Glee Club, under the direction of Professor Frederic Joslyn, held a Jubilee concert in the grand ballroom of the Plaza Hotel in New York City. The concert was sponsored by the Alumnae for the benefit of the Silver Jubilee Fund. Sara LaBarbera of the Class of 1947 served as accompanist, and Dolores Trumpler of the Class of 1948, with her beautiful soprano voice, rendered several solos.

The climax of the Jubilee Year was reached in April, centering around the feast of Our Lady of Good Counsel. Cardinal Spellman had been asked to officiate at a Pontifical Mass. But he was not able to do so, having been invited by the venerable Archbishop of Melbourne, the Most Reverend Daniel Mannix, to help him celebrate the centenary of his archdiocese and the establishment of the hierarchy in Australia. However, Cardinal Spellman asked the Community's dear friend Bishop James E. Kearney to represent him at the Jubilee celebration and sent his special blessing for the occasion.

On Friday, April 23, a Triduum was begun by Bishop Kearney in preparation for the feast of Our Lady of Good Counsel. On each of the three days the Bishop preached a special sermon, centering around "The Blessed Virgin, Our Life, Our Sweetness and Our Hope".

The Alumnae were invited to return to their Alma Mater for the Mass and Communion Breakfast on Sunday, April 25th. Bishop Kearney celebrated Mass and preached the sermon. About 250 members attended and wholeheartedly took part in the singing. A special Silver Jubilee leaflet missal was printed containing the hymn to Our Lady of Good Counsel with a new stanza added:

> *"These four short years we nestled 'neath thy mantle,*
> *Those were days when life was young and free,*
> *With grateful hearts, we sing again thy praises*
> *In this hour of joyful jubilee:*
> *Dearest Mother, we are still thy children,*
> *Wending homeward, old scenes to renew;*
> *And praying once again before thy altar,*
> *O Mother, tell me, what am I to do?"*

Each member of the Alumnae present received a silver medal of Our Lady of Good Counsel.

On the feast of Our Lady of Good Counsel, April 26, 1948, a solemn Pontifical Mass was celebrated by Bishop Kearney representing His Eminence Francis Cardinal Spellman. At the end of the Mass His Excellency expressed the *"regrets of the Cardinal at his inability to be present to render in person his congratulations and to convey his blessing to Mother Mary Aloysia, the foundress of the College, to the faculty and the students on the magnificent story of the past 25 years and of his appreciation of the part Good Counsel College plays in the Archdiocese."*

Bishop Kearney then offered his own personal congratulations to the foundress of the College *"on the manner in which she has borne the responsibility that the late Cardinal Hayes placed upon her shoulders on a memorable afternoon 25 years ago when he said, 'There ought to be a college here,' and later announced at the Academy graduation that a college would be opened in September of that year 1923."*

Monsignor Arthur J. Scanlan, pastor of St. Helena's Church in New York City, preached, outlining briefly the growth and progress of the College during the past 25 years. He recorded the material, intellectual, cultural and spiritual advantages afforded to the students at Good Counsel, calling attention to the growth of the College from its original seven students to nearly 400 registered in 1948. He particularly called attention to the College's spiritual mission: *"Good Counsel boasts today that she has brought her students nearer to God and Our Blessed Mother -- after all, what better test is there of the spirit here at Good Counsel than the knowledge that in the 25 years, 80 vocations to the religious life have developed through Our Lady of Good Counsel?"* Over 75% of that number entered the Sisters of Divine Compassion. Monsignor Scanlan then paid tribute to all those who had been associated with the College from the beginning, especially to His Eminence Cardinal Spellman and to His Excellency, Bishop Kearney of Rochester who had been a true friend and benefactor through a quarter of a century, to Mother Mary Aloysia who bore the burden of the problems and difficulties of the beginning and who brought the College to the place it enjoys today among the accredited colleges of the nation.

Monsignor Scanlan did not forget those who were no longer with us, but, who had played such an important part in the development of the College. He mentioned Cardinal Hayes at whose suggestion and encouragement the College came into existence, the honorary Presidents Monsignor Patrick N. Breslin and his brother Monsignor Joseph A. Breslin; tribute was paid to Sister Mary Edmund Glynn, the first Dean, to Sister Mary Berchmans Byrne, Sister Mary Philomena Corridon and Sister Mary Augustine Bowie who had served the College so well and faithfully.

After the Mass a Jubilee luncheon was served for the clergy in the administration building, while the numerous guests were accommodated in Preston Hall.

Among the guests who came to celebrate the Silver Jubilee were representatives from Church, State and the educational world. Fifty-two members of the clergy graced the occasion. Jay R. Crowley, Supervisor of Adult Education, represented the University of the State of New York. Bernard A. Durand came for the Mayor of the City of White Plains. College presidents and deans conveyed the good wishes and congratulations from 16 different institutions. Other friends of long-standing, including members of the Guild of Our Lady of Good Counsel, were also present.

With an overflow of feelings of gratitude and thanksgiving, Mother Mary Aloysia expressed her sentiments in the following words, in a letter to Monsignor Arthur J. Scanlan:

"The good people of White Plains and of the neighboring towns and villages, the mayors, the heads of schools and their associates, -- our public officials, -- those in the medical and other professions, -- all, without exception, have been most loyal and friendly and helpful on all occasions. We have no words to express our gratitude to each and every one of these friends. Especially do we offer prayerful gratitude to God for the priests and ecclesiastics who have worked with us and shared our joys and sorrows during these twenty-five long years.

His Excellency Bishop Kearney, and your own self, dear Monsignor, have labored ceaselessly and at great personal sacrifice for the welfare of the college, its faculty and its students -- not only since its foundation but even before it came into existence. We are deeply grateful, dear Monsignor, and we pray daily that God will reward you with His choicest gifts and favors for all you have done for us."

The students had their share in their own Jubilee celebration on Tuesday, April 27. On this day, the 110th anniversary of the birth of Mother Mary Veronica, the students, arrayed in academic attire, attended a Gregorian sung Mass in the college chapel offered up in Thanksgiving by Monsignor John J. Hartigan, honorary President. Bishop Kearney presided and preached the sermon.

Bishop Kearney, in his sermon, dwelt on the notion of a dreamer's dream come true, though Mother Mary Veronica was no longer on this earth to see that dream become a reality:

"Today we celebrate our Mother's birthday and I think that sentence in itself carries all the sentiments that are in your hearts and in the hearts of all of us who have the privilege of calling Good Counsel, Alma Mater.

It was just 110 years ago today that a little baby was born in the lower part of the island of Manhattan in what was then known as "little old New York". That baby grew up to womanhood and at the age of 30 received the gift of faith and was received into the Catholic Church. That young woman began to have dreams of the future, and as a poet tells us, the dreamer lives on forever while the worker dies in a day. After 110 years one of the dreams of that child that was born 110 years ago is certainly realized today because we are conducting these thanksgiving services over the mortal remains of that dreamer. I refer to Mother Mary Veronica, the foundress of this community. Her dream was to devote her life to the service of young women. Her dream was to organize in this diocese, which she grew to love, a community whose principal work would be interest in the spiritual welfare of young woman-hood. -- She was deeply concerned about the development of the character of young women."

In paying tribute to Mother Mary Aloysia, the Bishop goes on to say:

"The Foundress of your college is one whom God has blessed with the privilege of nursing it year after year, of remaining very close to it and giving it the blessing of her outstanding leadership and personality. Those of us who have been intimately associated with this college from its very beginning are deeply appreciative of everything that has been done by the members of the faculty, the magnificent spirit that has always characterized the student officers in cooperation with the student body, but there is not one of us who has lived intimately with this college who does not realize that the personality and spirit of Mother Aloysia has been the great secret of its outstanding success and its universal acceptance in

this community and in the Archdiocese at large. So, in this Holy Sacrifice of the Mass, therefore, we pause -- to give thanks to God, to Our Blessed Lady, and to the President of the College, Mother Mary Aloysia.

Thanks be to God the story of 25 years of education at Good Counsel has been a very impressive story because so many of your classmates -- have come back to her to use in the college or the community the gifts that they received as they knelt in this chapel or as they stood in the classrooms of the college, -- the willingness of girls like yourselves to enter into the picture to become dreamers, as Mother Veronica was a dreamer, and dream of days when in some classroom they would influence the hearts and souls of other girls.

That my dear girls is the challenge of the Silver Jubilee -- Good Counsel must carry on the programs; Good Counsel must continue to influence the lives of young women in the next generation as she has done in the past. Good Counsel cannot do it unless girls of the next generation can furnish the fine flower of womanhood that the last quarter of a century at this college has furnished -- with that prayer in our hearts, with that sincere hope that you yourselves will realize the lessons of this jubilee, we commit dear old Good Counsel to the next quarter of a century."

The various activities, on the remaining days leading up to graduation, all tended toward the celebration of the Silver Jubilee. On April 30, the Junior-Senior supper and dance was held in Preston Hall.

Children's Day was celebrated in great style on Saturday, May 15. More than 100 youngsters, sons and daughters of the alumnae, the youngest being only one month old, romped on the campus enjoying the clowns, pony cart, Maypole, fishing pond and other amusements.

Commencement Week opened on Sunday, May 23, with the baccalaureate sermon at 3:30 p.m. delivered by the Most Reverend William A. Scully, coadjutor Bishop of Albany, the uncle of one of the graduates, Mary Anne Scully. This was followed by solemn Benediction. The Alumnae held a reception and tea at 5:00 p.m. in Preston Hall for the seniors, to welcome them to the Association, which now numbered 765 members.

Monday, May 24th, opened with a solemn Baccalaureate Mass at 9:00 a.m. celebrated by Monsignor John J. Hartigan, honorary President of the College. Class Day exercises were conducted on the campus at 3:00 p.m. in a lovely setting under the trees. For the occasion the students composed a special Jubilee song:

Good Counsel we've a prayer for thee
On thy Silver Jubilee.
Good Counsel we have thanks for thee
On thy Silver Jubilee.
For her whose courage gave thee birth
Our grateful chant ascends from earth
On thy Silver Jubilee.
From grateful hearts thy praises ring
On thy Silver Jubilee.
My thanks to thy loved shrine I bring
On thy Silver Jubilee.
For bringing God so near to me,
For making Mary dear to me
I vow to keep true faith with time,
On thy Silver Jubilee.

The banquet for the Seniors was given by the Juniors at 7:00 p.m. in Preston Hall, followed by the Senior-Junior traditions. The students of the College took advantage of this occasion to present a silver vase to Monsignor Hartigan in honor of his Silver Jubilee as a priest.

Tuesday, May 25, was chosen for Commencement Day for the Jubilee class, as the 25th day of each month during the year was a special day of prayer and thanksgiving for the founding of the College 25 years ago. Bishop James E. Kearney presided as a representative of Cardinal Spellman who was still on his extended trip to Australia. To show his interest and esteem for the College, Cardinal Spellman had attended every commencement since his coming to New York in 1939, with the exception of that in 1943 when as Military Vicar he was visiting military and naval units abroad on a trip which extended from February to the middle of July. That year he commissioned His Excellency the Most Reverend Stephen J. Donahue, the Auxiliary Bishop of New York to represent him.

Though he could not be present at the Jubilee Commencement, he took time out before leaving on April 23 to send the following letter to the class of 1948. The letter from the Cardinal's Residence was dated April 20, 1948:

Dear Friends:

It is with the deepest regret that I shall not be with you on Commencement Day because, more than a year ago, I accepted an invitation from Archbishop Mannix of Australia to attend the centenary exercises of the establishment of the Catholic Church in the great Archdiocese of Melbourne. In addition to my visit to Australia, I shall see many of our missionaries in the Philippines,

China and Japan, so that I know that you will understand the reason for my absence. Spiritually, I shall be with you as I pray for your future steadfastness in the faith and your devotion to the principles that have been taught to you during your college years. Please convey my congratulations to your parents on this happy occasion which is also a joyous one for them as they see in you the answer to their own prayers and hopes.

Asking God and His Blessed Mother to guide, encourage, and help you upon the rest of your journey through this mortal life and with my heart's blessing, I am

> *Very sincerely yours in Christ,*
> *(signed)*
> *Francis J. Spellman*
> *Archbishop of New York*

To the 1948 Class
of Good Counsel College

In choosing his representation for the Jubilee commencement, the Cardinal could not have done better than to ask our dear devoted and longstanding friend Bishop Kearney to officiate in his stead.

The exercises were held in the auditorium because of rain, but the rain did not dampen the joyous spirit of the day. The hall was filled to capacity with students, faculty and parents and friends of the graduates. The 64 candidates for degrees, arrayed in academic gowns, proceeded with dignity to take their assigned places. Their caps bore the silver tassel which they had received at Investiture and worn at all formal occasions over the four years as the distinguishing mark of the Jubilee Class.

The graduates were presented to Bishop Kearney by Monsignor John J. Hartigan, honorary President of the college. The Bishop in his address recalled the opening of the college 25 years ago when he joined the first faculty as an instructor of religion. He paid tribute to Mother Mary Aloysia, President and founder of the College, on whose ideals of scholarship and Christianity the College was based. He urged the young women to be strong and to go forth to fight for the preservation of Christian principles in all walks of life, in the home, in society and in the political arena.

"Those today blessed with a Christian education must stand against the organized efforts to keep God out of education. Under the false interpretation of the separation of church and state, there are those who seek to drive God from any place in public life. You

*face a demand not made upon previous generations to stand and
defend the ideals of Christian civilization."*

With his congratulations and final blessing, the Bishop brought to
a close the year of Jubilee for the Class of 1948.

The Second President & Further Expansion

In the fall of 1948 Good Counsel College launched its 26th
academic year with a large freshman class of 122 students and a total
enrollment of 387. Enrolled in this class were students from many parts
of the world -- from Peru, Nicaragua, Columbia, Cuba, Puerto Rico,
Newfoundland and the Philippine Islands, as well as from several states
of the Union. Of the 70 students who graduated in 1952, over 75%
belonged to this original freshman class, four members attaining high
honors.

Speaking at the general assembly of the College on September 20,
1948, Mother Aloysia welcomed the new freshmen and presented the
newly appointed President of the College, Sister Mary Dolores. Rising
to a warm ovation, Sister Mary Dolores repeated Mother Mary Aloysia's
welcome. The College had been established on a firm foundation, she
said; *"my task is a comparatively simple one. It is only for me to carry
forward and safeguard the work begun by Mother Mary Aloysia. The first
class on the road to the Golden Jubilee has the grave responsibility of
maintaining the high ideals already established during the first twenty-five
years."*

The Investiture, with cap and gown, for the twenty-sixth freshman
class took place at a very impressive ceremony on Friday, November 12,
1948. Bishop James E. Kearney presided and delivered a challenging
address, explaining that wearing the cap and gown of Good Counsel
College imposed upon each student three grave responsibilities: to the
past, the present and to the future.

At the opening of the Annual Bazaar on November 13th, the
alumnae were invited to attend a dinner at which Mother Mary Aloysia
was to be honored after 25 years of guiding the college through rough
days and fine days. In greeting Mother Mary Aloysia, the Alumnae
presented her with a check of $3,500.00 for the Silver Jubilee Fund. A
few days later, she received in the mail another check for $2,500.00 from
an Alumna who wished her name to be withheld. Bishop Kearney's gift
for the Silver Jubilee was a complete set of white vestments trimmed
with blue, which were worn at all the Jubilee Masses.

The eventful Silver Jubilee year of 1948 came to a close on Carol Night with its colorful pageant.

The students were delighted with the choice of Sister Mary Dolores as their new President. Myriam Coust, of the Class of 1946, wrote from Havana, Cuba, *"They could have never chosen a better person for it, and I am sure all the girls must be proud and very happy."* Another wrote, *"How very nice for Good Counsel. Things are sure to hum now."*

The new President set to work to prepare herself for her administrative position. A round of attendance at meetings, conventions and seminars followed her appointment, while all the time ideas were maturing in her mind that would set the College on a more efficient course. In 1949 she introduced faculty ranks with an equitable salary scale. She organized the curriculum into a departmental structure, setting a chairman over each department.

In the midst of all this activity, on July 2, 1951, Sister Mary Dolores was elected Mother Superior General of the Community. Never afraid to innovate and experiment with new ideas which might improve the educational experience of the students, Mother Mary Dolores also addressed the academic structures at the college. In 1956 she reorganized the curriculum, abandoning the old major - minor plan in favor of fields of concentration. The new curriculum concluded a reading seminar in the junior year and a coordinating seminar in the senior year, in preparation for comprehensive examinations to be taken by seniors in their fields of specialization.

Board of Advisors

In trying to solve the many problems that arose in connection with the administration of the College, Mother Mary Dolores felt the need for advice coming from outside, since all the seven members of the Board of Trustees belonged to the Congregation of the Sisters of the Divine Compassion.

Therefore, in 1956, she established an Advisory Board made up of ten members, later increased to twelve, in 1969. She invited friends of the College with experience in business, education, law and public life to form a Board to act in an advisory capacity to the President.

In the fall of 1956, Mother Mary Dolores announced the names of the ten charter members of the new Advisory Board: Right Reverend Monsignor Arthur J. Scanlan STD, Pastor of St. Helena's Church, Parkchester, New York; Mr. William A. Berbusse Jr., President of William A. Berbusse Inc., Builders; Mr. Roy J. Deferrari, Secretary

General of the Catholic University of America; Mr. John B.J. Gerety, Attorney at Law; Mrs. Genevieve Hunter, Director of the Archdiocese Vocational Service; Mr. Conrad Kellenberg, Vice President of the Brevoort Savings Bank, Brooklyn; Mrs. Anna O'Reilly Kniphuisen, Alumna of Good Counsel College, Class of 1927; Mr. Dominic Pastorelle, Vice President of the County Trust Company, White Plains; Mrs. Ruth V. Sands, First Vice President of the Atlantic and Pacific Tea Company; and Mr. Edward R. Shiebler, Promotion Manager of Community Counseling Service.

In the beginning, the members of the Board were consulted individually as the need arose. By 1967 it was felt that a more formal structure was needed, involving one or two meetings a year, while still retaining the privilege of consulting with individuals as the need arose.

As the years went by, the names of other distinguished citizens were added to the list of advisors: Mr. Raymond T. Bogert, Vice President of the National Bank of Westchester (In 1969, Mr. Bogert became a member of the Board of Trustees of Good Counsel College); Mr. William J. Casey, Attorney, Tax Lawyer, father of Good Counsel Alumna, Bernadette Casey of the Class of 1965 (Mr. Casey became a Trustee of Good Counsel College in 1969); Mr. Carl J. Delfino, Councilman of the City of White Plains; Mr. Brian Donnelly, Assistant General Manager, Westchester-Rockland Newspapers; Miss M. Lavelle Dwyer, Alumna of Good Counsel College, Class of 1963, Systems Engineer, Data Processing Division, IBM; Mr. George Hils Ferrenz, Architect, of the firm of Ferrenz and Taylor; Mr. J. Frank Halahan, Senior Vice President of the National Bank of Westchester (Mr. Halahan was named a Trustee of Good Counsel College in 1969); Mr. Thomas R. Horton, Director of University Relations for IBM (Mr. Horton became a Trustee of Good Counsel College in 1969); Miss Frances Kelly, Good Counsel College Alumna, Class of 1957, President of the Alumnae Association, Secretary to the Chairman of the Board of IBM; Mr. Walter McCarthy; Reverend Laurence J. McGinley S.J.; Honorable Edwin Michaelian, County Executive, White Plains, New York; Honorable Ogden R. Reid, House of Representatives, Congressman; Miss Virginia Schoman, Alumna Good Counsel College, Class of 1942; Mr. Allan B. Stevens, Allan G. Stevens & Son, Inc.; Honorable Carl A. Vergari, District Attorney, Westchester County; Mr. Schach A. Van Steenberg, Founder of the Middendorf, Colgate & Co., Member of the New York Stock Exchange, husband of Carol Carmody, Alumna of Good Counsel College (Class of 1927) (In 1969 Mr. Steenberg became one of the lay Trustees of Good Counsel College); and Mr. Allen Wagner, General Foods, father of Corinne Wagner, Good Counsel Alumna (Class of 1949).

During the tenure of Mother Mary Dolores as President of Good Counsel College, the student enrollment increased steadily, the number of faculty increased, and new courses were added to the curriculum. In 1957, Mother Mary Dolores inaugurated the extensive college building program, beginning with Aloysia Hall. Later followed Mater Dei Hall in 1964, Madonna Library and the Leo I. Kearney Sports Building in 1965. Dannat Hall and an addition to Preston Hall of a new dining room were both completed in 1968.

Along with the erection of the new buildings went an extensive renovation of five existing structures. The campus was also enlarged by the acquisition of four pieces of property on Crane Avenue. The following purchases were made: 31 Crane Avenue in 1964; 27 Crane Avenue in 1965; 82 North Broadway, St. Clair's Hall, in 1966; and 33 Crane Avenue in 1968.

In the fall of 1968 the Montessori School was introduced and located at 33 Crane Avenue, with a qualified teacher and all the necessary equipment. It was named the Caroline Montessori School in honor of Mary Caroline Dannat Starr, the Foundress of the Sisters of Divine Compassion.

The pressure of business soon took its toll on the already delicate health of Mother Mary Dolores. A serious illness made necessary a short stay in the hospital, but she bounded back with vigor and was able to continue her work of guiding and planning the erection of five major buildings, along with all the other necessary work in connection with the efficient running of the College until 1970. At that time, in accordance with the decree of the General Chapter of the Community held in 1968, that "Sisters will offer their resignation to the Superior between the ages of sixty-five and seventy", Mother Mary Dolores submitted her resignation as President of the College. Her request to retire as of March 1, 1970, after twenty-two years as President and forty-one years of exceptional service to the college was accepted by the Board of Trustees at its meeting held on February 18, 1970.

Diamond Jubilee of the Sisters of the Divine Compassion

July 2, 1961, marked the Diamond Jubilee of the founding of the Congregation of the Sisters of the Divine Compassion. The year opened with a special Mass of Thanksgiving offered by His Excellency Bishop James E. Kearney of Rochester. In the presence of a large gathering in the Church, the Bishop extolled the work of the Sisters in the cause of

Catholic education and thanked God for permitting the community to grow and flourish.

All the events of the year tended toward the Jubilee celebration. One of the first steps taken by Mother Mary Dolores, President of the College, was to give the Alumnae a chance to share in the celebration by their contributions toward beautifying the Church by installing pews.

The Alumnae were delighted with the suggestion and came forward with a ready response.

Before the Jubilee Year was over, the project was brought to a successful conclusion: the Sisters' stalls and the individual chairs and kneeling benches were removed and replaced by pews, each bearing a plaque with the names of the donors.

"Echoes of Good Counsel"

As part of the Diamond Jubilee celebration, the Sisters' choir of 50 voices, under the direction of Paul Shields, produced a long-playing stereo record, featuring sacred music, both Gregorian and polyphonic, along with American folk songs.

Sally Denny of the Class of 1956 told the story in an article for The Reporter Dispatch which appeared on Saturday, September 9, 1961, under the title "Nuns' Choir Records Sacred Music":

"Echoes of Good Counsel", an LP stereo disc, has recently been produced by the 50-voice Sisters' choir. It was made at the College of Our Lady of Good Counsel through the facilities of Capital Records.

The recording, which features sacred music and American folk songs, is the choir's first recording. Appropriately, the record has been presented to the order which this year is celebrating the 75th annivers-ary of its founding. On November 25th, the choir will sing the Mass of Thanksgiving in St. Patrick's Cathedral, celebrating the diamond jubilee of the Sisters of the Divine Compassion....

Mr. Shields, assistant professor of music at the college, has been working enthusiastically with the nuns' choir and noted that many of its members have accomplished voices.

The director said he is always surprised when people ask him, "Do these sisters just pray and sing all day?"

Since most of the choir members teach in the various parochial schools operated by the order (a number of them are college professors), they have relatively little time for singing.

Rehearsals are limited to once-a-week and for special occasions, twice-a-week.

Before joining the college faculty in 1957, Mr. Shields studied Gregorian chant and liturgy under Dom Gajard, O.S.B., Choir-Master at the Solesmes Abbey in Sarthe, France. He holds a choir-master's degree in the American Guild of Organists and has written a book "Outline Course in Music", which covers sacred and secular music.

In directing the sisters' choir, Mr. Shields stresses perfection in Gregorian Chant and polyphonic music. He is assisted by Sister Mary Celine, a kindergarten teacher at Good Counsel Academy and student at the Pius X School of Music, Manhattanville College, Purchase.

"Echoes of Good Counsel", recorded in three different places at the college, illustrates a remarkable blending of voices in both chant and harmony. The a cappella selections were made in the crypt of the college chapel; the accompanied sacred music done in the choir loft with organ.

It ends with a selection of traditional folk music, recorded in the library of the convent. Sounds of chapel bells are dispersed between sections throughout the record.

For the individual numbers included in the record, see Appendix 2.

The Centum Club

As a mark of appreciation and to give a special vote of thanks to the Sisters of the Divine Compassion on the occasion of the Diamond Jubilee of the founding of the Congregation, a group of alumnae banded together to devise a plan whereby a substantial sum might be presented to the College each year. The idea originated with Marie Todd Martine and her sister Evelyn Todd Mittelholzer, both of the Class of 1933. The society, known as the Centum Club, was composed of 100 chosen members of the alumnae, those who through the years had evidenced a deep loyalty and devotion to Good Counsel College. Each member would contribute $10.00 annually so that the sum of $1,000.00 could be presented to the President of the College each year, to be used at her discretion for the benefit of the College.

The first presentation was made on Saturday, November 11, 1961 and was a complete surprise to Mother Mary Dolores, who wrote:

"It is seldom that I receive so pleasant a surprise as the check which was presented to me this morning by your representative. Your devotion to Alma Mater has always been outstanding, and this additional expression of it is very deeply appreciated.

As the labors and the burdens of the college increase with the ever growing student body, it is a consolation to know that there is a devoted and loyal Alumnae, who make us realize that our efforts for Catholic Education are not in vain. They are our greatest asset.

But I want you especially to know that I am most mindful of your personal sacrifice as a member of the Centum Club.

May Our Lady of Good Counsel obtain for you and yours many blessings from her Divine Son.

With prayerful gratitude, I am

Devotedly in Our Lady,
Mother Mary Dolores

The Centum Club was faithful to its promise and each year, beginning in 1961 and continuing up to 1968, was able to make its contributions of $1,000.00 to the President's Fund.

The 100 members of the Alumnae chosen deemed it an honor and a privilege to belong to the Centum Club and responded generously. From among the many expressions of appreciation only a few can be mentioned.

Kathryn Leonard '29, Executive Director of the Talbot Perkins Adoption Service writes: *"I am glad to become a member of the 100 Club under the conditions you stipulated in your letter. Good Counsel College has had a profound influence on my life, and I shall always be grateful that I attended Good Counsel and not some other college. In these days of confusion, lowering of standards, unethical practices, immorality and amorality, it is a source of great strength and confidence to be able to fall back on the sound training and scholarship I received at Good Counsel."*

Catherine Nacey Ott '43: *"I was quite pleased to be numbered among the 100 picked to belong to the society you are forming for the benefit of Good Counsel College. It gives many of us the opportunity to do something really big for the college, which we probably could not do as individuals. I am enclosing my check and request that you definitely consider me as one of your members. Thank you again for this opportunity to express to the college my heartfelt thanks for all they have done for me."*

Margaret Arctander O'Brien '36: *"I do think you have a splendid thing going. It is an ideal way to make a substantial gift without the usual pressure or fuss."*

Donata Lombardi True '30: "*Bless you for giving me a chance to do something within my means in the way of supporting Good Counsel. I am happy that you included me in your list of the Committee of one-hundred.*"

The President's Fund made it possible to purchase equipment for the College which otherwise would not fit into its budget. Each year, in thanking the members of the Centum Club, Mother Mary Dolores mentioned the specific gift that was purchased, thus giving the alumnae the satisfaction of knowing exactly how the money was spent. By means of the President's Fund, the following items were added to the college equipment: a Pitney-Bowes Postage Meter Machine, an automatic typewriter, and an addresso-graph machine.

The Centum Club terminated its existence in 1968 when the Annual Alumnae Fund was established to support the vast building program undertaken by Mother Mary Dolores. This pioneer annual giving group, which in its short life had contributed $8,000 to the College, joined wholeheartedly the new Annual Alumnae Fund.

Over the years, from its inception in 1968 through 1981, the Annual Alumnae Fund contributed a total of $332,396.81 to the College.

The Fathers' Club

The Fathers' Club conducted several special events early in the fall of 1961, to commemorate the Diamond Jubilee of the founding of the Sisters of the Divine Compassion. On Sunday, September 10th, a Father-Daughter Communion Breakfast was held. Mass was celebrated by Father Leonard Della Bedia, and the Sisters' choir provided the music under the direction of Paul Shields. Following the Mass, breakfast was served in the Preston Hall dining room where Father Della Bedia addressed the two hundred and twenty fathers and daughters present.

Another contribution of the Fathers' Club was a Diamond Jubilee Dinner and Dance held at the Glen Island Casino in New Rochelle, on Saturday evening, September 23rd. Dinner was served in the main dining room at 8:00 p.m., followed by dancing to the music of Nick Mara's orchestra. Mr. James P. Faughnan, father of Mary Ann Faughnan '63, was the general chairman of the affair. The dance was most successful, with over 170 couples attending.

Bazaar

A gala Diamond Jubilee Bazaar began on October 28th and continued through the week to November 5th. The activities opened with a dinner for the Alumnae in Preston Hall. His Excellency the Most Reverend James E. Kearney presided as guest of honor. A completely furnished Hope Chest donated by Bishop Kearney was the main attraction among the sweepstake prizes.

The Prestonian

A special issue of The Prestonian in November 1961 was prepared to mark the Diamond Jubilee, featuring articles outlining the history and development of the educational and other works of the Sisters of the Divine Compassion. The issue carried several articles of interest, such as:

"Religious Community Develops from Apostolate to the Young"
"Memorable Events 1886-1961"
"Original House on Tilford Estate Has Long and Interesting History"
"Hand House Now Serves as Library"
"Foundation of College Dates from 1923, Established by Mother Mary Aloysia"
"Publication of Biography of Foundress"
"Founders Room in New Wing of Convent Contains Many Mementos"
"Sister Mary Aquino Recalls Days Spent with Mother Mary Veronica"
"Today (1961) Community Staffs 3 High Schools, 11 Elementary Schools and a College"

Mass at St. Patrick's Cathedral

The climax and crowning event of the Diamond Jubilee year came on November 25, 1961, with a Solemn Pontifical Mass of Thanksgiving celebrated in Saint Patrick's Cathedral at 9:30 a.m. by the Most Reverend John J. Maguire, Vicar General and Auxiliary Bishop of the Archdiocese of New York. His Eminence Francis Cardinal Spellman presided at the Mass, with the Right Reverend Monsignor Terence J.

Cooke, Chancellor of the Archdiocese as Archpriest, the Right Reverend John T. Halpin as Deacon, and Reverend Thomas P. Cahill as Subdeacon. The Master of Ceremonies was Right Reverend Monsignor Thomas A. Donnellan, Chancellor of the Archdiocese.

Assisting the Cardinal as Assistant Priest was the Right Reverend Monsignor John J. Hartigan, Honorary President of Good Counsel College. The Deacons of Honor were the Right Reverend Monsignor James A. Boyle and the Right Reverend Monsignor John J. Corrigan. The Master of Ceremonies was the Right Reverend Monsignor Edwin B. Broderick, the Cardinal's secretary.

The Most Reverend James E. Kearney, Bishop of Rochester preached the sermon. The Cathedral was beautifully decorated for the occasion under the direction of Frank G. Simeola, Landscaper.

The Mass was attended by the entire Community of the Divine Compassion, clergy and the Religious of various orders, students of the College and other schools, members of the Fathers' Club and the Mothers' Guild, invited guests and friends of the Community.

The Sisters' Choir, directed by Paul Shields, provided the singing. Before the Mass, Mr. Shields rendered organ selections by Purcell, Frescobaldi and Bach, and the Sisters sang Bach's "Jesu, Joy of Man's Desiring". At the conclusion of the Mass the Te Deum and Aiblinger's "Jubilate Deo" were sung; afterward, the Sisters were greeted individually by Cardinal Spellman.

After the conclusion of the ceremonies at St. Patrick's, the Sisters of the Divine Compassion and the other religious were transported by car and bus to Preston High School in the Bronx, where luncheon was served, catered by Thomas Fox & Sons.

It was a day of joy never to be forgotten and ended with a prayer of thanksgiving in every heart.

At the request of Mother Mary Ethelburge, Monsignor Thomas A. Donnellan was able to obtain the Papal Blessing for the Community through the Apostolic Delegate, Archbishop Egidio Vagnozzi.

November 13, 1961

Reverend and dear Mother:

On the occasion of the Seventy-Fifth Anniversary of the Sisters of the Divine Compassion, it affords me genuine pleasure to inform you that our Most Holy Father, Pope John XXIII, has graciously deigned to impart his Apostolic Benediction as a pledge of divine favor and a token of his paternal benevolence. It is the express wish of His Holiness that this Blessing be shared by the members of the Community and by the friends who join with them in celebrating this memorable day.

*The increase of foundations truly testifies to the remarkable
zeal and unfailing self-sacrifice of the many dedicated women who
have followed the call of a religious vocation. Of greater importance but known only to Almighty God and to the countless souls
are the spiritual and corporal works of mercy performed by the
Sisters daily in ministering to the Christ they see in others.*

*With prayerful good wishes for the years ahead, and with
renewed congratulations for the past fruitful years, I remain*

Sincerely yours in Christ
E. Vagnozzi
Apostolic Delegate

Mothers' Guild

The celebration of the Diamond Jubilee continued on into the
Spring of 1962. On Sunday, March 11th, a special function for the
combined Fathers' Club and Mothers' Guild was held in the Chapel of
the Divine Compassion at 3:00 p.m. Reverend Vincent Nugent, C.M.,
Professor of Sacred Doctrine at St. John's University, gave an address
on the forthcoming Ecumenical Council, followed by Solemn Benediction of the Blessed Sacrament, after which all repaired to Preston Hall
for a Tea and Reception.

The Mothers' Guild sponsored a Spring Fashion Show, Bridge and
Luncheon on May 8 at the Schrafft's Restaurant in Eastchester. Over
500 members attended to honor the Sisters in their Jubilee year. Mrs.
James Faughnan was in charge of the arrangements.

Vox and Vestigia

The Vox Studentium, the literary magazine of the students of Good
Counsel College, brought out a Diamond Jubilee issue in 1962, the
special Jubilee feature of which was an article by Sister Mary Teresa,
R.D.C. entitled "Through the Glass Darkly". In it she described the
struggle of Mary Caroline Dannat to gain a sure footing on the ground
of the true Faith.

The Class of 1962 lovingly dedicated their yearbook Vestigia to the
Sisters of the Divine Compassion in honor of their Diamond Jubilee. In
the dedication article, outlining the development and work of the
Community, they likened the growth of the Order to the gradual
perfecting of the diamond in all its phases from a rough stone to a

colorful and brilliant jewel: *"The diamond is recognized universally as the peer of gems. So, too, are our Sisters of the Divine Compassion marked by the reflection of God's love."*

Near the end of the Jubilee year, Patricia Wortman, President of the Student Council, presented to Mother Mary Ethelburge, Superior of the Community, a gift of $4,000 in the name of the students, in recognition of the Seventy-Fifth Anniversary of the founding of the Sisters of the Divine Compassion.

The Fruit of His Compassion

One of the outstanding and significant events of the Jubilee Year was the publication, in the Spring of 1962, by Pageant Press of the book The Fruit of His Compassion, written by Sister Mary Teresa Brady, R.D.C. In this definitive biography of the Foundress of the Community, Sister Mary Teresa contributed a loving and lasting memorial to Mother Mary Veronica.

His Eminence Francis Cardinal Spellman graciously consented to write the Foreword which concluded with the words:

"It is appropriate that in this diamond jubilee year of the foundation of the Sisters of the Divine Compassion that this biography of their foundress, Mother Mary Veronica be published. I pray that the spirit of compassion so nobly lived by Mother Mary Veronica will continue to animate her spiritual daughters and those to whom they minister with such Christ-like concern."

The book traces the life of Mary Caroline Dannat Starr from her birth in New York City on April 27, 1838 to her death in White Plains on August 9, 1904. The first part of the book deals with her early life, her conversion to the Catholic faith and her charitable works as a lay woman among the poor in New York City, leading up to her crowning achievement, the founding of a religious community, Sisters of the Divine Compassion, which came into existence in 1886 with the cooperation of Monsignor Thomas G. Preston, her spiritual director. Several chapters tell the story of the purchase of the White Plains property in 1890 to which was transferred the motherhouse and novitiate, the establishment of a school for girls at Good Counsel, the building of the Church in 1895 and the founding of the Catholic Girls Club. The last chapter, "Following in Her Footsteps", relates the progress and growth of the Community, the expansion of its apostolate in education, culminating with the work for the higher education for women at Good Counsel College.

In the annual "Best Book Contest" for 1962, Pageant Press Inc., announced that Sister Mary Teresa, had been awarded second prize for The Fruit of His Compassion.

"The Valiant Woman"

On May 9th, the College held its own celebration in honor of the Diamond Jubilee. The Most Reverend John J. Maguire, Vicar General of the Archdiocese of New York, celebrated Mass in the College Chapel at 11:00 a.m. for the faculty and students, followed by a luncheon served in Preston Hall.

The main event of the day took place at 8:15 p.m. when the College students presented a pageant in the auditorium.

"The Valiant Woman" was a dramatic poem in blank verse, constructed along classical Greek lines, written by Sister Mary Alacoque Marshall and Sister Mary Consuela McGrory. The verse called for a choral speaking group, which was under the direction of Roberta Curry, teacher of Speech and Dramatics; an interpretive dance group, the choreography being the work of Mary Coretti, a junior student in the College; and a choir for singing the music especially composed for the pageant by Paul Shields, Choir Master and Instructor in Art and Music.

The theme of the Valiant Woman was triply expressed: the valiant woman of the Old Testament, a valiant woman of the New Testament, Saint Veronica, and a valiant woman of our own times, Mother Mary Veronica, Foundress of the Congregation.

The pageant covered three episodes in Mother Mary Veronica's life, leading up to the foundation of the Religious Order. The first episode, "The Call", traced the events in the life of Mary Caroline Dannat Starr which led to her acceptance of the call to the religious life. The second part, "The Response", outlined the answer of Mother Mary Veronica and mentions several phases of her early work. The final episode, "Fruition and Thanksgiving", acclaimed the gratitude of the Community for its existence of over seventy-five years.

The sets and costumes were very simple, permitting the audience to concentrate on the imagery and meaning of the poetry. The members of the chorus were clothed in robes of light pastel shades, reminiscent of classical Greek simplicity. The backdrop on the stage showed the Shield of the Religious of the Divine Compassion with a suggestion of the gates of the college chapel.

"The Valiant Woman" was acclaimed by all who witnessed it as an outstanding and brilliant success, including Richard S. Hendey, Mayor of White Plains, who called it *"an excellent and professional performance."*

Third President of Good Counsel College
Charles E. Ford: September 1970 - February 1972

Upon the resignation of Mother Mary Dolores as President of Good Counsel College in February 1970, a Presidential Search Committee was set up by the Board of Trustees. Members of the Committee were drawn from the trustees, administration, faculty, students and alumnae. In the meantime, Sister Helen Coldrick, Assistant Professor of Modern History, was appointed by the Board of Trustees as Acting President as of March 1, 1970.

The Committee composed of the following members began its work at once. The trustees were represented by Dr. Thomas Horton, Chairman, William J. Casey and Frances Kelly. Two members were drawn from the faculty, Claire Magowan, Assistant Professor of English, and Sister Rosemary McCabe, Assistant Professor of Art. The Alumnae were represented by Virginia Curry, Class of 1959. Marianne Rafter, '71, and Cheryl Johannan, '72, represented the students. Mother Louise Marie Cutler, Chairman of the Board of Trustees and an Alumna of Good Counsel College, was an ex-officio member of the Search Committee.

The group worked diligently during the spring and summer, evaluating the numerous applicants. One stood out as being highly qualified, Dr. Charles E. Ford; added to his fine background was the recommendation of Brother Gregory Nugent, President of Manhattan College.

Dr. Ford was officially appointed President of Good Counsel College by the Board of Trustees on September 10, 1970. The announcement was made to the College Community on Friday, September 18, by Mother Louise Marie Cutler. He began his work at once. Dr. Ford was the third President of Good Counsel College and the first layman to hold this office. He took up residence on the campus, living with his family at 33 Crane Avenue.

At the time of his appointment Dr. Ford was 39 years old, a native of Vineland, New Jersey. He was Director of the Center for Christian Higher Education at St. Louis University. He graduated from Temple University, Philadelphia, Pennsylvania. He received his M.A. degree from St. Louis University and his Ph.D. from Washington University, both located in St. Louis, Missouri.

He had wide teaching experience, having taught at the University of Detroit and St. Louis University. He had been a visiting Professor at Washington University and also at the University of Missouri. His background in administration was rich and varied. At St. Louis University, Dr. Ford was assistant to the Dean of the College of Arts and Sciences and Director of the Evening Session and of Student Teaching. Formerly he was Vice President of Fontbonne College, St. Louis, Missouri, a college for women founded in 1923.

The official Inauguration of Charles E. Ford, as third President of Good Counsel College took place at Commencement, Monday, June 7, 1971.

During his brief administration, which lasted only a year and a half, he succeeded in bringing about some innovative changes. Among the most dramatic may be mentioned the change of name, the secularization of the College and the introduction of co-education.

On September 1, 1971, President Ford informed the College community that he had been authorized by the Board of Trustees to petition the Board of Regents of the State of New York to change the name of the College from Good Counsel College to The College of White Plains. Action on this petition was taken up at the Regents meeting held on September 24, 1971. The petition was approved and the new name went into effect by a revision of the Charter dated September 24, 1971.

The question of the name was one of the oldest concerns of the College. When it was founded in 1923 by Mother Mary Aloysia, several names were suggested and considered, among them Preston College, White Plains College, Good Counsel College. The last mentioned was wisely chosen as Cardinal Hayes advised us to stay with Our Lady of Good Counsel, who since 1890 had played such an important part in developing the spirit at Good Counsel.

Reaction to the name change was wide and varied, but for the most part favorable. County Executive Edwin G. Michaelian said that "*The new name identifies an educational institution bearing a proud heritage and tradition. While the college will be known as The College of White Plains, its mission will still be to provide good counsel to those who seize the opportunity for higher education in our community.*"

Mayor Richard S. Hendey of White Plains said he "*was tremendously pleased. All of us at City Hall feel honored that this distinguished college has adopted White Plains in its new name.*"

Some among the Alumnae were saddened by the change. The name Good Counsel recalled for them many cherished memories of devotion to Our Lady of Good Counsel and happy days spent under her protection. The students, however, took the change in stride. There were many who regretted the change, but others saw in the new name a chance of attracting a wider range of applicants.

Mother Louise Marie explained that the name change was due in part to the fact that "*Since its founding in 1923 the college has been geographically very close to the heart of White Plains. Academically, the administration and the faculty have served the educational needs of over 2,588 students from Westchester and all parts of the Country. We sincerely hope that the name The College of White Plains, which will focus on the location of the college, will also indicate the more dynamic thrust of the college in serving White Plains and Westchester County.*"

Dr. Ford, in an official statement to the College community, stated, "*The College of White Plains has been for nearly 50 years and will continue to be, closely connected with the community in which it is located. There has been nearly unanimous support, both within and outside of the college for the move. While no single aspect of an institution can necessarily alter its nature, it is anticipated that The College of White Plains will attract an increased involvement and support of our educational efforts.*"

"*Good Counsel Goes Public - To Expand Higher Learning.*" Such was the headline of an article in The Reporter Dispatch in 1971. During the first year of his presidency, Dr. Charles E. Ford brought a secular tone to the College in preparation for the possible reception of State aid. When Aloysia Hall was built, each classroom was equipped with a Crucifix, Our Lady's statue had a prominent place, and at the entrance door a small holy water fount was placed, giving a thoroughly Catholic atmosphere to the building. Now all such objects were removed. While it is true these were only accidentals, yet their removal left a void. Some felt the College was 'selling out' and compromising itself.

A concentrated effort was made for the College to become public-oriented by the introduction of a Continuing Education Center, the opening of the College to Community groups as a meeting place, and the addition of more lay members to the administration. The thirteen members of the Board of Trustees was composed of five religious women, two lay women and six laymen.

By a revision of the charter dated June 25, 1971, Good Counsel College was permitted to admit male students. The Board of Trustees gave unanimous approval to the admission of male students on a part-time basis -- that is, men were permitted to carry as many as twelve credit hours and to pursue all the programs of the College, but were not, at this time, to be considered candidates for the degree.

The first young men registered for courses during the summer session of 1971. By September 1972, The College of White Plains was officially recognized as co-educational. In the Class of 1973, two young men had the distinction of being the first males to graduate from The College of White Plains. By June 1975, the number of male alumni had risen to 21.

After a year and a half of service as President of The College of White Plains, Dr. Charles E. Ford presented his resignation. This act came as a surprise to the Board of Trustees, who had expected that his tenure would be of longer duration. The following notice from Dr. Ford, dated February 23, 1972, shook the entire community.

"I wish you to know that I have informed the Board of Trustees of The College of White Plains of my resignation, which will take effect February 29, 1972. The Board has appointed Dr. Katherine M. Restaino as the Acting President of the College.

The reasons I stated in my letter of resignation center upon the opportunity that has been presented to me for professional advancement which reflect my own longstanding interests and experiences in higher education.

I wish to thank the members of the faculty, administration, student body, and Board who have made my tenure as President a pleasant one. I wish it also to be known that I do not leave with any criticism implied within the college or in the direction in which this institution is progressing. Great progress has been made in the past several years. Reorganization of the Board of Trustees, formation of an internal governance system, the reform of academic programs, and the development of new academic opportunities were all opportunities to which I am deeply committed and which I believe represent worthwhile contributions to the college and its students.

May I urge you to assist all of the college officers as they seek to perform their duties, but especially the Acting President, Dr. Restaino, who comes to this position with excellent qualifications and, in my judgement, an opportunity to move the college still forward to higher levels of educational effectiveness.

Thank you for your support."

Charles E. Ford

Dr. Ford was asked to reconsider. However, an opportunity, nearer to his interests, opened up at Sacred Heart University in Bridgeport, Connecticut, where as Vice President he was to administer the entire academic program.

The Board of Trustees accepted the resignation of Dr. Ford as President of the College, effective March 1, 1972, and expressed its appreciation and gratitude for his dedicated service to the College during his tenure as President in the administrative re-organization and in the expansion of the Board of Trustees. He was commended for his innovative changes that have been vital factors in the forward thrust of the College during the past eighteen months. The Board then appointed Dr. Katherine M. Restaino, Dean of the College, as Acting President.

Fourth President of the College of White Plains
Formerly Good Counsel College
Katherine Marie Restaino: January 1973 - June 1975

Katherine Marie Restaino has the unique distinction of filling several roles at Good Counsel College, first as a student and an Alumna, Class of 1960, then as Professor, Dean, and finally President of the College.

Katherine M. Restaino was born in Brooklyn, New York, on November 14, 1937, the daughter of John Joseph and Katherine Marie Fischetti Restaino. She received her early education in Brooklyn's Public School 104, from which she graduated in 1951. She then attended Bay Ridge High School from September 1951 to February 1954. The family having moved from Brooklyn to Westchester County, Katherine completed her secondary school education at Pleasantville High School, graduating in June 1955. She chose to register at Elmira College, Elmira, New York, where she remained for one year, 1955-56.

Little did Katherine realize what would be the outcome when she transferred as a sophomore to Good Counsel College in September 1957. She began her work in earnest, carrying a heavy schedule. Despite this fact she was able to maintain her name on the Dean's List for each of the six semesters she spent at Good Counsel. As the days and weeks passed she grew into a real "Good Counsel girl"; she states that the *"Junior year was the best year because I really began to feel at home at Good Counsel. The highlights of that year are those rich in old traditions - - the Junior-Senior Bouquet, Pine Walk and an unusually exciting Saint Patrick's Day. The best moment for me in senior year was delivering the Salutatory address at the Commencement."*

During the whole course of her college career, Katherine was productively active. She was elected President of the Literary Club, was a member of The Prestonian staff and contributed articles to Vox Studentium. She had several poems published. The Atlantic Monthly

Creative Writing Contest for college students gave honorable mention and merit awards for her contributions for two successive years. When the College Literary Club held a Symposium during the Catholic Book Week in February 1960, one of the outstanding presentations was a paper delivered by Katherine Restaino, entitled "Books to Develop Us Spiritually".

Katherine graduated from Good Counsel College on May 26, 1960, with a B.A. degree in English and a Teacher's Certificate. Her record was so outstanding that she was admitted to two honor societies, Kappa Gamma Pi, National Honor and Activity Society of Catholic Women's Colleges, and Delta Epsilon, National Honor Society for Students, Alumni and Faculty of Catholic Colleges and Universities.

Miss Restaino was awarded two Assistantships to the Graduate Departments of English at Fordham University and Villanova University. She chose to attend Fordham University, where she obtained her Master's degree in English in 1962. She continued her graduate studies in English at Fordham in preparation for the Doctorate, which she was awarded in 1966.

In the meantime, Katherine met her future husband, Bernard Francis Dick; they were married in July 1965. She chose to retain her maiden name in her public life; as she explained, "*I wanted my maiden name on my Ph.D. degree as a thank you to my parents (Mr. and Mrs. John J. Restaino of Hawthorne) and because I'm very proud of my Italian-American heritage. I had also been teaching for three years and was known as Dr. Restaino. On the practical side, we both thought it would be confusing to have two Dr. Dicks in the family. We both wanted to retain our separate identities.*"

Dr. Restaino gained valuable teaching experience at Mercy College, Dobbs Ferry, where she taught English for seven years, and served as Director of the Honors Program. Other experiences were obtained as a Graduate Assistant at Fordham University (1960-63) and as a staff member of the Writers Conference at Iona College (1964-67). She held membership in several organizations, among them the Modern Language Association of America, America Comparative Literature Association, National Council of Teachers of English and the American Association of University Professors. Katherine was an avid reader, and succeeded in having 21 book reviews published in her major field of interest.

It was with this rich experience and background that Dr. Restaino returned to her Alma Mater in September 1970 as Associate Professor of English, the beginning of a most distinguished career at Good Counsel College.

Her administrative ability was soon recognized, and she was appointed Director of Freshman Studies by Dr. Charles E. Ford, effective March 1, 1971. Before the school year was ended, another promotion came to Dr. Restaino. Sister Mariam Moran, who had been Dean since 1960, was now named Vice President for College Relations. The obvious choice to replace her was Dr. Restaino. In June 1971, Dr. Ford requested the approval of the appointment, the matter was considered by the Board of Trustees, and at the meeting of the Executive Committee held on July 12, 1971, her appointment as Academic Dean was approved. This was the first time in the history of the college that this office was held by a laywoman.

She entered upon her work enthusiastically, covering the various phases of college organization -- admissions, the library, the registrar's office, the faculty, and most important, the curriculum. Working through committees she was responsible for the smooth running of the entire college organization.

Things came to an abrupt halt when, in late February 1972, Dr. Ford suddenly and unexpectedly announced his intention to resign from the Presidency and to leave the College for a position more in keeping with his interests. The Board of Trustees asked Dr. Restaino to assume the position of Acting President as of March 1, 1972. In the interim, a search committee was set up to find a new President.

Katherine embraced her new assignment with vigor. She said, "*I plan to be a very active Acting President*", and indeed she was. She faced important issues with courage and confidence. As Academic Dean, she had become familiar with a number of areas under the jurisdiction of the President, such as the application for Bundy Aid, the Master Plan and the Budget preparation.

Word came in December of the successful outcome of the application for Bundy Aid. In a memorandum to the entire college community, dated December 27, 1972, Dr. Restaino made the following announcement:

> "*The College of White Plains has received a marvelous Christmas present in the form of Bundy Aid. In a letter dated December 22, Commissioner Nyquist informed the College of a favorable decision on its application for funding. In the concluding paragraph of his letter Commissioner Nyquist said:*
>
> > *'It is my hope that the funds provided by this program will assist the College of White Plains to continue its important contribution to higher education in New York State.'*"

After a search that went on for almost a year, Dr. Restaino was finally chosen, out of over 200 applicants, to be President of The College of White Plains. Her recommendation and subsequent election by the Board of Trustees took place Thursday evening, January 11, 1973, and was announced the following day by Dr. Thomas R. Horton, Chairman of the Board. The formal inauguration of Katherine M. Restaino as fourth President of The College of White Plains took place at Commencement, Monday, May 28, 1973.

Among the hundreds of letters of congratulations that came pouring in upon the announcement of the news of her appointment as President of The College of White Plains, one seems of special significance in the light of what was to happen two years later. The following letter dated January 22, 1973 came from Dr. Edward J. Mortola, President of Pace University.

Dear Dr. Restaino:

My warmest congratulations and good wishes to you as President of The College of White Plains. I have been aware of the fine work you have been doing in moving the college along since you became Academic Dean, and I simply want to tell you that your Board is to be congratulated on finding so fine a solution to its problem of determining the right leadership for The College of White Plains.

As neighbors in Westchester, and as sister institutions in New York, I am sure that we will have many occasions to work together on behalf of our own institutions and higher education generally.

I should also identify a parochial interest of mine by indicating that I am happy to know that another Fordham graduate heads an institution in New York State.

> *Sincerely,*
> *Edward J. Mortola*
> *President*

A few days later Dr. Restaino replied:

Dear Dr. Mortola:

Thank you for your letter of encouragement. I look forward to meeting with you at some time to discuss recent developments in private higher education, both in New York State and Westchester County. Dr. Thomas Horton, Chairman of our Board of Trustees, has mentioned some of your ideas concerning cooperative ventures.

With all good wishes, I am

> *Sincerely,*
> *Katherine M. Restaino*
> *President*

Her first week in office was spent in San Francisco at the Convention of the Association of American Colleges. She returned refreshed and eager to begin her new role as President. Preparation for the visit of the Middle States Association of Colleges and Secondary Schools engaged her attention over the next several weeks. The visit took place on April 12, 1973; the outcome was satisfactory, and The College of White Plains was maintained on the accredited list of the Association.

Another matter that needed immediate attention was to find a new Academic Dean since Dr. Restaino had retained this position along with her role as Acting President.

Search for a new Academic Dean began in February. Dr. Restaino hoped that the position would be filled by June 1, 1973, but such was not the case. The search continued over the summer, without success. September arrived and still no Dean had been found. Dr. Restaino then asked Sister Helen Coldrick, Assistant Professor of History, if she would be willing to fill the position of Acting Dean. Sister consented to do so. Though she loved teaching, Sister Helen explained, *"because of my dedication to the College I was very happy to do so. Basically, I'm here because I was asked under emergency conditions. I'm happy I can be of service, and I am looking forward to returning to the classroom."*

However, Sister Helen was not able to return to her "first love", teaching, for over a year. It was not until the end of the school year that a new Academic Dean was found. Dr. John M. O'Brien assumed the post on June 1, 1974. The following Monday he sent this message to his colleagues:

"I am most pleased to assume the office of Academic Dean at CWP. During the next few weeks, I shall work at familiarizing myself with the campus and the College community. I hope to meet with as many individuals as possible and would like to extend a personal invitation to you to drop by my office for an informal chat. Please feel free to drop in or arrange an appointment through Joanne Fairchild."

> *Yours sincerely,*
> *John M. O'Brien*
> *Academic Dean*

The following announcement, made by Dr. Restaino, President, appeared in "News Release" for September 13, 1974:

"John M. O'Brien joins the college community as Academic Dean. Dr. O'Brien, holder of the Ph.D. degree from the University of Southern California, comes to CWP from the City University of New York where he served as Special Assistant to the Vice Chancellor for Faculty and Staff Relations. Dr. O'Brien is a former American Council Education Administrative Fellow. In this

capacity he served an internship at the University of California at Berkeley as Assistant to the Chancellor."

Relieved of the responsibilities as Dean, Dr. Restaino could now devote her full attention to the demands of her new office as President. She worked tirelessly for the advancement of the College, for the improvement of its academic program, and its service to the larger community of the City of White Plains and Westchester County.

Among the highlights of the administration of Dr. Restaino may be mentioned the following:

The restructuring of the academic program: the individual departments were abolished in favor of the broader divisional structure. Five divisions were chosen, each with its own chairman, elected to serve for a two year period. The divisions were: Arts and Letters, Human Studies, Science and Mathematics, Education, and Business.

New degree programs were introduced, including an interdisciplinary major in Children's Studies and an associate degree in Applied Science in Banking.

New and interesting courses were added, for example: Local History and Irish Studies, both in History and Literature.

Two late semesters were started, one in November, the other in March, leading to the launching of the first Satellite Center at Brewster, New York, in March 1974; this continued with great success for five sessions.

Many new administrative and faculty appointments were made.

Standards for faculty promotion and tenure were established.

Relations between the College and the local community were enhanced. The celebration of the 50th Anniversary of Good Counsel College of White Plains initiated frequent interchange with its neighbors as all were invited to share in the festivities. The College also cooperated closely with the White Plains Public School system in the implementation of a paraprofessional training program. College facilities and personnel were available for the program throughout the year. In addition, space was provided in the College for local community organizations to meet and conduct their programs.

In a letter to Sister Mary Basil, dated March 17, 1980, Dr. Restaino sums up her experience as an administrator:

"I remember most vividly the excitement of the years in which Good Counsel College became the College of White Plains. Those years were probably the most challenging, and sometimes most frustrating ones in the College's history. The events which led to

my appointment as President of the College were certainly unusual and were not anticipated by anyone, let alone myself. I saw my work as an attempt to move the college in a direction more compatible with the trends in higher education. But it was my hope during those years to try to keep alive the traditions and history symbolized by Good Counsel College. The challenge of those years included the design of the Master Plan, the restructuring of the academic departments into divisions, and the development of new programs. The two greatest moments of my term as president will always be the day the college received word that it qualified for Bundy Aid and the September we began our Liberal Studies Program. The sight of all those nurses in white uniforms rushing into Aloysia Hall is something that I will never forget. The introduction of that program with its initial enrollment of over 100 students was a turning point for the college. Through Sister Berchmans' direction, that program became the medicine the college needed for survival.

The most challenging period in my term as president occurred during the last six months when the consolidation with Pace University was being designed and discussed. That was a very difficult period for the entire college family. It was crucial because in the end it enabled the Board of Trustees to find a way to continue the college and to let the campus develop into the exciting place it is today."

When Dr. Restaino agreed to accept the position as President of the college, she did it with the understanding that it would be for a short term. Now the time had come when she felt she must move on. At the meeting of the Board of Trustees held on February 4, 1975, she announced her desire to relinquish the Presidency of the College at the end of the academic year in June 1975. The Board accepted her resignation with regrets, but with deep gratitude for the many outstanding contributions she had made to the college. The next day her decision was made known to the college community in a memorandum from Dr. Horton, Chairman of the Board of Trustees:

"As you may know, when we asked Dr. Restaino to assume the top post, she indicated then her willingness to do so for a short term. She now feels that her academic career interests lie outside a college presidency. Her contributions to CWP both as Academic Dean and President have included development of the College's Master Plan, qualifying the College for New York State aid, organization of the divisional structure, strengthening the College's relations with the Westchester community, and academic develop-

*ment through both new programs and significant expansion of
continuing education. We all owe her a great debt and wish her
well as she makes plans for her future."*

Dr. Restaino continued to work faithfully and diligently during the
remaining months of her administration.

At the Commencement held on the campus, Friday, May 23, 1975,
the last before the consolidation with Pace University, The College of
White Plains bestowed upon Katherine Marie Restaino its highest
honor, the Mater Boni Consilii Medal, in grateful appreciation of her
devotion and service to the College. The citation for this distinguished
alumna of Good Counsel College, was read by Sister Loretta Carey,
Secretary of the Board of Trustees.

The Golden Jubilee of Good Counsel College

The academic year 1973-74 marked the Golden Jubilee of the
founding of Good Counsel College. This was an occasion which called
for a special celebration.

Planning for the Golden Jubilee celebration dated back to January
1971. Dr. Charles E. Ford, then President of the College introduced a
program called "Campus 73" to give everyone in the entire community
a chance to express his opinion in preparation for the celebration of the
50th Anniversary of the founding of the College. Nine committees were
formed representing every phase of college life, faculty, students, library
and administration.

Immediate planning for the great event began early in the fall of
1973. Dr. Katherine M. Restaino, President of the College, discussed
possible ways of observing the 50th Anniversary with trustees, College
officials, and other members of the College community. A special
committee was formed to work out the details for a gala celebration.
The Golden Birthday Planning Group consisted of the following
members: Sister Miriam Moran, Sister Helen Coldrick, Sister Rita
Dougherty and Carolee Berg, Dean of Students. They contacted faculty,
students and alumni concerning involvement and creative contributions
for the great event.

A slide and film show was presented on Thursday evening,
November 29, 1973, in the Tudor room in Preston Hall. The program
to commemorate 50 years in the life of Good Counsel provided much
fun and laughter for the audience as they reviewed the old films starring

graduates, faculty and members of the administration of yesterday and today. The program was sponsored by the <u>Vestigia</u> staff.

<u>The Prestonian</u> featured several articles during the year calling attention to the Jubilee. Nancy Louden of the Class of 1975 contributed an article entitled "Celebration Encourages Evaluation", in the October 26, 1973 issue, in which she called attention to the value of personalized education made possible by the small college such as the one founded by Mother Mary Aloysia in 1923. Another article, by Mandy Beaton, in the April 22, 1974 issue of <u>The Prestonian</u>, entitled "Happy Birthday CWP", outlined briefly the history of the founding of Good Counsel College.

Through the kindness of Mr. William Jaeger, Director of WFAS Radio and a member of the President's Council, a series of one-minute radio spots, highlighting the fiftieth year of the college were broadcast over a period of six weeks beginning in November 1973. The messages were taped on Wednesday, November 14, 1973 at the President's Council breakfast. Those participating in the session included from the Board of Trustees, Dr. Thomas Horton, Dr. Anthony Marano, and County Executive Edwin Michaelian; from the President's Council, Mayor-elect Carl Delfino; Edward Dowdall, former Executive Director of the White Plains Chamber of Commerce; Reverend Wesley Konrad, Pastor of Grace Episcopal Church; Monsignor Charles J. McManus, Pastor of St. Bernard's Church; Israel Moss, Director of the Anti-Defamation League of Westchester; and Daniel O'Brien, Vice President of the National Bank of North America. The series concluded with a tape by Sister Miriam Moran. The messages were interesting and diversified in approach, highlighting the history of the College and its programs and offering congratulations from Westchester County leaders in business and industry.

Another event to celebrate the Golden Jubilee of the founding of the College took place on March 30, 1974 in the form of a cocktail party given by the Board of Trustees. Prominent citizens of White Plains and Westchester County were invited to join the Trustees in the celebration.

The Alumni Association was happy to take part in the celebration by preparing a cookbook entitled "Our Favorite Recipes", with the following dedication:

"This book commemorates the 50th Anniversary of the Founding of The College of White Plains. These recipes have been donated by Alumni and members of the college community, Board of Trustees, President's Council, Administration, Staff, Faculty and Friends. As we celebrate our Alma Mater's Golden Birthday, we hope this cook book will bring much enjoyment to the homes of all who use it."

The climax of the celebration came with a giant birthday party extending over the weekend of April 26, 27, and 28, 1974. The College opened its doors to all of Westchester County, inviting all to participate in the celebration. Special invitations were sent to our immediate neighbors on Crane Avenue. It was a gorgeous weekend; the weather was perfect, with sunshine, blue skies, and magnolias in bloom. Festivities began on Friday, April 26, 1974, the feast of Our Lady of Good Counsel, with a reception for the Alumni Association and the presentation of the Golden Gift in Preston Hall.

On Saturday evening, April 27, a more spiritual expression of our great joy in celebration was offered at 6:00 p.m. with the Liturgy of Thanksgiving offered by Monsignor Daniel Flynn. Both living and deceased members of the College Community were remembered and enfolded in prayer during the celebration of the Holy Sacrifice of the Mass.

As an introduction to the Mass, a beautiful slide presentation was prepared by Sister Mary Celesta Kelley, in order to bring to mind some of the people who in God's providence helped to build the College and nurture its growth. Also depicted were students of the past and the present who came to Good Counsel to learn and to grow in mind, heart and body.

The Carnival, on Saturday, April 27, lasted all day from 10:00 a.m. to 11:00 p.m. with rides, clowns, balloons, games and refreshments. There were booths for books, arts and crafts and a white elephant sale. For the main attraction the College hired the "Wonderful World Shows", a carnival from upstate New York, run by Eugene Simpson with Ferris wheel, merry go-round and bouncing and tumbling on an air mattress inside a 20-foot-high balloon called "The Moon Walk". All this provided great fun and laughter for the little folk and for the not-so-little folk.

Local talent provided entertainment, among them the Irish Dancers, the White Plains High School Dance Group, Peekskill Drama Workshop, Folksingers Adrienne and Christie, and a Marionette show.

One of the special features of the Carnival weekend was the Children's Theatre presentation of "Tarradiddle Tales" by Flora Atkins, for ages 5 to 95. Three performances were given in Preston Hall Theatre, two on Saturday and one again on Sunday, for the enjoyment of all, both young and old.

The whole atmosphere at Good Counsel was that of a country fair. Through Saturday and Sunday the College campus resounded with "rinky-dink" mechanical music, happy laughing children and hundreds of welcome guests. It was estimated that over 4,000 people visited the White Plains College campus to take part in the 50th Anniversary Birthday Party.

"College Birthday gets A+", so wrote J. Franklin Jones, staff writer for the <u>Reporter Dispatch</u> in an article which appeared in the paper on Monday, April 29, 1974.

The Merger With Pace University

As early as February 4, 1975, the Board of Trustees of The College of White Plains had begun to raise the question of some type of affiliation with another institution. A Task Force was appointed, under the direction of Mr. Robert McCarthy, to study the question of alternatives for the College.

Early in March, Dr. Edward Mortola, President of Pace University, approached the trustees regarding the possible merger of the two institutions. His plan included the erection of the Pace Law School on the White Plains campus. Conversations continued between representatives of Pace and The College of White Plains, which resulted in the offer to explore this possibility further.

In the meantime, another offer came from Mercy College. The President, Donald Grunewald, approached Dr. Horton suggesting conversations concerning a merger with that institution. After discussing the matter with the Board of Trustees, it was agreed that this course of action would not be pursued, and President Grunewald was thus informed by Dr. Horton.

The proposed merger with Pace University continued to develop and make progress. However, other contacts were made with Iona College and Manhattan College, neither of which showed an interest in a merger. Fordham University did express an interest and was willing to pursue the subject if there was a mutual interest on the part of The College of White Plains. The matter was brought before the Board and discussed. An agreement was reached by the Executive Committee that it was not feasible to deal with two possible mergers at the same time. A motion was passed that the Executive Committee would recommend to the Board of Trustees that the Pace merger proposal be accepted and that the necessary steps be taken to bring about the merger. The members of the Executive Committee present at that time voted unanimously for this proposal.

By this time, rumors began to circulate about a possible merger with another institution, causing unrest in the college community. Dr. Horton felt that an official announcement was in order; therefore, he asked Dr. Restaino to inform the College community on the progress of the discussions taking place between The College of White Plains and Pace

University. The following notice was sent to the College community by Dr. Restaino on April 15, 1975:

"For several years The College of White Plains has been involved in an assessment of its role in private higher education in Westchester County. The Board of Trustees has been considering several alternatives which would help the College further develop its academic offerings and services to the students.

One such alternative is a merger with Pace University. Preliminary discussions have been held and will continue because of a number of favorable factors, the most important of which is the preservation of The College of White Plains as a unique community within the larger university's framework.

Newspaper reporters have become aware of the discussions and a story will be carried in the local papers today. Dr. Thomas R. Horton, Chairman of the Board, has asked me to inform you of the preliminary discussions and to assure you that these matters are simply under study. No firm decisions of any kind have been made. Furthermore, The College of White Plains will continue to preserve its special nature and academic purpose."

Frequent meetings of the Board of Trustees continued over the spring months. Preliminary elements of a proposed merger with Pace University were drawn up and discussed, and amendments suggested. Many conferences followed. The amendments were spelled out and studied carefully by The College of White Plains. Both Dr. Charles H. Dyson and Dr. Edward J. Mortola agreed that the amendments would be acceptable to Pace.

Finally, on May 30, 1975, came the announcement:

"Pace University and The College of White Plains have voted to consolidate into one institution. The announcement of this important development in higher education was made by Dr. Charles Dyson, Chairman of the Board of Pace, and Sister Loretta Carey, Chairman of the Board of The College of White Plains."

One of the last acts of Dr. Restaino, before leaving the College on June 6, was to inform the College community and the alumni of the final decision of the Board of Trustees to accept the merger with Pace University.

Dear Members of the College Community, After several months of discussion and consideration, The Board of Trustees of The College of White Plains has reached a decision on the proposed consolidation between The College of White Plains and Pace University. The Board has voted to consolidate, and the appropri-

ate documents will be submitted to the Board of Regents of the State of New York.

This action is truly a significant step in our college's development. The unique feature of this consolidation is the preservation of our identity as The College of White Plains within the structure of Pace University.

The coming months will involve much effort and creativity on the part of all members of the college community as we work towards the continued development of our college.

With all good wishes, Katherine M. Restaino, President

A similar letter was sent to the alumnae and alumni.

Not everyone was pleased with the outcome. There came a few dissenting voices. A group of eight Sisters, four of them trustees, the others, members of the administration, felt that the merger was not in the best interest of the College which would lose it autonomy. Others felt that the increased student population in the College would make it difficult, if not impossible, to run the grammar school and high school adjacent to a busy college campus. On June 7 they sent a petition to the State Board of Regents to stop the consolidation. A hearing on the petition was held on Wednesday, June 25, before the Committee of Higher and Professional Education of the Board of Regents. Despite the objections brought forward by these Sisters, the Board of Regents, by a vote of 9-1, approved the merger at its meeting held on June 27, 1975.

The Regents ruling was to become effective on July 15 with the condition that certain amendments already approved by The College of White Plains be adopted by Pace University.

In the interim, between the departure of Dr. Restaino on June 6, and the selection of a new White Plains Campus Administrator, someone had to be appointed to carry on the business of the College. Sister Miriam L. Moran was chosen to fill this important and delicate position, as acting President. This was announced by Sister Loretta Carey, the new Chairman of the Board of Trustees on June 6. On July 2, 1975 Sister Miriam informed the White Plains community:

Dear Colleagues,

It is with a genuine sense of achievement as well as a realistic sense of new responsibilities that we write to tell you that the consolidation of The College of White Plains and Pace University has been approved by The Board of Regents, effective July 15, 1975. Confirmation of the Regents' action was received on Friday, June 27, 1975.

Much work lies ahead of us to achieve reconciliation with those who have opposed the consolidation -- to make the consolidation work -- to produce from it the maximum benefit for all parts of our united institution. We are all now part of a larger and more diversified university. Within that diversity our objective is to achieve unity and solidarity of purpose.

To all who have helped, encouraged, prayed for this day, our heartfelt thanks.

Sincerely,
Miriam L. Moran R.D.C.
Acting President
The College of White Plains

On July 10, 1975, the Board of Trustees of Pace University held a special meeting at which they voted unanimously to approve the various amendments to the original plan of consolidation with The College of White Plains. This action cleared the way for the emergence of a new institution. Dr. Edward J. Mortola, President of Pace University, expressed his appreciation for the action of the Pace Board. He expressed his belief that the consolidation would preserve and strengthen The College of White Plains. He said, *"Pace will devote its efforts to this goal."*

Sister Loretta Carey, Chairman of the Board of Trustees of The College of White Plains, called the Board's approval *"a signal achievement that will assure the future development of The College of White Plains."*

Dr. Mortola also announced that Dr. Edward B. Kenny, Associate Dean of the University, had received the approval of the Board as Acting Vice President and Dean of the White Plains Campus. Dr. Kenny had been associated with Pace for a number of years as a member of both the faculty and administration. A resident of Westchester County, Dr. Kenny assumed his new duties at The College of White Plains of Pace University on July 15, 1975.

On Tuesday, July 15, Dr. Mortola came to the White Plains campus with a group of University officers, providing an opportunity for the administrators of both institutions to become acquainted. A warm welcome was given to our new associates. A series of meetings and discussions followed throughout the day.

On July 23, 1975, Dr. Mortola wrote a letter addressed to all the members of The College of White Plains, including students and alumni. In it he explained many of the details of the consolidation and its significance for The College of White Plains:

138

Dear Faculty, Staff and Student Associates of The College of
  White Plains of Pace University:
    You have, I feel sure, been following the progress toward the
joining of The College of White Plains and Pace University into
one consolidated institution. During the past six months, many
meetings involving trustees, administrators, faculty, staff, students,
and alumni have taken place. A remarkable degree of understand-
ing, agreement, and support has developed. The result has been
that with the consolidation of the two institutions, which became
effective July 15, there already existed a sense of unity that I hope
I may be able to transmit to you and share with you in the spirit
which motivated and made the consolidation possible.
    Many questions of detail will arise in the future. Some of these
may be answered by this letter, but most important, I wish to
explain to you the general nature of the consolidation and its
significance for The College of White Plains. From the very first of
the many discussions and written commitments concerning the
consolidation, it has been stressed that The College of White
Plains is to be preserved in its nature, name, and mission. That
commitment is binding. It will not be abrogated. The nature of an
institution is dependent upon its purpose and the way in which its
trustees, faculty, staff and students recognize and pursue that
purpose. Basic to the consolidation is the agreement to preserve the
entire College of White Plains board as an influential advisory
group; to constitute the Board of the consolidated institution so
that one-third of its membership shall be drawn from The College
of White Plains; to retain faculty and staff; and to preserve the
liberal arts programs of study of the College.
    In the final analysis, it is the human resources -- administra-
tive, faculty, and students -- that constitute the critical factor in
preserving the nature and character of a college. We intend to
build upon this important element of The College of White Plains -
- to retain it and to enhance its future. The presence of strong
liberal arts programs on the New York and Pleasantville campuses
of Pace University will in no way diminish the need for the
determination to maintain and enhance the liberal arts program of
The College of White Plains. Indeed, it is anticipated that each will
support the other and result in greater service to the students of all
parts of the University. In addition, Pace's professional programs
will be made available, as appropriate, in accordance with student
interest and need.

It seems important to reiterate the fundamental concept of the consolidation that has taken place. The objective is to blend the strength of the University with the intrinsic academic value of The College of White Plains and help to preserve and develop that institution through a sharing of the resources of the two institutions. A larger institution and a smaller one will become one entity in which trustees from both will continue to share fully in the responsibility to chart the course for the consolidated university while retaining the nature and identity of the smaller college. This is a unique objective and a seldom found achievement.

The commitments made in seeking to define the way in which the objective of preservation and perpetuation of The College of White Plains would be achieved included the retention of staff and faculty, honoring of all existing contracts, participation of The College of White Plains faculty administration and students in the Pace University Senate, maintenance of the fee structure for the new and continuing College of White Plains students during the academic year 1975-76, and providing for student choices of designation, either Pace University or The College of White Plains of Pace University, for diplomas to be awarded in the next few years.

We shall seek to increase full-time and part-time enrollment thus making possible the scheduling of a more diversified program of course offerings. A law school will open in September 1976, and graduate level courses will be offered in September 1975. Parking and building facilities will be improved, and staff, in critical areas such as counselling and student personnel, will be increased. In addition, Pace personnel in specialized areas will be available to all students on all three campuses of the University.

Working together, we hope to capitalize on the strength that exists at The College of White Plains and create an even more exciting environment than circumstances have permitted in the past. Our theme, as you will see in advertising soon to appear, is that The College of White Plains 'is thriving.' It deserves to be, for the sake of its students and faculty and because of all that its history implies.

I welcome this opportunity to communicate with you and look forward to an early day in September when we may meet personally.

> *Sincerely,*
> *Edward J. Mortola*
> *President*

A Certificate of Consolidation was received in the office of Dr. Edward Mortola, President of Pace University, on September 22, 1975. Receipt of the Certificate was the final step in the long process leading up to the Consolidation of The College of White Plains with Pace University.

New Jersey Alumnae Chapter

Brooklyn, Long Island Alumnae Chapter

Mother Mary Dolores - Cardinal Spellman 1966

Silver Jubilee of Good Counsel College 1948

THE ALUMNAE ASSOCIATION
OF GOOD COUNSEL COLLEGE

The Alumnae Association of Good Counsel College was established in 1927 by the members of the first class to graduate from the College. This small group of 10 young ladies, filled with love for their Alma Mater, and wishing to express their gratitude, came together to form the Alumnae Association. The following officers were elected:

Marguerite C. Dolan, President
Margaret F. Reynolds, Vice President
Carol C. Carmody, Secretary
Wanda J. Graboski, Treasurer

Under the auspices of Mother Mary Aloysia, President of the College, the new association spent the first months of its existence setting up a strong foundation for a permanent and effective organization.

The Alumnae Association was founded in order that the spirit of the College might be kept alive, that the friendships of college days might be sustained, and that the union of all graduates might strengthen the Catholic ideals of its members and make them instruments for spreading these ideals through the world.

With one or more of these purposes in mind, the Alumnae Association engaged in various activities:

1. Fall meeting held at the College to outline the activities for the year.
2. Days of Recollection and prayer.
3. Alumnae Supper and night at the Bazaar at Good Counsel.
4. Formal dance held in a New York City hotel.
5. Winter meeting held in January in New York City.
6. Annual Bridge held in the winter in a New York City hotel.
7. Communion Breakfast in the spring held at the College.
8. Children's Day held in May at the College.
9. June meeting held at the College for election of officers and reception of new members into the association with banquet for the graduates.

The chief source of information concerning the Alumnae in the early days was supplied by The Prestonian. It carried a special column called "Alumnae Gleanings" and reported other important events as they occurred.

In September 1942, the Alumnae began the publication of a Newsletter, the first of which appeared in a three-column mimeograph form edited by Alice Lehmann '39. Year by year the Newsletter improved in form and content. In 1946 the printed copy appeared. This now became the best source of information concerning the members of the Alumnae. Since not all were able to attend the meetings, the Newsletter was a means of uniting the members of the Association and keeping alive the spirit of the College.

Among the many Editors of the Newsletter who worked so diligently to obtain news and to report it so faithfully, may be mentioned Janet Bussell '40, who continued to serve in this position over a good number of years.

Alumni Jubilee Reunions

In the spring of 1952, Good Counsel College began the beautiful custom of celebrating the Silver Jubilee of the classes. Graduates were invited to return to Alma Mater for a weekend of activities. Dinner was served on Saturday evening at which members of the faculty were invited guests. Year after year, whenever possible, His Excellency Bishop James E. Kearney planned to be present. On Sunday morning a special Mass was offered for the Jubilee class, followed by a Communion Breakfast.

This event continued to take place each year, beginning with the Class of 1927 whose Silver Jubilee occurred in 1952. The practice of celebrating the 40th Anniversary was introduced in 1967 with the Class of 1927. The members of the class were invited as special guests to the annual Communion Breakfast sponsored by the Alumnae Association. The Breakfast followed the Mass, celebrated this year by the Most Reverend James E. Kearney, retired Bishop of Rochester, on April 2, 1967. The Class of 1942, marking its 25th Anniversary, were the guests of the College for the entire weekend. Each member of the class received an engraved silver charm from Mother Mary Dolores.

At a later date the 20th, 10th and 5th Anniversaries were added as a means of honoring a greater number of Alumnae.

PRESIDENTS OF THE ALUMNAE ASSOCIATION
GOOD COUNSEL COLLEGE

Marguerite C. Dolan '27	1927-1930
Mary F. Fearon '28	1930-1931
Mary R. Corley '27	1931-1933
Una Falls '31	1933-1935
Mary A. Drury '32	1935-1938
Kathryn White '31	1938-1939
Marie E. Todd '33	1939-1941
Doris Dowd '36	1941-1942
Katherine Shepard '31	1942-1944
Rita V. Burns '34	1944-1946
Virginia T. Hyland '29	1946-1947
Margaret A. Higgins '37	1947-1949
Florence M. Simpson '43	1949-1951
Margaret M. O'Brien '43	1951-1952
Una Falls Gavin '31	1952-1953
Geraldine Grant '30	1953-1954
Eileen Slater Blake '45	1954-1956
Madeline J. Dinger Schaeffer '34	1956-1960
Jeanne J. Farnan '49	1960-1961
Jeanne A. Nolan Sinnott '51	1961-1963
Rosemary R. Leddy Quinn '43	1963-1966
Frances M. Kelly '57	1966-1970
Virginia A. Curry '59	1970-1972

PRESIDENTS OF THE ALUMNAE ASSOCIATION
THE COLLEGE OF WHITE PLAINS

Barbara M. Seitz '63	1972-1974
Judith E. Paladino Anson '63	1974-1976

PRESIDENTS OF THE ALUMNI ASSOCIATION
THE COLLEGE OF WHITE PLAINS
OF
PACE UNIVERSITY

Cynthia S. Acconci Schwanderla '56	1976-1978
Gwen E. King Snyder '59	1978-1980
JoAnne B. Stack '49	1980-1983
Barry L. Kennedy '80	1983-

Gifts of the Alumnae

Window in the Church

In the spring of 1933, Mother Mary Aloysia had stained glass windows installed in the Church. Many generous friends came forward to help finance the project, among them the Alumnae of Good Counsel College, at that time numbering 158 members.

The beautiful window depicting the Child Jesus in the Temple was the gift of the Alumnae of 1933, presented in loving gratitude to Mother Mary Aloysia, Foundress and First President of Good Counsel College.

Pews in the Church

In connection with the celebration of the Diamond Jubilee of the founding of the Sisters of the Divine Compassion in 1961, Mother Mary Dolores, President of the College, invited the Alumnae to take part in a project of installing pews in the Church. In June 1961 she sent the following letter to the alumnae:

Dear Alumna,

There is something within the heart of every one of us that makes us want to be remembered. Perhaps that is one of the many reasons why young people are so notorious for carving their names on desks! We are not recommending any such action, but we do have a plan to offer by which you may carve your name permanently in the House of God.

For "four long years" you knelt, perhaps daily, before the tabernacle here in the college chapel of the Divine Compassion. It was here in the silence of the Chapel that you spoke so intimately with Our Lady of Good Counsel. Certainly, if there is any place where you are remembered, and where you want to be remembered, it is here.

Encouraged by the frequent suggestions of our friends, and motivated also by concern for the comfort of our congregation, we have decided that the college chapel must be equipped with pews. Our dear friend, Bishop Kearney, expressed the opinion, with which we readily agree, that many alumnae would doubtless welcome the opportunity of having their names engraved upon plaques as seat or pew donors. It seems to me that the excellence of this plan speaks for itself, and that further words are unnecessary.

· May our beloved Lady of Good Counsel inspire you to great generosity in beautifying her chapel and yours, and may she protect you always.

Sincerely in Our Lady
(signed) Mother M. Dolores

The project was launched with enthusiasm and the blessing of Bishop Kearney with the words, "*May the devoted 'Seat of Wisdom' bring you many seats for those who seek her wisdom at Good Counsel.*"

The Alumnae responded generously, many deeming it a privilege and an honor to have a part in beautifying the Church, as a few quotations from responses to the appeal will show:

Marie Todd '33 wrote, "*Thank you very much for giving me this wonderful chance to get a little closer to Our Lady of Good Counsel. I am deeply grateful. Evelyn and I are so excited about the Church.*"

Rosemary Leddy Quinn '43, "*If each alumna feels as I do about the college and the chapel, I'm sure you will receive a substantial return.*"

Jeanne Fornan '49, "*We thought it was a wonderful idea to offer the members of the alumnae an opportunity to participate and we sincerely hope they will respond generously. We know the chapel will look lovely when the work is completed and we will be anxious to see it.*"

Loretta Long Carey '35, "*It is indeed a great privilege and pleasure for me to be able to participate in this noble cause. The happiest days of my life were spent in the chapel.*"

Mary Ann Cohan '54, "*What a wonderful opportunity for the alumnae to be remembered by Our Lady of Good Counsel. By all means I would like to donate a seat in the chapel.*"

Joan Bellucci '60, "*I wanted to thank you and Good Counsel College for everything you have done for me. When I received your letter concerning the chapel pews and seats, it seemed like a splendid way to say "thank you".*"

Vivian Greco '61, "*I wish I could give more to the college that gave me the four happiest years of my life. I feel very honored to be given the privilege of donating a seat in the college chapel.*"

Practically every class, from that of the first of 1927 to the Class of 1961, made contributions for either a pew or a seat. The names of the donors are engraved on plaques attached to the pews, a happy reminder of the days they spent time in prayer and adoration in the beloved chapel, at the feet of Our Lady of Good Counsel.

The Ostensorium

As a mark of love and gratitude, the Alumnae presented a gift to the Community on the occasion of the Diamond Jubilee of the founding of the Congregation. At the suggestion of Bishop James E. Kearney an ostensorium was chosen as the gift and approved wholeheartedly by the Alumnae.

The Ostensorium was manufactured from the gold and silver contributed by the Alumnae, students and friends of the college. The monstrance is adorned on the top with the pectoral cross that was presented to Bishop Kearney when he was consecrated Bishop of Salt Lake City. The only other precious jewels used came from the class rings of the first eleven classes. Eleven brilliant stones are set in a circle, five beautiful sapphires and six deep red garnets. We are happy to record the names of the donors:

Carol Carmody Von Steenberg '27	Irene Rogalin '32
Helen McGuiness Curry '28	Marie Todd '33
Edith O'Shaugnessy Flintoft '29	Eileen O'Donovan '34
Katherine Mergardt '30	Eve Lenk Wenz '35
Una Falls Gavin '31	Clair Joyce '36

Margaret Bender '37 - Donated by Mrs. Bender in memory of her daughter who died suddenly on January 6, 1935. Margaret would have been a member of the Class of 1937.

The Ostensorium was completed in the fall of 1939. The presentation took place at the Alumnae reunion supper held on November 11, 1939, at which Bishop Kearney was a guest of honor. Marie Todd, President of the Alumnae Association, made the presentation in the name of the Alumnae. Monsignor Joseph Breslin, speaking in his capacity as Honorary President, accepted the gift for the College, and praised the generosity of the Alumnae.

Children of the Alumnae

Children's Day

A new tradition was founded on Saturday, April 27, 1940, when the Alumnae brought their little children to Preston Hall for an afternoon party. The children ranged in age from 3 months to six years. The Alumnae and their little ones were received and welcomed by His Excellency James E. Kearney, Bishop of Rochester, and Mother Mary Aloysia. After the party all the guests were invited to go over to the College Chapel where Benediction of the Blessed Sacrament was given by Bishop Kearney, assisted by Father R. Rush Rankin, S.J. Children's Day had been delightfully established.

Each year, thereafter, the Alumnae returned to their Alma Mater with their children. It was a day looked forward to with much joy. On Saturday, May 17, 1941, there were representatives from each class. A committee of college students was organized to arrange the program of games to be played. Toys and favors were distributed among the children. Again the day was brought to a close with Benediction of the

Blessed Sacrament in the College Chapel. Whenever possible, Bishop Kearney planned to be present. He took great delight in meeting his former students and blessing their children.

The years went by quickly. Soon these little children reached college age and their mothers returned to register their daughters at the college they loved so well. A sure proof of their loyalty and devotion to the college was shown by the fact that a great number of Alumnae wished their daughters to experience the same college life it was their happiness to enjoy.

Alumnae Daughters

The list of Alumnae daughters is long and distinguished. The year 1951 saw the arrival of the first two young ladies, Bettie Ann Kehoe, the daughter of Evelyn Dolan Kehoe of the Class of 1927, and Avalon Kniphuisen, daughter of Anna O'Reilly Kniphuisen, Class of 1927. Later in 1956, Mrs. Kniphuisen sent her other daughter Anne to the College, not only to become a student, but to enter the religious community of the Sisters of the Divine Compassion.

Space does not permit recording all the daughters of the Alumnae, but a few deserve special mention.

Helen McGuiness Curry of the Class of 1928 sent two daughters to Good Counsel: Virginia Ann Curry, an excellent student who graduated cum laude in 1959 to become a distinguished member of the Alumnae and the President of the Association from 1970 to 1972, and Ellen Rose Curry who graduated magna cum laude in 1963. She was awarded a Fellowship in Chemistry by St. Louis University and an Assistantship in Chemistry by Loyola University in Chicago. Despite these tempting offers, Ellen returned to Good Counsel to enter the Community of the Sisters of the Divine Compassion on October 7, 1965.

Margaret Hoolahan Landers of the Class of 1931, entrusted her two daughters to Good Counsel, Carol Ann Landers and Mary Elizabeth Landers. Carol Ann was President of the Student Council and graduated in 1959.

Mary O'Brien Lyons of the Class of 1932 deemed it an honor to send her three daughters to her Alma Mater: Mary Veronica Lyons who graduated in 1962, Patrice Ann Lyons who graduated in 1963, and Rose Therese Lyons who graduated in 1965. After graduation, Patrice Anne continued her studies and obtained her Masters Degree in French Literature from Syracuse University. She then decided to pursue law as a career. She entered the Georgetown University Law Center and received her law degree, Juris Doctor. She is now following a very successful law career. She is distinguished member of the Alumnae Association and was chosen as the Alumna of the Year in 1979.

Among the freshmen registered in September 1965 were seven daughters of Alumnae: Denise M. Blewett, daughter of Gloria Carreras Blewett, a cum laude graduate of the Class of 1944; Joan Darragh, daughter of Helena Donnelly Darragh, Class of 1942; Frances Grainger, daughter of Loretta Pfeifer Grainger, Class of 1940; Suellen Koelsch, daughter of Muriel Clark Koelsch, a cum laude graduate of the Class of 1935; Mary Rita McElroen, daughter of Rita Cashin McElroen who graduated magna cum laude in 1934; Barbara Quin, daughter of Margaret Casey Quin, Class of 1942; and Margaret Robbins, daughter of Margaret Lyons Robbins, Class of 1941.

Several of these young ladies distinguished themselves in turn during their college days. Denise Marie Blewitt was enrolled in the College Honors Program. She was chosen valedictorian of her class and graduated magna cum laude in 1969. She was awarded the Mother Mary Veronica Memorial Medal for general excellence. Denise was admitted to Kappa Gamma Pi, the National Scholastic and Activity Honor Society of Catholic Women's College. She was also admitted to Delta Epsilon Sigma, the National Honor Society for Catholic men and women's colleges. Miss Blewitt was offered a Graduate Assistantship in Mathematics by Indiana University and a Research-Teaching Assistantship in Mathematics by the University of Southern California.

Frances Marie Grainger was named to Who's Who in American Colleges and Universities. To be eligible for this honor, a senior must have been on the Dean's List each semester and have held an office in Student Government, Class or Club. Frances was a member of the College Honors Program, was on the Dean's List for four years and held several offices. She graduated in 1969 and was awarded the Leo I. Kearney Memorial Medal for Theology. She was admitted to two Honor Societies, Kappa Gamma Pi and Delta Epsilon Sigma. Miss Grainger was offered several graduate assistantships: from the University of Virginia, a National Institute of Health Pre-Doctoral Fellowship in Biochemistry; from Ohio State University, a Teaching Assistantship in the Department of Chemistry; and from New York University, a National Institute of Health Fellowship in Environmental medicine.

Three other young ladies in this group completed their studies and graduated in 1969: Joan Helena Darragh, B.S.; Suellen A. Koelsch, B.S., who also received a New York State Teacher Certificate in Mathematics; and Mary Rita McElroen, B.S.

The Alumnae Association Chapters

At a reunion held at the College on Sunday, September 27, 1931, the Alumnae were the guests at a dinner given by the faculty in the new dining room of Preston Hall, which had just been completed. After the dinner, a tour of the new building was made. All were delighted with what they saw.

Following the tour, the regular fall meeting of the Association was held, at which it was decided that a series of functions be sponsored by members of the various localities -- Westchester, New York City, New Jersey, Brooklyn and Long Island.

The total number of Alumnae at this time had reached 92. It was felt that activities of the Alumnae could be carried on more effectively by the smaller groups, where the members were known to each other. Thus the idea of Alumnae Chapters came into focus. Some of these Chapters had already been organized while the members were still students in the College.

The New Jersey Chapter

One of the earliest and most active was the New Jersey Chapter which was organized at its first meeting on November 18, 1926. The following officers were elected: Marguerite Dolan '27, President; Margaret Wall '27, Vice President; Evelyn Dolan '27, Secretary; Kathryn Dunn '30, Treasurer.

The members of the group were determined to implant the true spirit of Good Counsel in the hearts of the future students of their Alma Mater, and to keep the students from New Jersey more closely united. During the following years, they carried on a number of activities for the benefit of Good Counsel College. Each year they sponsored a Bridge held at the home of one of the members. On March 5, 1927, the first such affair was held at the home of Catherine Collins '29, of Elizabeth, New Jersey. All the students were invited and attended in good numbers.

The original officers of the Jersey Chapter having graduated from the College, the remaining students from New Jersey got together in June 1927 to elect new officers to carry on the works of the Chapter. The following students who had just completed their sophomore year were elected: Roseclaire Stanton '29, President; Helen E. Tarrant '29, Vice President; Catherine M. Collins '29, Secretary; Elizabeth A. Kennedy '29, Treasurer.

The New Jersey Chapter continued to flourish, each year welcoming new students who came to the college from New Jersey.

As these students graduated, their Chapter continued as an active group of the Alumnae Association. Through the interest and zeal of Marie Todd '33, the Jersey Chapter was able to receive constant publicity in the Jersey papers. On the other hand, the pages of The Prestonian continued to record the many activities of the College branch of the New Jersey Chapter.

The Brooklyn-Long Island Chapter

Another Alumnae Chapter which had its roots in the organization established by the students in 1926 was the Brooklyn-Long Island Chapter. The early pages of The Prestonian tell of the numerous programs of this very active Chapter, carried on with great success under the direction of its presidents: Mary Fearon '28, Grace Dodworth '27, Helen Keenan '29, Dorothy Kiernan '33, Alice Hogan '34.

One of the chief aims of this Chapter was to support the Missions and to obtain funds for the building program. As a Chapter of the Alumnae Association, Brooklyn-Long Island continued to make its contribution to the College over the years. By 1971, the Alumnae residing in Long Island had become so numerous that it was decided to divide the Chapter into five different Chapters, two in Nassau County, two in Suffolk County, and one comprising Brooklyn and Queens County. The organizational meeting was held at the home of Elizabeth Shannon Mahon '49, in East Northport. Those present at the meeting included: Madelyn Avallon Sacchia '51, Susan Hines '70, Dolores Trumpler '48, Elizabeth Mueller Ford '51, Mary Elizabeth Herman Moore '50, Mary Lou Gaffney Synoldt '58, Elizabeth Dwinell Tolan '59, Mary Zupo Skrolly '60, Elaine Johnson McKeon '61, and Sister Mary Leona Fechtman '34.

The pages of the Alumnae Newsletter tell of the continued activities of the alumnae from Long Island.

The New York City Chapter

References to the New York City Chapter of the Alumnae appear quite early and frequently in the pages of The Prestonian. On Friday, April 13, 1934, the Chapter held its annual dance at the Waldorf Astoria in New York City, which was attended by a good number of Alumnae as well as by students from the College.

This Chapter carried on many successful functions during the years. One of special interest was the Christmas party on Sunday, December 20, 1942, given to the little children of Our Lady's Institute in Fordham. The tiny tots, ranging in age from 2 to 5 years, provided all the entertainment. They sang songs, recited and told stories, much to the delight of all present. Our good friend Leo I. Kearney played Santa

Claus with such great skill that his disguise fooled even some of the members of the Alumnae present. After the party, the Alumnae enjoyed refreshments served by the Sisters. Credit for the success of this party went to the careful arrangements made by Miriam Roche '39, Thelma Ryan '39, and Rita Burns '34.

A similar party was given again in 1943, becoming an annual event thanks to the interest and enthusiasm of Vera McNamara Ford '35 and Ethel Grainger '40.

The New York Chapter continued to flourish during the 40's, then followed a period of decline lasting too many years. In 1960, there were repeated demands for its revival. A meeting was scheduled in the spring of 1961, held at Keating Hall, Fordham University. Under the leadership of Catherine Nacey Ott '43, the New York City Chapter was completely reorganized and began again a vigorous life of activity.

The Westchester Chapter

The Westchester Chapter began to function in 1936. It flourished for a while but was disbanded during the War years. It was brought to life again and reorganized in 1944 by Margaret O'Brien '43.

During the first years of its existence, the Westchester Chapter, under the Presidency of Regina Cashin '36, held various activities, the proceeds of which were given to the Jubilee Fund, in honor of the Golden Jubilee of the founding of the Sisters of the Divine Compassion.

After its reorganization in 1944, the Westchester Chapter continued to be very active. Each year a reception was given to welcome new members and monthly meetings were held in the Bronxville Library.

Among the members of the Alumnae who were zealous in promoting the activities of the Chapter may be mentioned just a few: Joanne Kennedy '34, was Chairman of a dance held at the Rye Country Club on June 11, 1937; Dolores Koch Palmer '35, was President of the Chapter in 1946; Dorothea Herrick Cope '43, was Chairman of a successful Bridge held in 1946; Virginia Henchy '49, helped to activate the Chapter in 1952; Patricia Young Oleson '49, of White Plains, was Chairman of a Bridge and Fashion Show held in Preston Hall on April 10, 1953; and again the next year, the Westchester Chapter held a very successful Spring Bridge and Fashion Show in Preston Hall on April 23, 1954, under the Chairmanship of Kay Manning Blackmore '41 and Eleanor Delaney '45. The Chapter met again at the Town Tavern in Bronxville on May 19, 1954 to elect new officers, choosing Frances Keegan '51 as President.

The Westchester Chapter continued to flourish and to make its contribution to the welfare of the college. As Westchester Alumnae, Good Counsel College graduates are also members of the Council of

Women's College Clubs in Westchester County. Margaret O'Brien '43 became very active in this group.

Because of the vast extent of its territory and the large number of its members, it was decided in the spring of 1966 to organize the Westchester Chapter into area clubs (Yonkers, White Plains, etc.), each smaller unit to have its own officers and to be responsible for its own activities. The Yonkers Club, with Dolores Gray Carey '39 as President, launched into a period of activity. The White Plains Club was organized by Cynthia Acconci Schwanderla '56, who introduced a series of interesting lectures held over a period of time.

The Westchester Chapter was responsible for the new Alumnae Office established in St. Joseph's House by Mother Mary Dolores in the Fall of 1965. It was under the expert supervision of Virginia Curry '59, until the appointment of Sister Mary Leona Fechtman '34 as Director of Alumnae Relations in 1968.

The Upstate New York Chapter

A group of students from the Rochester Diocese often met with Bishop Kearney at breakfast when he came to Good Counsel to say Mass or attend one of its functions. A close friendship began to spring up among these students. To strengthen these bonds, the idea of forming an Upstate Chapter was discussed with Bishop Kearney, who was delighted with the idea and gave them every encouragement, since the number of students attending the College from the Rochester area was growing.

Betty Schneider '47 and Theresa Kelley '49 looked into the matter systematically. They obtained from the Registrar's Office a list of the names of all the students from the Rochester Diocese as well as those from Buffalo, Watertown, Elmira, Dansville, Syracuse and Auburn. Armed with this information, they formed a committee and met on a lovely afternoon in August 1945 at the Rochester home of Betty Schneider who acted as chairman, with Theresa Kelley as co-chairman from Auburn.

The founding committee was made up of the following members: Elizabeth Schneider '47, Chairman; Theresa Kelley '49, Co-Chairman; Patricia Burke '47, from Kenmore; Jean Hartman '47, from Hamburg; Jeanne Schneider '48, from Rochester. Kathryn Thomas '51 from Elmira, who had registered for the freshman class at the College in the fall, was also invited to attend the meeting. Bishop Kearney had been invited but was unable to attend that day. However, he called and wished the group success in their endeavor to set up a Chapter and gave them his blessing. The little group did succeed in establishing a strong foundation for a "gem" of a Chapter, which was very dear to the heart of Bishop Kearney.

Thus the Upstate Chapter came into existence and began to function as these students returned to College in September 1945. When they graduated the Alumnae Association welcomed this new Chapter and its members into the organization. Through the years, it continued to be one of the most active groups. Regular meetings were held which often began with Mass celebrated by our devoted friend Bishop Kearney, who remained as the guest of honor at the luncheon which followed. Not only did he attend many of their meetings, but the Bishop offered a special Mass twice a year for the members of the New York Upstate Chapter.

The Rockland County Chapter

An Alumnae Chapter for the Rockland area was formed in October 1963 by Jean Fordrung Stellato '58. The meeting was held at her home in Pearl River; 15 members of the Alumnae were present. It was agreed that the group should meet periodically throughout the year at the home of one of the members. In December 1963, an organizational meeting was held at the home of Marie Tummolo '59 in Pomona, at which Jean Fordrung Stellato was named Chairman. Other officers elected were Rita Willett Raywid '50 as Publicity Chairman and Marie Tummolo as Secretary.

In the spring of 1964, another meeting was held at the home of Eileen Madison Dolson '47 in Monsey to discuss the role of this Chapter in the general Alumnae Association. It was decided that one of the chief aims of this group was to promote the knowledge of Good Counsel College by participating in College Nights at the County High Schools and by having Teas for prospective freshmen.

The officers elected for 1965-66 were Co-Chairmen Theresa Nassisi Helbeck '59 and Jean Fordrung Stellato, Mary McAuliffe Rothaupt '46, Treasurer, and Eileen Madison Dolson, Secretary.

Two special events were planned for that year, a fund raising cocktail party in October 1965 and an evening of recollection in March 1966 to which all local Alumnae of Catholic Women's Colleges in Rockland County were invited. This event was conducted at Marydell Convent in Suffern, New York.

By the fall of 1966, the number of Alumnae had increased to 2,074 members, scattered over a wide area of the United States. To serve this large number more effectively, the Alumnae Association planned to concentrate more on the formation of area Chapters during the year 1966. Catherine Nacey Ott '43 was appointed to the new position of Chapter Coordinator. It was her duty to lend assistance to groups wishing to form a Chapter or area club. She served as liaison officer between the Executive Board and the various Chapters.

The Albany Chapter

The Albany Chapter was initiated by Claudette Stroble '65, who felt that the Capital District should have a Chapter of its own so that the many graduates from Good Counsel living in the area could get together and work for the College. The group began to function in the winter of 1967. They attended College Fairs to meet with prospective students who wished to "go away" to school, but, not too far away, so that trips home could be arranged economically. They stressed the advantages of attending Good Counsel, a college near enough to New York City to be able to participate in and enjoy its many cultural and educational opportunities.

The Albany Chapter was also very helpful in finding challenging jobs for recent graduates living in the area.

The Connecticut Chapter

In 1969, a Connecticut Chapter was established in the Waterbury area. The initial meeting was held in November 1969 at the home of Joanne Marchetti Pannone '61, in Oakville. The Alumnae who attended the formation meeting of the Connecticut Chapter included Loretta Longo Heller '60, Patricia Dwyer Mellitt '58, Kathleen Gleeson Cosgriff '61, Sister Mary Berchmans Coyle '42, Kathleen Alicky '53, Sister Helen Coldrick '54, Sister Mary Leona Fechtman '34, and Jeanne Marchetti Pannone '61.

Alumnae Fund Raising

From the earliest days of its establishment the Alumnae of Good Counsel College adopted as one of its objectives the support of the works of the College by contributing funds.

A special memorial fund drive was started in 1954 to honor Mother Mary Aloysia, Founder and first President of Good Counsel College, who died on December 29, 1953. Her passing was mourned by all, the community, the students in the College, and especially by the Alumnae who remembered her gentle presence which added a special warmth to every College function.

To show their appreciation, they enthusiastically supported the drive that would make possible the erection of a fitting and lasting memorial to be named in her honor as a constant reminder and inspiration of her life of dedication and service. Funds began to arrive year after year, slowly but surely.

A more extensive drive was launched in 1957 under the jurisdiction of the Community Counselling Services. It involved not only the Alumnae but the whole community, the Father's Club, the Ladies' Guild, students in the College and schools and the friends and relatives of the Sisters. As a result, sufficient funds were available by January 1958, to start construction on Aloysia Hall.

The Good Counsel Development fund continued to make its contribution, the Alumnae having no small part in the program through its Centum Club, thus making possible the vast building program carried on by Mother Mary Dolores during the years 1958-1968.

The Centum Club closed its accounts in 1968 and joined forces with the more pretentious fund raising project for annual giving known as the Annual Alumnae Fund. The total amount presented to the College over the years 1968-1981 reached the sum of $332,396.81. This generous contribution helped in no small way to defray the expenses of the vast building program carried on during the years 1958 to 1968.

ALUMNI ANNUAL FUND

Year	Co-Chairmen	Amt. Contributed	# of Alumni	%
1968	Margaret O'Brien '43 Catherine Nacey Ott '43	$26,560.00	788	46%
1969	Gloria Riverso Agro '55 Diane Riverso Regan '59	23,629.00	650	38%
1970	Margaret Hanley '63 Patricia Brennan DeFlorio '63	25,749.00	736	45%
1971	Gwenyth Kriss '53 Rita Kriss Frong '58	24,126.50	619	34%
1972	Margaret Pritchard '36	18,234.33	515	32%
1973	Denise Duquet McAnanly '57 Lucille Duquet Landry '59	25,012.11	651	39%
1974	Mary Corley Taylor '27 Shaileen Shanley '73	29,056.56	650	36%
1975	Cynthia Acconci Schwanderla '56	20,531.04	700	33%
1976	Salley Reid Lennon '53 Barbara Worm Donnehy '53	25,099.00	660	29%
1977	Gioia Gilgano '55 Margaret Foley Spellman '55	20,291.60	655	27%
1978	Marilyn Weigold '65 Claudette Strobel '65	19,944.02	621	24%
1979	Julia Hogan Picot '64	25,555.14	669	26%
1980	Janet A. Bussell '70	25,009.01	660	24%
1981	Jeanne Ahern Madison '70	23,599.00	808	29%
TOTAL AMOUNT CONTRIBUTED		**$332,396.81**		

Scholarships

The College of White Plains Alumni Association Executive Board announced a new program of Alumni Scholarships in September 1977, which were to be made available to relatives of the Alumni.

Three partial scholarships were thus awarded for the year 1978-79 to students at the College of White Plains of Pace University. One student received a $1,000 award, the other two received $500 each.

Each year the Alumni Association makes available $2,000 in scholarship funds for qualified students recommended by the College office of financial aid. First preference is given to relatives of the Alumni. An Alumni Scholarship Committee determines the number of recipients and the amount of the award granted to each student. Individual scholarships may range from $500 to $2,000. In addition, the Alumni Association also provides money for books to aid needy students in purchasing their college texts.

Cookbook

To commemorate the Fiftieth Anniversary of the founding of Good Counsel College, the Alumnae Association produced a cookbook entitled Our Favorite Recipes. The printed book became available in the Spring of 1974. It contains 300 excellent and varied recipes submitted by alumni, administrators, faculty, staff, trustees and friends. Each recipe is identified with the name of the person who submitted it. Its arrival on the campus caused a great deal of excitement and enthusiasm. The book sold for $3.50. The project proved to be a great success.

Wedgewood Plates

A beautiful set of four plates depicting several campus views -- the Church, Preston Hall, the first classroom building and the high school was a project launched by the Alumnae Association in the 1950's. Whether used for serving food, or just to hang on the wall, these lovely plates are an asset to any home.

Good Counsel College Charm

In 1959, the Alumnae Association joined with many other colleges throughout the country by having the College crest put on a lovely 14-carat hand-enameled charm in true College colors. The work was done by Marchal Jewelers, Fifth Avenue, New York City.

Alumnae Office

An office for the Alumnae Association was opened in St. Joseph's House on October 1, 1965, by Mother Mary Dolores. The room was situated on the first floor at the east end of the building. It had its own separate entrance. The room was furnished through the generosity of Bishop James E. Kearney, who contributed a gift of $1,000. Other contributions came from Mother Mary Dolores and the Westchester Chapter of the Alumnae.

The office was under the supervision of Virginia Curry and other members of the Westchester Chapter. The Alumnae took great pride in their office, which became the center of lively Alumnae activity.

Sister Mary Leona Fechtman '34 was appointed Director of Alumnae Relations in 1968 by Mother Mary Dolores. She took her place in the new office and supervised all the activities of the Alumnae Association. The room continued to be a center of activity and a source of information and service. On the walls of the new office, Sister Mary Leona displayed the pictures of the Presidents and Deans of Good Counsel College. The whole atmosphere of the room spoke of her love and interest in the College and its Alumnae Association, and each one of its members, familiarly known as "our girls". So great was the activity stemming from this office that the house began to be referred to as Alumnae House, overshadowing its official name, St. Joseph's House, given to it by Mother Mary Veronica in 1894.

Sister Mary Leona held the office of Director of Alumnae Relations for 14 years. She retired in 1982 and was succeeded by Jeanne Nolan Sinnott '51 who served as Director until 1984, when the position was taken by Cynthia S. Acconci Schwanderla, a graduate of Good Counsel College in 1956 and a former President of the Alumni Association for two years, 1976-1978.

Recognition Award

In the spring of 1975 the Alumni Executive Board introduced the subject of an award to be given each year for outstanding achievements to one or more members of The College of White Plains Alumni. A committee of five was appointed to set up the criteria for the award and to make recommendations to the Alumni Board. All the members of the Alumni Association were invited to submit comments, suggestions and the names of candidates for consideration.

The criteria for the award as established by the five member committee are as follows:

The College of White Plains Alumni Association "Outstanding Alumnus Award" shall be presented to one or more individuals who meet the following criteria:

1. *A living graduate of the college.*
2. *One who has been supportive of the college.*
3. *A person who has distinguished himself/herself by notable accomplishments in the business or professional world; and/or who has made a significant contribution to society, the community or fellowman.*

At its annual meeting in May 1976, The College of White Plains Alumni Association made the initial presentation of the newly established "Outstanding Alumnus Award" to two distinguished alumnae, Rosemarie DiLallo '52 and Virginia Schoman '42. These two women were selected by the awards committee from a large group of nominees who met the requirements for the award.

Alumni Association of the College of White Plains Recipients of the Alumna of the Year Award

1976 - Rosemarie DiLallo '52 & Virginia Irene Schoman '42
1977 - Marilyn Weigold '65
1978 - Bernadette Marie Bartels '55
1979 - Patrice Ann Lyons '63
1980 - Maria Stack Kinsella '47
1981 - Colleen A. Kelly '55
1982 - Sister Mary Leona Fechtman '34
1983 - Maureen Toomey Hillpot '51
1984 - Sister Mary Basil Hayes '27
1985 - Nancy Louden '75

The Guild

The Guild of Our Lady of Good Counsel was founded by Mother Mary Aloysia in 1941. The members of the organization consisted of the mothers or guardians of the students of the Academy and the College, as well as of the Alumnae. The aim and object of the Guild is to assist the Sisters of the Divine Compassion in any way possible, by financial support, and to promote interest in their works.

The list of first Officers of the Guild, who were to serve for a period of two years, is as follows:

President	Mrs. Joseph J. O'Reilly
1st Vice President	Mrs. Charles V. Lehmann
2nd Vice President	Mrs. Joseph F. Mazac
Recording Secretary	Mrs. Charles E. Healy
Corresponding Secretary	Mrs. George Sinnott
Treasurer	Mrs. George Higgins

Monsignor Joseph A. Breslin, Honorary President of Good Counsel College, acted as Spiritual Advisor.

Over the years the Guild has worked diligently and has made many generous contributions, thus enabling the Community to carry on its educational program more effectively. At the present time Mother Mary Ethelburge serves as the Moderator of the Guild.

The present Guild is an outgrowth of an earlier organization, known as the Auxiliary of Our Lady of Good Counsel, established in 1913 by Mother Mary Aloysia. Its members were made up of friends and benefactors of the Community who took a great interest in all its works and were willing to lend support especially in securing funds for the building of the unfinished wings of the convent.

Mother Mary Aloysia, R.D.C.
First President of Good Counsel College

Mother Mary Dolores, R.D.C.
Second President of Good Counsel College

Dr. Charles E. Ford, Third President of Good Counsel
with Sr. M. Teresa Brady; Sr. M. Charles Moran, Dean;
Sr. M. Basil Hayes; Terence Cardinal Cooke

Dr. Katherine Restaino
Fourth President of Good Counsel College

Sr. Mary Carmelita; Rev. Thomas P. Cahill;
Mother Mary Compassio; Msgr. Joseph Breslin; Sr. Mary Liguori;
Bishop James Kearney; Mrs. Helen Gerety; Mother M. Aloysia;
Sr. Mary Cyril, Dean; Msgr. Joseph Clune; Dr. Leo I. Kearney

Sr. Mary Basil; Sr. Mary Trinitas; Sr. James Marie (Ellen McGrath);
Sr. Mary Alice; Sr. Mary Liguori; Mother Mary Ethelburge;
Sr. Mary Teresa; Msgr. Charles McManus; Mother Mary Dolores;
Sr. Mary Leona; Sr. Mary Charles (Miriam Moran);
Sr. Mary Dolorita (Rita Dougherty)

Bishop James E. Kearney

Dr. Leo J. Kearney
Grand Marshall, Commencement Day

Mr. John J. Gerety; Mrs. Helen Gerety;
Professor Iole Gardella; Professor Elena Chavez

Sr. Mary Basil
Grand Marshall, Commencement Day 1975

OUTSTANDING FIGURES IN THE HISTORY OF GOOD COUNSEL COLLEGE

Mother Mary Aloysia, R.D.C.
Founder and First President
of
Good Counsel College

Mother Mary Aloysia (Catherine Ann Kelly) was born in Boonton, New Jersey, on January 17, 1869, the daughter of William and Mary Murphy Kelly. She received her early education in the schools of Brooklyn and New York City.

As she grew into womanhood, she felt that she had a vocation to the religious life. She consulted Father Matthew Taylor, pastor of her parish, the Blessed Sacrament. Father Taylor, discerning a true spirit, sent her to see Mother Mary Veronica in White Plains, with the comment, "*She is a young lady with positive character, yet mild, docile and gentle. She will make a very good and efficient religious.*"

On June 14 she left her home and arrived in White Plains at the convent which had been purchased just the year before. Here she made a retreat in preparation for the step she was about to take. Mother Mary Veronica received her into the young community as a postulant on June 19, 1891 at the age of twenty-one.

Sister Catherine began her life as a Sister of the Divine Compassion in the House of the Holy Family located at 132 Second Avenue in New York City. She was the last postulant to be received during the lifetime of Monsignor Preston. The day on which she applied for admittance into the community was the very day on which Monsignor Preston was stricken with the illness that resulted in his death on November 4, 1891. Sister Catherine, the postulant, was present at his bedside to receive his final blessing just a few days before he died.

Sister Catherine received the habit on April 2, 1892 and was given the name Sister Mary Aloysia. She pronounced her first vows on April 2, 1894 and her final and perpetual profession on Sunday, November 18, 1899.

Sister Mary Aloysia worked closely with Mother Mary Veronica in carrying out her early assignments. She was one of a staff conducting classes at the House of Nazareth in White Plains, had charge of the little boys in St. Stanislaus House, and performed the duties of sacristan, helping to get the newly completed Church ready and preparing the altar for the first Mass celebrated there on April 26, 1897. She performed a similar function for the solemn consecration of the Chapel of the Divine Compassion on May 31, 1897.

When the House of Nazareth was incorporated in October 1901, its name changed to Good Counsel Training School for Young Girls, and Sister Mary Aloysia was assigned to teach the girls in the Training School.

In February 1902, Mother Mary Veronica initiated a new pioneer work by establishing a club for working girls in New York City in the House of Our Lady of the Wayside at 37 Eighth Street and St. Marks Place. Finding the house too small for the ever increasing number of girls who joined the Catholic Girls' Club, Mother Mary Veronica sold the house at St. Marks Place in March 1904 and purchased two pieces of property uptown, situated at 52-54 East 126 Street. She named it Our Lady's House. Sister Mary Aloysia and Sister Mary Joseph Scheuer were appointed to the work.

With the death of Mother Mary Veronica on August 9, 1904, Sister Mary Clair was elected Superior. In the fall of 1904, the new Superior appointed Sister Mary Aloysia as Novice Mistress, a position she held until her own election as the third Superior General of the Sisters of the Divine Compassion.

Upon her election as Superior, Mother Mary Aloysia immediately embarked upon her favorite work of education. One of her first tasks was to reorganize Good Counsel Training School for Young Girls. She renamed the school the Academy of Our Lady of Good Counsel. By 1914 the high school department was added.

Another work that engaged her attention was the building of the convent, one wing of which had been completed and occupied in 1908. Funds were lacking, but through the prayers of the Sisters and the financial aid of the Auxiliary of Our Lady of Good Counsel, by 1922 she was able to resume the work on the other three wings of the convent.

During her early days as Superior, Sisters were sent to the parishes in White Plains and St. Mary's in Katonah to conduct classes in catechism to children attending public schools. Out of this last came the first parochial school staffed by the Sisters, opened in 1921. Other parochial schools followed: St. Lawrence O'Toole, Brewster, in 1927; Our Lady of Mt. Carmel, Elmsford, in 1929; St. Frances de Chantal,

Bronx, in 1930; St. Bernard's, White Plains, in 1932; and St. Joseph's, Croton Falls, in 1949.

In 1926, Mother Mary Aloysia purchased a beautiful piece of property in Throggs Neck on Long Island Sound known as the Huntington Estate. The large house on the land became the new House of the Holy Family when the Sisters and the girls took possession in August 1927, the property at 136 Second Avenue having been sold in the spring.

In 1916 came a request from Father Patrick N. Breslin, pastor of Our Lady of Mercy Church Fordham, to conduct a day and evening business school and kindergarten. The work was officially started on February 1, 1917 under the name of Our Lady's Institute. Sister Mary Reparata introduced a unit of the Catholic Girls' Club. The house also served as a residence for working girls. The project continued to flourish for over 38 years and supplied several vocations to the community. It was finally terminated in 1954.

While providing for the education for the children in the various schools, Mother Mary Aloysia did not neglect the education of the Sisters. In cooperation with Fordham University, a plan was worked out by which extension courses could be offered at White Plains. In the summer of 1919, Father Matthew L. Fortier, S.J., Director of the Summer Session, permitted Marietta Riley, a Fordham professor, to conduct courses at Good Counsel for the Sisters in preparation for the degree of Bachelor of Arts. Upon completion of the requirements, Fordham University conferred the Bachelor's degree upon the successful candidates. Having obtained the Bachelor's degree, several Sisters then registered at Fordham University to continue their studies for the Master's degree. Father R. Rush Rankin joined the Fordham faculty in 1920. He took a deep interest in the education of the Sisters and continued to advise Mother Mary Aloysia on the choice of courses for higher degrees. Mother Mary Aloysia, herself, attended the extension courses offered at Good Counsel and later continued her graduate work at Fordham University. She obtained a Bachelor's degree in 1921, a Master's degree in 1922, and a Doctor of Philosophy in 1926.

The crowning work of Mother Mary Aloysia in the cause of Catholic education was the founding of Good Counsel College in 1923, at the express wish of Patrick Cardinal Hayes, then Archbishop of New York.

A project that engaged the attention of Mother Mary Aloysia during the spring of 1933 was one dear to her heart. A.L. Brink Studios had installed the beautiful stained glass windows of Our Lady of Good Counsel in Preston Hall in 1931. She now contracted with this company to install eight stained glass windows in the Chapel of the Divine Compassion. Special attention was given to a window depicting St.

Veronica offering her veil to Christ on the way to Calvary. A photograph of Mother Mary Veronica was given to the artist to serve as a model for the face of Saint Veronica, so that a very satisfactory resemblance of the Foundress of the Community is now enshrined in the window.

In 1947, she established a new high school in the Bronx, naming it Preston High School in honor of Monsignor Thomas S. Preston, Founder of the Community. Two more parochial schools were added to the list of those conducted by the Community, St. Joseph's School, Croton Falls, in 1949, and Sacred Heart School, Hartsdale, in 1953.

In 1948, after 25 years of a very effective administration as President of the College, Mother Mary Aloysia handed over the task to Sister Mary Dolores Hayes. Mother Mary Aloysia never lost interest in the College, but continued to watch over its progress with loving solicitude. Over the next five years she witnessed the rapid growth in enrollment, until God called her to her eternal reward on December 29, 1953.

Mother Mary Dolores, R.D.C.

Mother Mary Dolores Hayes was born on May 10, 1900, in Ballincollig, a little town southwest of Cork City in the County of Cork, Ireland, the first child of Patrick J. Hayes and Margaret Josephine Blake Hayes. Her parents returned to the United States with their infant daughter in August 1900 and settled in New York City.

Mary began her early education at the School of Our Lady of Perpetual Help in Brooklyn, New York, where she was enrolled for the first and second grades. She continued her elementary and secondary education at the Academy of Our Lady of Good Counsel.

While living at Our Lady's Institute in New York, she enrolled in night classes in accounting at Fordham University. Wishing to serve others in a more meaningful way, she prepared herself for a nursing career by attending the Rhode Island Hospital in Providence from September 1924 to November 1926. However, feeling a strong desire to serve God in religious life, she made application and was accepted as a postulant on December 8, 1926. She received the habit of the Sisters of the Divine Compassion and the name Sister Mary Dolores on August 15, 1927. She made her first profession on July 2, 1929 and pronounced her final vows on July 7, 1934.

She received her B.S. degree from Good Counsel College on June 6, 1929. Fordham University awarded her the M.A. degree in Philosophy on June 13, 1934, and she received her Ph.D. in Philosophy from the Catholic University of America on May 29, 1942.

Sister Mary Dolores joined the faculty of Good Counsel College in 1928. She taught courses in science along with her specialty, philosophy. Her rich background in science enhanced by her preparation for a nursing career made her a most able and effective science teacher. After a two-year absence from teaching, while preparing for her doctorate, she returned to Good Counsel in the fall of 1942 and was named Chairman of the Philosophy Department.

To encourage students interested in philosophical thought, she established the Aquinas Philosophy Club, to *"create a greater interest in philosophical problems and by study and discussion to see the practical applications of Thomistic principles to the problems of every day life."*

Sister Mary Dolores continued her teaching apostolate until 1948, when in September came the official announcement that the Board of Trustees had appointed her President of the College. She continued in this position through twenty-two years as President totaling forty-one years of exceptional service until her retirement on February 18, 1970.

In 1964 Mother Mary Dolores had introduced a new honor, the Mater Boni Consilii Medal, the highest award that the College could bestow on persons she wished to honor for outstanding achievement and service to the College. She herself was the recipient of the award upon her retirement, when at the 1970 Commencement the College asked His Eminence Terence Cardinal Cooke to confer on her its highest honor, with a glowing citation.

One more honor was bestowed upon Mother Mary Dolores by Pace University when, at the commencement in May 1979, she was awarded the Honorary Degree of Doctor of Humane Letters.

Since her resignation as President of the College, Mother Mary Dolores has been actively engaged as Treasurer for the community of the Sisters of the Divine Compassion, with residence at the Motherhouse, Good Counsel Convent in White Plains.

Dr. Leo T. Kearney, K.M.

Leo I. Kearney was born in Red Oak, Iowa, on April 19, 1883, first child and son of William Patrick Kearney and Rosina O'Doherty Kearney. Two more sons were born into the Kearney family, James Edward, the future Bishop, on October 28, 1884 and William J. in 1887. The family moved to New York City some time after 1886 to reside in Saint Agnes Parish.

Leo received his early education in the public schools of New York City. He attended DeWitt Clinton High School and graduated with the class of 1901. Wishing to prepare himself for teaching, he enrolled at the New York Training School for Teachers and graduated with a license to teach in the New York City schools in 1903. He obtained a B.S. degree from Teachers' College, Columbia University in 1915. He continued his studies at the Graduate School of Fordham University and was granted his M.A. degree in 1926.

Mr. Kearney's first assignment as a teacher was to Public School 51 in 1904. After a few years in 1907 he was transferred to P.S. 25 in Manhattan where he taught for many years. He became Assistant Principal at P.S. 40 in the Bronx in 1917. Then in 1924 he was appointed Principal of P.S. 18 in Manhattan.

On Holy Saturday, April 7, 1917, Mr. Kearney married the lovely Mona Sheridan. The ceremony took place in St. Agnes Church and was performed by Father James E. Kearney, the brother of the bridegroom, who at that time was Assistant Pastor of St. Cecilia's Church.

In 1927 Mr. Kearney was appointed Assistant Director of the Bureau of Reference, Research and Statistics of the Board of Education of the City of New York, a position he held until 1949. He joined the faculty of Fordham University in 1919 where he taught courses in Education and Teaching Methods, until he retired in 1960 at the age of 77, after 41 years of successful teaching.

Good Counsel College welcomed Mr. Kearney to its ranks in 1925. For 35 years he rendered invaluable service in the classroom in preparing future teachers until ill health forced his retirement in 1960. Mr. Kearney's service to Good Counsel was not limited to the classroom. He took delight in participating in every activity and function, rendering a willing and cheerful hand in each and every task.

Despite his devotion to the work of education in the schools, Mr. Kearney found time to take an active part in the life of his parish and Community. He was held in high esteem by the members of the Saint Vincent de Paul Society, which he served for over sixty years. At the time of his death in 1966, he was Vice-President of the Bronx Council, having formerly been its President. He was untiring in his work for the betterment of youth.

The list of his services is long and varied. He was an official of the Public School Athletic League in the early days, judged Amateur Athletic Union and Knights of Columbus indoor track meets from 1920 to 1961, was Principal of the Recreation Playground season from 1909 through 1917, and Supervisor of Contests in the Playgrounds from 1914 to 1917. He served also as Supervisor on the Lecture Bureau and Assistant Examiner for the New York Board of Education. He was teacher and Principal of the Knights of Columbus Business School on West 96th Street, an evening school for adults and for soldiers after World War I.

In 1949 the Church, recognizing the outstanding contributions of Mr. Kearney for his many years of service, honored him with the distinction of membership in the Knights of Malta. Francis Cardinal Spellman bestowed on him the Maltese Cross, the insignia of the Order.

If Professor Kearney loved Good Counsel College; the College in turn loved him and seized upon every occasion to honor him. In 1950, upon his completion of 25 years of service to the College, he was tendered a testimonial dinner and reception by the President and Faculty on Sunday evening, January 15. Then a few days later on Thursday, January 19, another tribute was given to Professor Kearney, beloved teacher and friend, by the College students in Preston Hall.

The students also wished to voice their appreciation for this wonderful teacher and friend. In the February 1950 edition of The Prestonian this lovely tribute appeared:

A Tribute to Mr. Kearney

Tonight our memories wander through these silver years,
Made luminous with fruitful deeds of sterling worth,
But greatness lies not in the gleam of outward things --
It hides within the soul, hence radiates its strength
So let us go beyond the praise of men, and plunge
Into the very depths of his nobility.
How admirable are the traits we find; among which glows
The lovely gift of friendship, lavishly bestowed.
A friend of youth, he spent himself that he might mould
The pliant minds of those who hold tomorrow's world.
A friend of his co-workers in the field of Christ,
He taught the humble beauty of self-sacrifice
A friend to all Good Counsel, he has shared the toils
That brought our Alma Mater to its present heights.

Nor is this gift of friendship limited to human spheres.
For was it not Divinity Who spoke these words:
Whate'er you do for one of these, My least, you do for Me?
And from another world, that Voice more beautiful
Than all earth's jubilee, entones these joyous words
"Behold my faithful friend!"

In the fall of 1953 Dr. Kearney began his 29th year as a familiar figure on the campus of Good Counsel. At the Investiture of the Freshmen, held on November 11th, Bishop James E. Kearney presiding, Dr. Kearney presented the 79 candidates for the cap and gown. The highlight of the afternoon, however, was when he himself was presented with the doctoral robes, the gift of the College, by Audrey Shiebler, President of the Student Council. In her address she lauded him as *"the epitome of the Catholic educator, loyal to God, his duties and his friends."*

Year after year Professor Kearney journeyed to Good Counsel for his classes in education, teaching such courses as Principles of Education and General Methods of Teaching. He held his last class in the Spring of 1960, at the age of 77 and after 35 years of service to Good Counsel College. Ill health forced his retirement.

Though his presence no longer graced the campus, Dr. Kearney was not forgotten by the College. On August 6, 1963, the feast of the Transfiguration, the Most Reverend John J. Maguire, Vicar General of the Archdiocese of New York, officiated at the ceremony of the groundbreaking for two new buildings to be erected on the campus.

Dr. Kearney was not able to be present for the laying of the cornerstone, but his wife took the trowel in hand and added her share in fastening this stone in place.

On Sunday afternoon, May 23, 1965, His Eminence Francis Cardinal Spellman officiated at the Blessing and Dedication of Madonna Library and the Leo I. Kearney Sports Building. Then, Cardinal Spellman presented Dr. Kearney the Mater Boni Consilii Medal, the highest honor the College has to offer.

There remained only a few more months in the life of Dr. Kearney. He spent his last days in patient suffering until God called him to his reward at the age of 82. He died on October 7, 1966, the feast of the Holy Rosary. At the time of his death he was survived by his wife, Mona Sheridan Kearney, his son Donald L. and two grandsons James E. and George J. Kearney, also his two brothers, the Bishop James E. Kearney and William J. Kearney.

Bishop James E. Kearney, D.D.

James Edward Kearney was born at Red Oak, Iowa on October 28, 1884. He was the second child and son of William Patrick and Rosina O'Doherty Kearney. An older brother, Leo I. Kearney, had been born on April 19, 1883. A third son, William J., was added to the family in 1887.

James Edward received his elementary and secondary education in the public schools of New York City. Upon graduation from high school, he felt a strong inclination toward the priesthood. His parents made no objection, but since he was so young, his mother advised caution. He greatly loved his mother and respected her counsel. He thus enrolled in the New York Training School for Teachers. Its two-year course including practice teaching, gave him a wide experience in the New York Public School System which served him well later when he was appointed superintendent of Catholic schools in the Bronx in 1931. Upon graduation from the New York Training School, he acquired both a City and a State license to teach.

In the fall of 1903, at the age of 19, he entered St. Joseph's Seminary, Dunwoodie, Yonkers. Due to his high qualifications he was ordained ahead of his class, on September 19, 1908.

Immediately after his ordination, the young Father Kearney was sent to the Catholic University of America to complete his last year of theological studies. Later, as bishop, he was happy to serve on the Board of Trustees of the University. Having completed his theological studies, he returned to New York in 1909 for his first assignment, as assistant pastor of St. Cecilia's Church in Manhattan. It was here that he developed his pastoral skills. In 1928, after 19 years of fruitful service, he left St. Cecilia's to become the founder of the new parish of St. Francis Xavier in the Bronx.

It was at this time that Father Kearney joined the faculty of Good Counsel College to teach courses in religion. Father Kearney's interest in and service to the College went far beyond his teaching in the classroom. He entered wholeheartedly into all the activities and important functions. Even before he joined the faculty, when still at St. Cecilia's, he attended, along with Mr. and Mrs. Leo I. Kearney, the first of the annual debates, held on February 22, 1924. Again on March 30, 1926, he gave an illustrated lecture on the Life of Christ.

When he became Bishop, his presence lent dignity and prestige to many a function.

Year after year, beginning in 1933 and continuing for 32 years, he presided at the Investiture Ceremony bestowing the cap and gown on the incoming freshman class. His talks on these occasions were inspiring, always highlighting devotion to Our Lady of Good Counsel.

His presence at the annual Bazaar gave encouragement and support to the alumnae and students. One of the big attractions each year was his gift of a well-stocked Hope Chest and a Thanksgiving Dinner with all the trimmings. An even more important gift, relying on a bishop's privilege, he would bestow a welcome holiday. His many visits over the years to his dear Good Counsel were an inspiration and a blessing.

Our Holy Father Pope Pius XI appointed him Bishop of Salt Lake City on July 1, 1932. James E. Kearney was consecrated as the fourth Bishop of Salt Lake City in St. Patrick's Cathedral on October 28, 1932, the anniversary of his 48th birthday.

Many problems faced the Bishop in this western Diocese, which included the whole state of Utah, the home of the Church of the Latter Day Saints, who greatly outnumbered the Catholics. The friendliness and tact of the Bishop soon succeeded in establishing a good rapport with his Mormon fellow citizens.

The students of Good Counsel College also took an active part in helping the Bishop in his mission work in Utah, holding several card parties in the Grand Ballroom of the Hotel Commodore in New York City. As a result of their labors, they were able to send the Bishop a substantial sum.

After a five-year stay in the Diocese of Salt Lake City, Pope Pius XI on July 31, 1937, transferred him to the See of Rochester to succeed Archbishop Edward Mooney, who had been promoted to Detroit. James E. Kearney now became the fifth Bishop of Rochester and the second New Yorker to fill this post.

James E. Kearney was installed in his new diocese by His Eminence Patrick Cardinal Hayes on November 11, 1937, the first bishop to be enthroned in the pro-cathedral of the Sacred Heart, the old Cathedral of St. Patrick having been sold and demolished earlier that year. Bishop Kearney was transferred to the See of Rochester near the end of the Great Depression, but soon the dark days of World War II followed. The Bishop took up the task of not only strengthening the spiritual needs of his flock at home but also supplying 42 Diocesan priests as Chaplains for the armed forces abroad.

Bishop Kearney was popular, respected, revered, and loved by both priests and laity. He was a friendly man, sociable, but always respecting the dignity of his episcopal office. He was a zealous pastor of his flock, making every provision for their spiritual welfare. He had a great devotion to Our Blessed Mother, dedicating his diocese to Mary on August 22, 1948. He encouraged his people to pray the Rosary and never tired of praising and honoring the Mother of God. He came to be known as "Our Lady's Bishop."

When Bishop Kearney reached the age of 68, he asked the Holy See for an auxiliary bishop. Pope Pius XII chose Lawrence B. Casey, the rector of the Sacred Heart Cathedral, who was consecrated and named Vicar General in 1953. Bishop Casey took over many of the administrative duties, thus relieving the Bishop in his arduous task of running the diocese. This turned out to be a most providential move, for in 1956 Bishop Kearney had to undergo a serious operation and a long period of convalescence. However, he made a complete recovery and was able to function for many good years to come.

Bishop Kearney attended the opening session of the Second Vatican Council in 1962. However, since he had reached the age of 78, his Auxiliary Bishop Lawrence B. Casey represented the Diocese of Rochester in the subsequent sessions of the Council.

On March 9, 1966, when Bishop Kearney was 81 years old, Pope Paul VI removed his faithful and loyal auxiliary Bishop Casey from his side to become the new Bishop of Paterson, New Jersey. In that same year the Pope issued a decree requiring all heads of dioceses to submit their resignations when they had reached the age of 75. Though still active and in good health, with no desire to retire, Bishop Kearney complied with the wishes of the Holy Father and sent in his letter of resignation. Pope Paul VI accepted his resignation and appointed Bishop Fulton J. Sheen as his successor.

Though now in retirement, Bishop Kearney spent three or four more very active years in the service of the diocese. He preached, confirmed, presided at graduations, attended dedications, funerals and so forth. Finally, failing eyesight and strength necessitated his move to Saint Ann's Home, which he had built in 1963. Here he remained for the last two years of his life, taking up his residence at the Home on March 28, 1975. Though in his 91st year, he still continued to preach to the residents and go out on occasional calls. He was always cheerful, understanding and approachable; a holy man, a gentleman. He lived through the episcopate of Bishop Fulton J. Sheen and into that of Bishop Joseph Hogan.

Failing strength and eyesight finally curtailed his activity and confined him to his room. With a mind still clear, he patiently accepted his suffering and dependence, until at last God beckoned him to his reward on January 12, 1977.

The students of the College loved and appreciated Bishop Kearney; the following poem written by Margaret Daly of the Class of 1960, expresses well the sentiments of the Good Counsel girls:

*To His Excellency the Most Reverend
James E. Kearney, Bishop of Rochester*

> *Royal son of Christ*
> > *with unfailing wisdom*
> > *and abiding strength*
> *You have instructed us.*
> *Friend of Our Lady*
> > *with Christian humility*
> > *and Marian love*
> *You have inspired us.*
> *Beloved Bishop*
> > *with selfless devotion*
> > *and loving kindness*
> *You have earned our gratitude.*

Sister Mary Basil Hayes, R.D.C.

Sister Mary Basil Hayes (Lucy Agnes Hayes) was born on December 11, 1901. She received her elementary and secondary education at the Academy of Our Lady of Good Counsel. She graduated from high school in June 1922 and received a medal for general excellence. Since the College was not yet founded, she went to the New York Training School for Teachers, from which she graduated in 1924 with a Teacher's Certificate issued by the New York City Board of Education. The following year she spent teaching in the New York City public schools.

She entered the Community of the Sisters of the Divine Compassion on August 15, 1925. She joined the original class in the College as a junior transfer student and graduated with the first class in 1927 with the degree of Bachelor of Science. She continued her studies in higher education at Fordham University in Education and Philosophy. She was awarded her M.A. in 1929 and her Ph.D. in 1936.

Sister Mary Basil taught in the Elementary and High School departments of the Academy of Our Lady of Good Counsel during the years 1925-1927. In 1927 she was assigned to teach in the College, teaching a variety of courses such as Biology, Mathematics, History and Philosophy of Education, Educational Psychology and Special Methods of Teaching.

In 1942, upon the death of Sister Mary Edmund, the first Dean of Good Counsel College, Sister Mary Cyril was named Dean and Sister Mary Basil became Assistant Dean. During the following years, Sister Mary Basil continued to serve the College in various capacities: Professor of Education, Chairman of the Education Department, Director of the Teacher Education Program, and Assistant Dean.

In 1971 she was appointed to the position of Director of Institutional Statistics by Dr. Charles E. Ford, then President of Good Counsel College, an assignment she held for 9 years (1971-1980). On February 1, 1980 she was named College Historian by Dr. Edward Mortola, President of the College of White Plains of Pace University.

At the College Commencement held on June 7, 1971, Sister Mary Basil was awarded the Mater Boni Consilii Medal for having rendered 44 years of service to Good Counsel College.

In 1975, Sister Mary Basil celebrated her Golden Jubilee as a Sister of the Divine Compassion. As a mark of respect and appreciation, the Class of 1975 requested that she act as Marshal for the academic procession of the Commencement held on May 23, 1975.

At this same Commencement, the Board of Trustees of the College announced that the Library would be renamed "Hayes Library", honoring Mother Mary Dolores Hayes, who had been President of the

College for 22 years, and Professor of Philosophy for 19 years, and her sister, Sister Mary Basil Hayes, who was still actively engaged in college administration.

At the College Commencement held on May 27, 1977, Sister Mary Basil received the Alumni Golden Anniversary Award, as a member of the first class of 1927. This event marked not only the 50th anniversary of the class, but also her 50 years of continuous service to the college.

Pace University also awarded Sister Mary Basil Honorary Membership in the Twenty Year Club, as a woman *"Who since 1927 has served The College of White Plains and its predecessor Good Counsel College with devotion and singular benefit to students and colleagues."*

Sister Mary Philomena, R.D.C.

Sister Mary Philomena (Frances Mary Corridon) was born in New York City on September 16, 1882, the daughter of Michael Corridon and Mary McDermott Corridon who had come to the United States from Ireland around 1872 and settled in New York City. Here, Frances received her early education.

Feeling a strong desire to serve God in religion, she entered the young Community of the Sisters of the Divine Compassion on October 26, 1902 at the age of twenty. The convent at this time was located in Saint Joseph's House. Frances received the habit of the order and the name sister Mary Philomena on July 2, 1903. She pronounced her first vows on May 1, 1906 and her final profession on the feast of St. Veronica, February 4, 1914.

She was one of the last candidates to be admitted by Mother Mary Veronica. As a novice she had the privilege of praying at the bedside of the Foundress during her final illness which terminated with her death on August 9, 1904.

The sterling qualities of the young sister were recognized by her superiors, who placed her in positions of trust and responsibility. While still a novice, she supervised the work in the sewing room and later in the laundry. After her profession she spent a short time at Our Lady's House in New York City but returned to the Motherhouse at Good Counsel to take care of the wardrobe for the girls in residence. Then on June 19, 1909 she was placed in the important position as Director of the Training School. On January 23, 1910, the newly elected superior, Mother Mary Aloysia named her Director of St. Joseph's guest house, which position she held for many years.

In 1913, when the Auxiliary of Our Lady of Good Counsel was organized by Mother Mary Aloysia, Sister Mary Philomena became its Moderator. She also served as Procurator for the Community. In these positions her lovable and outgoing qualities made many friends and supporters for the Community.

When the College was established in 1923, the first resident students lived in St. Joseph's House, along with the other guests. Sister Mary Philomena had the added responsibility of looking out for the physical welfare of her young charges, who came to love and respect her.

When Preston Hall was completed and ready for occupancy in the fall of 1931, the most likely choice for Director of this new and important work fell on Sister Mary Philomena. That she was successful in this position was well attested to by the outpouring of love and appreciation that was manifested at the time of her death. After a short illness of several weeks, she went to her eternal reward on April 10, 1939.

The Requiem Mass was celebrated by Monsignor Joseph A. Breslin, and the eulogy delivered by Bishop James E. Kearney. The burial took place in the crypt of the Chapel of the Divine Compassion.

This humble woman who desired no acclaim was honored in death beyond all that she ever hoped for or expected. Bishop Kearney in his eulogy said in part:

"Sister Mary Philomena will be greatly missed, not only by members of the Community and the students, but also by a host of friends for her sympathetic interest and lovable qualities, and also on account of the responsible positions she filled so efficiently for many years. . . .She summed up in her life all that we consider worthwhile in a servant of God. She personified all that is finest and noblest and most admirable in the tradition of the Sisters of the Divine Compassion."

A very beautiful and handsome brass lectern, the gift of Bishop Kearney and his brother Mr. Leo I. Kearney, now stands as a solid memorial in the Chapel of the Divine Compassion, a tribute to *"Sister Mary Philomena who contributed in no small degree to the creation of the Spirit of Good Counsel"*.

Sister Mary Edmund Glynn, R.D.C.

Sister Mary Edmund (Margaret Dolores Glynn) was born in Rutsonville, Ulster County, New York on July 18, 1886, the daughter of Peter Glynn and Catherine O'Connell Glynn. Both of her parents were born in Ireland, but came to America and settled in New York State. In 1895, when Margaret Dolores was nine years old, the family moved to Middletown, New York, where she attended the Ursuline Academy. Later she enrolled at the Middletown School of Commerce from which she graduated. She began her career as a teacher in the Middletown schools. She was also employed as a bookkeeper. In November 1903, Miss Glynn moved to New York City and took up residence at Our Lady's House. Here she became acquainted with the Sisters of the Divine Compassion and was introduced to the Foundress, Mother Mary Veronica, to whom she became greatly devoted. She was impressed by the good work being accomplished by the young community and admired their zeal and religious spirit. After six months working as a stenographer, she began to feel a strong desire to serve God in the religious life, and asked to be admitted to the congregation. She entered the Novitiate, then located in St. Joseph's House in White Plains, on May 22, 1904. She was the last postulant to be admitted by the Foundress, who died the following August.

On May 24, 1905, she received the habit of the Order and a new name, Sister Mary Edmund. She made her first profession on November 7, 1905, and on the feast of Our Lady of Good Counsel, April 26, 1917, pronounced her final vows.

Sister Mary Edmund began her life work of education as early as September 1904. While still a postulant she was assigned to teach the girls in the Good Counsel Training School. When the Academy was established by Mother Mary Aloysia in 1910, Sister Mary Edmund was given the tasks of organizing the curriculum for the grade school and later for the high school.

Sister Mary Edmund loved the Academy children, particularly the Spanish girls who were so far from home and needed her mothering. The children, in turn, loved and respected her, giving her the title of the "Black Robed Chief". She loved nature and all God's creatures. Her techniques in the classroom were innovative. She used many devices to stimulate study, dividing the class into the "flowers" and the "birds", encouraging the fourth graders to write poetry, and introducing classes in stenography and typewriting for the pupils in the sixth grade.

She was named principal of the high school in 1921 and held this position with distinction until Good Counsel College was founded in 1923, when she became its first Dean.

Having obtained her B.A. from Fordham University on June 16, 1921, she continued her studies for higher degrees at the University. She was awarded the M.A. on June 15, 1922, and her Ph.D. on August 14, 1925.

Sister Mary Edmund's health, never robust, was always of great concern to her superiors, but she could never be induced to take rest and relaxation. In the summer of 1940, a serious illness confined her to the infirmary. She received the loving care of Sister Mary Berenice, the Community nurse, and her own sister Helen who was a registered nurse came to Good Counsel to care for her. By the end of the summer she was able to leave the infirmary to spend a little time for rest and recuperation at the home of her sister in Middletown. However, the period of quiet rest was brought to an abrupt close by the fatal accident of her sister. The shock of the tragedy deeply affected Sister, but her resignation and submission to God's will enabled her to return to her work in the College.

Commencement Day, Friday, June 5th, dawned bright and beautiful. Forty-three students received their degrees from the hands of Archbishop Spellman, bringing the number of Alumnae up to 494. This was the last commencement to be witnessed by Sister Mary Edmund. At the end of the exhausting day she collapsed. The few remaining days of her life were spent in prayer in preparation for her final examination. At the age of 56, God called her to receive the reward of a life spent in humble and faithful service. The rest she denied herself in life was finally won on June 16, 1942.

The second issue of the College Year Book Vestigia was dedicated to Sister Mary Edmund, the first Dean. M. Elizabeth Wilson of the Class of 1928 expressed the esteem of the students as follows:

Sister Mary Edmund

"To her whose wisdom and solicitude
Have been devoted without limit
To nurture in our minds sound principles
That we be fit to represent our Alma Mater,
Whose thoughtful care has ever been
A beacon light to guide our ships of ignorance
Safe within the harbor of right knowledge,
Whose personal concern for each of us has been
The norm by which we judged our worth,
We dedicate this book.
May it, for years to come, remain
A monument of our esteem."

Sister Mary Cyril, R.D.C.

Sister Mary Cyril (Anna Veronica Gallagher) was born in New York City on January 14, 1890, the daughter of Michael James Gallagher and Margaret Woods Gallagher. Both parents were born in County Tyrone, Ireland, and in the latter part of the 19th century settled in New York City.

Anna received her early education in the public schools of New York City. She attended Hunter College from which she received her B.A. degree in 1913. After graduation, she was engaged as a teacher.

As early as 1915, Anna began to think of entering the religious life. Inspired by the work being carried on by the Sisters of the Divine Compassion, particularly that of the House of the Holy Family, Miss Gallagher asked to be admitted to the Community. She was received as a postulant on September 8, 1918. Sister Anna began her religious life at a very difficult time, as a good number of the children in the Academy were down with Spanish influenza, as were many of the Sisters.

The eager postulant entered into all the activities of the day. She received the habit of the Sisters of the Divine Compassion on March 4, 1919 and was given a new name, Sister Mary Cyril, for Saint Cyril of Alexandria, the great champion of Mary as the Mother of God. After completing her novitiate, she pronounced her first vows on February 4, 1921, and made her final profession July 5, 1926.

Given the opportunity for further study at Fordham University, she was awarded her M.A. on June 15, 1922 and the Ph.D. in August 1925. Her special fields of study were in mathematics and philosophy.

Sister Mary Cyril's first assignment was to the high school department of the Academy of Our Lady of Good Counsel, where she taught for five years, from 1918 to 1923. When the College was established in the fall of 1923, Sister Mary Cyril became one of the first members of the faculty, as Professor of Mathematics and Physics. In 1925 she was named Assistant Dean, rendering valuable service to the Dean, Sister Mary Edmund. She continued to serve in this capacity until 1942, when upon the death of Sister Mary Edmund, she became the Dean of the College.

In 1960, after 42 years of remarkable service to the Community and the College, often beyond the call of duty, Sister Mary Cyril retired at the age of 70. Her remaining years, in poor health, were spent in cheerful resignation, to the edification of all who came in contact with her.

On April 20, 1968, Sister Mary Cyril celebrated her golden jubilee. On this joyous occasion she received a special apostolic blessing, which gave her consolation during the few remaining days of her life. God called her to her reward on August 16, 1968 at the age of 78.

A Requiem Mass was celebrated on Tuesday, August 20th, attended by numerous friends, relatives, students and alumnae. Many expressions of condolence came pouring in, showing the love and admiration for this simple, humble religious, among them the following lovely little tribute, composed by Sister Mary deLourdes:

Sister Mary Cyril

Her body bent, with struggle spent
She heard the welcome words;
*   "Arise, my love, and come away"*
And she replied, "My Lord"
Cheerful in the loneliness
Of long years lived apart
From all our busy life where once
She gave her mind and heart.
Brilliant -- with simplicity
Holy -- yet with wit
And hundreds of college women today
Are better because of it.
Dear Sister, we rejoice with you
Even as quick tears start.
Flights of Angels sing thee to thy rest
O noble heart.

Reverend Richard Rush Rankin, S.J.

Father Rankin was a sincere and devoted friend of Good Counsel College from its very inception. A man of vision and ideals, he was always ready with his sound advice and wise counsel. No detail was too small for his consideration. For over twenty-five years he served the College in various capacities: Retreat Master, Professor of Religion and Sociology, Visiting Lecturer. He made many a sacrifice in order to be present at important functions of the college.

On September 19, 1923, the very first day in the history of the College, it was Father Rankin who addressed the seven pioneers on the advantages of attending a small college, a Catholic college -- one under the eyes of Our Lady of Good Counsel. He presided at the first Investiture and those following in the early years, inspiring each entering class with his words of wisdom and wise counsel. It was Father Rankin who suggested the name The Prestonian for the College newspaper, and it was he who guided the editors of the paper in their first attempts at journalism.

Father Richard Rush Rankin was born on January 26, 1881 in Jersey City. He received his early education in his native city at St. Mary's Academy and St. Peter's High School. He attended St. Peter's College, from which he graduated in 1899 at the age of 18, as class Valedictorian. The same year he entered the Jesuit Novitiate at Frederick, Maryland. He pronounced his first vows in 1901. Having completed his classical and philosophical studies in 1907, his first assignment was to Georgetown Preparatory School in Washington, D.C., where he taught Latin, Greek and English. His next assignment was to Loyola High School in New York City, where he remained for four years. During the summer of 1912 he began his theological studies at Sacred Heart Seminary, Woodstock, Maryland, in preparation for his ordination to the Priesthood. He was ordained by James Cardinal Gibbons of Baltimore in 1915 at the age of 34.

In 1917 he was appointed Army Chaplain and served in this capacity overseas for two years. Father Rankin was decorated in France for gallantry in action and received the Croix de Guerre. The United States Army awarded him two Silver Stars for distinguished service. He received a personal Citation from General John J. Pershing on July 18, 1918. Father Rankin was discharged from the Armed Forces with the rank of Captain on August 27, 1919. The following year he began his services at Fordham University, where he achieved distinction in the field of Social Services. He was regent of the Fordham Graduate School for seven years. Later, his interest in social work led to his assignment as Director of the Fordham School for Social Services. During this period he gave invaluable help and direction to Mother Mary Aloysia in the education of the Sisters in preparation for the founding of Good Counsel College.

In 1926 Father Rankin, Dean of the Fordham Graduate School and Director of the Summer Session, was transferred to Georgetown University where he was to occupy the Chair of Philosophy in the School of Foreign Service. He held this position for two years. From 1928 to 1931 he was Dean of the College of Arts and Sciences while still directing the activities of the Georgetown Graduate School.

After a serious illness which occurred around this time, Father Rankin returned to teaching at St. Peter's College, his Alma Mater. For the next fifteen years he carried out his assignment as Professor of Ethics, Religion and Sociology, sharing his time with Good Counsel College where he taught Philosophy and Sociology.

During these years he engaged in an extensive correspondence with Mother Mary Aloysia, advising her on all aspects of college life: courses of study, speakers to be engaged, books for the library, plays for the Dramatic Club, means for making the yearbook financially possible.

In 1948 a severe illness forced his retirement. He returned to Georgetown University Infirmary where he remained until his death on August 19, 1949. The news of his passing brought sadness to the heart of his numerous friends, the Jesuit communities at Fordham, St. Peter's and Georgetown, but especially to his friends at Good Counsel College.

A touching tribute appeared in the Vestigia of the Class of 1950:

"The beloved name of the Reverend R. Rush Rankin holds a special place in the brilliant roster of men and women who have shared in the making of Good Counsel College...

Two faces of Father Rankin's personality, soldier and priest -- his strength and his gentleness, his valor and his humility, his love of right and his intense love of God, his leadership and his simplicity -- all united in the man himself, are what we shall always remember in the priest we loved so well."

John William Fuchs

John William Fuchs was born in Stamford, Connecticut, on February 12, 1899, the son of John William Fuchs and Theresa Vollmer Fuchs. He received his early education in the Stamford public schools. However, for the seventh and eighth grades he was a pupil at St. John's Catholic School. He then went on to Stamford High School. He attended the University of Toledo, Ohio and graduated with a B.A. degree in June 1920 at the age of 21. He received his M.A. degree from Teachers College, Columbia University, New York City, in June 1933. to keep up with the newest trends in education he continued to take courses at Fordham University, Montclair State Teachers College, New York University and Bank Street College of Education.

Mr. Fuchs started his teaching career at the early age of 20 as a high school teacher, also serving as athletic coach. Later he became Principal of an elementary school, which position he held for 12 years. In 1935 he was named Superintendent of Schools in Palisades Park, New Jersey. He remained in this position for 24 years during which time he maintained a strong inservice education program in his schools. He was also an active civic leader, being a charter member of the local Lions Club.

Mr. Fuchs was always interested in athletics, being too light to engage in sports himself, he enjoyed coaching. He was instrumental in helping many poor bright boys to succeed by obtaining for them athletic scholarships to his Alma Mater, Toledo University.

During the summer months he and his wife Stephanie travelled extensively in the United States, Canada, Mexico, Europe and the British Isles, gathering information and pictures for classroom use.

With his rich background and experience in education and public service, Mr. Fuchs came to Good Counsel in the summer of 1959 in answer to an urgent need for a supervisor of student teaching. For 15 years Mr. Fuchs served Good Counsel College faithfully and well as Associate Professor of Education and Supervisor of Student Teaching. His loyalty, devotion and wholehearted dedication to his work helped to raise the standard of the student teaching experience to a high professional level. His concern for each student teacher and his capability in organizing the whole program did much to enhance the quality of our program in the eyes of the Public School officials and personnel of White Plains and Westchester County.

The death of Mr. Fuchs occurred on Monday, February 18, 1974, at the age of 75. The following Friday, his mother Theresa Vollmer Fuchs, who had a great influence on his life, was called to her eternal reward, at the ripe old age of 99. It seemed that the two were loathe to be separated.

Shortly after his death, his wife Stephanie made a generous contribution of $1,000 to the curriculum library which Mr. Fuchs had helped to build and organize. Mrs. Fuchs continued her interest in the College and at a later date made another donation of $1,000 in memory of her husband.

Mr. Fuchs was respected by all and loved and admired by his students. They paid tribute to him in the following memorial which appeared in the Vestigia for 1974:

"As teacher and educator, Mr. Fuchs inspired his students with wisdom and comprehension. He never failed to incite them to strive after that which is noblest for future achievement. His charm was that of a kindly and courtly gentleman. Outside of the classroom and in addition to his tasks as supervisor of student teaching, he was always a familiar figure on campus, manifesting a deep interest in the functions of the college community.

Mr. Fuchs has given guidance and help that have become a cherished memory. Through the years the success of many has been furthered by his personal concern and their projects made possible by his support. His active loyalty as a sincere and worthy friend has been an inspiration to all those who revered him."

Sister Mary Leona Fechtman, R.D.C.

Sister Mary Leona graduated from Good Counsel College with a major in French in 1934. The following September she returned to Good Counsel to enter the Community of the Sisters of the Divine Compassion. She joined the faculty of Good Counsel College in 1936, and served the college for forty-six years. In 1968 she was appointed Director of Alumnae Relations by Mother Mary Dolores, and served in that capacity for fourteen years, supervising the Alumnae office until her retirement in June 1982.

During these years, Sister Mary Leona conducted fourteen annual Alumni Fund Drives from which some $325,000 was realized for the support of the development of the College, its students, faculty and program needs.

One of Sister Mary Leona's best-loved responsibilities was serving as faculty advisor to the student staff of the yearbook, <u>Vestigia</u>.

Sister Mary Leona is a member of the Photographic Society of America. She serves on the Board of Directors and is an active participant in the Color Camera Club of Westchester, Inc. Numerous awards and ribbons have come to Sister for her fine photographic work.

Sister Mary Leona has rendered a great service as the mainstay and unifying force for many, many alumni members, during the very difficult transition years from Good Counsel College to The College of White Plains, to the College of White Plains of Pace University. In 1984, Sister Mary Leona received the Alumni Golden Anniversary Award bestowed by Pace University. This event marked the fiftieth anniversary of her graduation from Good Counsel College.

Sister Miriam L. Moran, R.D.C.

The students returning to the College in the fall of 1960 were surprised and pleased to find that a new Dean had been appointed. Sister Mary Charles (Miriam L. Moran), the third Dean of Good Counsel College, succeeded Sister Mary Cyril Gallagher, who had been Dean since 1942.

Miriam Lucille Moran was born in White Plains on June 16, 1922, the daughter of Martin M. and Ellen V. Brown Moran. She received her early elementary education at St. John's parochial school. She then attended the Academy of Our Lady of Good Counsel for her secondary education and in the fall of 1939 she began her college studies at Good Counsel College. While a student in college, she took part in the various activities, her special preferences being the debate team, dramatics and inter-collegiate activities. In her sophomore year, she was elected to the Supreme Council of the Sodality and Vice President of the Eastern Westchester Division.

Despite her many activities, she maintained a fine academic record throughout the four years with a double major in History and English. She graduated on June 3, 1943, receiving her B.A. degree Cum Laude. A scholarship assistantship at Fordham University allowed her to pursue graduate study in History. Her field was the 20th century, and her research interest was a study of the Soviet Union and the League of Nations. She was awarded her Master's degree on June 7, 1944. In the meantime she taught Current and Modern European History at the College from January 1944 to June 1944.

Miriam entered the Sisters of the Divine Compassion on September 8, 1944. She was welcomed by two of her classmates, both honor students, who had preceded her, Virginia Frances Brady, B.A. Summa Cum Laude and Louise Marie Cutler, B.S. Magna Cum Laude. As a postulant she had gained valuable experience teaching Biology in the Academy of Our Lady of Good Counsel.

Miriam was given the name of Sister Mary Charles, on April 3, 1945. She made her vows on April 8, 1947 and her final profession on April 8, 1950.

She was encouraged to pursue further graduate studies in History at St. John's University. Her special research area of interest was British Foreign Policy and the Union of Europe in the Post-World War II period. Sister Mary Charles was awarded her Ph.D. degree on June 16, 1957. She joined the College faculty as a full time teacher of History in 1946. From the beginning, she encouraged the study of International Relations and served as Moderator of an active International Relations

Club for the students. In 1947 she was named Chairman of the History Department. She continued in this position until she was appointed Academic Dean on September 3, 1960.

While serving as chief academic officer of the College for eleven years, Sister Miriam introduced a program of travel-study to enrich the learning opportunities of the students, broadened the course offerings in Russian language and literature, Latin America and Far Eastern studies. She encouraged seminars in the History and Philosophy of Science, supported successful applications for NSF grants for increased instrumentation in the science departments and brought a series of scholars to the campus, among them Oscar Halecki, the noted Polish historian, upon his retirement from a major American university.

Sister Miriam considers her most significant contribution to the academic life of the College the establishment of the Honors Program in 1961, which, though modified and developed through the years, is a vital part of the quality programs offered by The College of White Plains today.

Active in professional and community organizations, Sister Miriam became a member of a number of professional associations -- among them The American Association for Higher Education, The American Historical Association, The American Academy of Political and Social Sciences, American Catholic Historical Association, The White Plains College Club, Westchester County Association and the White Plains Chamber of Commerce.

With the many changes that were introduced in the organization of the College after 1970, Sister Miriam was called upon to fill several important positions. From 1971 to 1975 she served as Vice President for College Relations.

When the College of White Plains consolidated with Pace University in 1975, she served as Assistant Vice President for University and Community Relations at the White Plains campus of Pace University from 1975 to 1978. Then, at the request of President Edward J. Mortola, she accepted the additional post of University-wide Student Recruitment Coordinator and Vice President for University Admissions from 1978 to 1982. In 1982 Dr. Moran was appointed Vice President for Enrollment Management of Pace University, a position she held until 1991. She currently teaches History as Professor Emeritus at the College.

The Mater Boni Consilii Medal

The following citations for the Mater Boni Consilii Medal outline the contributions of a few of the other men and women who contributed to the development of Good Counsel College.

In 1964 Mother Mary Dolores introduced the Mater Boni Consilii Medal, by which the College could honor individuals whose exceptional achievement or outstanding service she deemed worthy of receiving the award, the highest honor that the College could give. In each case the College made use of some important occasion, such as commencement, investiture or the dedication of a building to bestow the honor.

Mater Boni Consilii Medal Recipients

Frederic Joslyn	June 5, 1964
Dr. Leo I. Kearney	May 23, 1965
Bishop James E. Kearney	October 24, 1965
Sister Mary Carmelita Connell	October 24, 1965
Francis Cardinal Spellman	June 3, 1966
Sister Mary Ambrose Cavanagh	October 29, 1967
John B.J. Gerety	May 30, 1968
George Hils Ferrenz	April 26, 1969
Monsignor John T. Halpin	June 2, 1969
Helen Green Gerety	June 2, 1969
Mother Mary Dolores Hayes	May 25, 1970
Sister Mary Basil Hayes	June 7, 1971
Sister Marie Therese O'Hearon	June 7, 1971
Sister Mary Liguori Mistretta	May 26, 1972
Shach A. Van Steenburg	May 26, 1972
Josephine P. Lange	May 26, 1974
Katherine M. Restaino	May 23, 1975
Sister Rita Dougherty	May 23, 1975

Frederic Joslyn

The first recipient of the Medal was Mr. Frederic Joslyn, who, in the presence of Cardinal Spellman, received the award at commencement, June 5, 1964, for thirty-seven years of devoted service as Director of the College Glee Club.

Citation

Associated with the college since 1927, Mr. Frederic Joslyn has generously dedicated his talent and tireless energy to the cultural enrichment of the students. Under his aegis, the College Glee Club has developed a high quality of performance and has made a significant contribution to the pursuit of beauty and the fine arts in the college community. It is with sentiments of the highest esteem and gratitude that Good Counsel College on this occasion pays tribute to Mr. Joslyn whose life has been distinguished by unswerving fidelity in the cause of Catholic education.

Sister Mary Carmelita, R.D.C.

On October 24, 1965, the Mater Boni Consilii Medal was bestowed upon Sister Mary Carmelita Connell, a member of the original faculty since its foundation in 1923 and still serving the College at that time as Professor of Biology. Sister Mary Carmelita died on May 27, 1976.

Citation

In grateful recognition of 42 years of devoted service, Good Counsel College today wishes to honor one of the first members of the College faculty, Sister Mary Carmelita. Initiator of the science program at the College in 1923, untiring mentor for the students who return as graduates from far-flung posts of useful service as physicians, research scientists, teachers and biology specialists in many fields of endeavor, Sister Mary Carmelita brought with her to her task as department chairman an inexhaustible fund of knowledge and skills, not only in the biological sciences but in the fine arts as well.

The number of her students admitted to medical schools and graduate schools all over the United States, attests to the high calibre of work produced under her able leadership in the biological sciences at Good Counsel College.

Sister Mary Carmelita will continue to hold a place of grateful remembrance in the hearts of subsequent generations of Good Counsel students who will build upon the foundations she has so generously laid for the future.

In recognition, therefore, of 42 years of outstanding service, Good Counsel College takes pleasure in awarding to Sister Mary Carmelita the Mater Boni Consilii Medal.

Sister Mary Ambrose, R.D.C.

Presentation of the Mater Boni Consilii Medal was made for the sixth time to Sister Mary Ambrose Cavanagh, Registrar of the College from its foundation in 1923. She had served the College well in this capacity for 44 years. Sister Mary Ambrose died on June 22, 1977.

The presentation took place at the Investiture Ceremony on October 29, 1967 in the Leo I. Kearney Sports Building. At the request of Mother Mary Dolores, she received the medal from the hands of Monsignor Charles McManus, Principal of Archbishop Stepinac High School, who presided at the ceremony.

Mother Mary Dolores read the following Citation:

Citation

We pause today in the midst of our Freshman Investiture Ceremony to honor Sister Mary Ambrose whose work as Registrar has assisted these young women in the process of admission to the College. This day is a memorable one in their lives, and it is a significant one in the life of Sister Mary Ambrose as we honor her for forty-four years of service. Sister has been an outstanding member of the college community since its beginnings in 1923. Unfailing in her devotion, loyal and self-sacrificing, she has cheerfully performed the tasks involved in welcoming applicants and their parents to the college. Through her hands have passed the ambitions and hopes of these young women. She has marked their progress through four years on campus and then followed their careers after graduation with her interest and prayers. Foreign students have always been her special concern and their correspondence with her and visits through the years testify their gratitude for her friendship.

With equal devotion did she perform her role as Moderator of the Sodality of Our Lady, sponsoring each year a Lenten play, the proceeds of which went to the Sodality Scholarship Fund. The yearly May procession honoring Our Lady was also under her loving direction.

It is especially fitting then, in the last days of Our Lady's month of the Rosary, that in tribute, we bestow upon her the medal of the patroness of the College. With deep consciousness of the debt Good Counsel owes her, we ask you Monsignor to confer upon Sister Mary Ambrose, the Mater Boni Consilii Medal.

John B.J. Gerety

Mr. John B.J. Gerety, our good friend and legal advisor for many years, was the seventh recipient of the Mater Boni Consilii Medal. He received the award from the hands of His Excellency the Most Reverend John J. Maguire, Coadjutor Archbishop of New York who presided at Commencement on Thursday, May 30, 1968.

Citation

We pause in the midst of our Commencement Exercises this afternoon, to honor Mr. John B. Gerety, a devoted friend and councillor of Good Counsel College since its inception; a man of exemplary life and great personal integrity. Mr. Gerety, a noted member of the legal profession in Westchester County, has also found time in his busy career to assume the role of college professor. Since 1932, he has lectured in the fields of Business Law and American Constitutional History at Good Counsel College. Through all these years he has maintained a kindly personal interest in students, alumnae and faculty. He has loyally supported college activities, assisting at the ceremonies of Tassel Turning and Induction of the Student Government, graciously chaperoning, together with Mrs. Gerety, innumerable student social affairs, and acting as marshal of the academic processions at Freshman Investiture and at Commencement. A member of the Board of Advisors, Mr. Gerety has proved a trustworthy legal advisor who has gratuitously given the benefits of his well-informed mind and sound judgment and counsel to the trustees and administrators of the College. Unselfish with his time and his talents, Mr. Gerety has been a loyal friend to Good Counsel, ever concerned with her best interests. It is with deep gratitude for his devoted years of service and loyalty, that we ask Your Excellency to confer upon Mr. Gerety, the Boni Consilii Medal.

George Hils Ferrenz

On a beautiful spring afternoon, April 26, 1969, the Feast of Our Lady of Good Counsel, the blessing and dedication of the new student dormitory, Dannat Hall, took place. After the ceremony all went in procession to the Leo I. Kearney Sports Building for a program which included the awarding of the Mater Boni Consilii Medal to Mr. George Hils Ferrenz, the architect. After reading the citation, Mother Mary Dolores asked His Excellency the Most Reverend Terence J. Cooke, Cardinal Designate, Archbishop of New York to confer the medal on Mr. Ferrenz. Overwhelmed with surprise he arose to accept the honor.

Mr. Ferrenz is a partner in the firm of Ferrenz and Taylor. He attended Wittenberg University and is a graduate of Ohio State University with degrees in architecture and architectural engineering. He has served the College well as architect for the six buildings erected from 1957-1969. He has remained a true friend, advisor and liberal benefactor over the years.

Citation

During today's ceremony of dedication of Dannat Hall, it is my happy privilege on the part of all at Good Counsel College to pay tribute to Mr. George Ferrenz, architect for the building and a sincere and loyal friend and advisor of the College.

Mr. Ferrenz's association with Good Counsel began in 1957. In the succeeding twelve years, he drew up plans and was closely associated with the construction and completion of six buildings on campus that relate to every phase of college life: the administration and classroom building, Aloysia Hall; a new wing on the convent, where the religious faculty live; the Leo I. Kearney Sports Building where we are now gathered for this ceremony; the important intellectual center of the campus, Madonna Library; the dining room addition to Preston Hall; and finally, the beautiful students' residence Your Eminence has just blessed, Dannat Hall.

Professional skill, wholehearted dedication, and warm, genuine, personal interest have characterized Mr. Ferrenz's relationship with us in all these projects of the Development Program. He has actualized for us through physical structures our dreams and aspirations for the students of the college, but he has also shared deeply in those dreams and aspirations.

In grateful acknowledgment of his professional contribution, his personal dedication, and his many benefactions to the college, we ask Your Eminence to confer on Mr. Ferrenz the Boni Consilii medal.

Monsignor John T. Halpin

On June 2, 1969, His Eminence, the newly-created Cardinal Terence Cook, returned to Good Counsel to preside at Commencement. The College made use of this occasion to award the Mater Boni Consilii Medal for distinguished service to Monsignor John T. Halpin.

Father Halpin joined the College faculty in 1951 as Professor of Philosophy, teaching such courses as Ethics, Metaphysics, Natural Theology and the History of Philosophy. The time he devoted to the College in no way interfered with his chief ministry as pastor of St. Frances de Chantal parish, Bronx, New York.

At the Commencement of Good Counsel College on June 4, 1958, His Eminence Francis Cardinal Spellman made a surprise announcement: that Father Halpin had been made a Monsignor. In the fall on October 27, 1958, the College in turn honored Monsignor Halpin at a formal testimonial dinner in Preston. After 18 years of continual and exceptional service, the college again wished to honor him by bestowing its highest award, the Mater Boni Consilii Medal. Mother Mary Dolores read the following:

Citation

Today, it is my happy privilege to pay tribute to Monsignor John T. Halpin, devoted friend of Good Counsel and Professor of Philosophy at the College since 1951.

Thirty-eight years of Monsignor Halpin's fifty-one years of priesthood have been spent in close association with the Sisters of the Divine Compassion: first, at Our Lady of Mercy parish in the Bronx, then at St. Mary's parish in Katonah, and now in his present post as pastor of St. Frances de Chantal Church in the Bronx where the Sisters teach the sixteen hundred children enrolled in his school.

Monsignor Halpin's association with the College has extended over the past eighteen years. He has taught the junior and senior courses in philosophy, and has generously given time, interest, and counsel to a generation of students enrolled in the college. Among their college memories are not only his classroom lectures, but also his presence at so many academic functions, his homilies at Mass and Sodality receptions, his popular review sessions before final examinations. Monsignor's priestly interest in the students has extended beyond their four years here, and he has followed their careers, officiated at their weddings, and baptized their children.

The administration and faculty of the College regard Monsignor with deep and sincere affection, thoroughly aware of the personal spirit of self-sacrifice that has enabled him, in the midst of so many other duties and claims upon him, to prove such a sincere and devoted member of the Good Counsel family. It is, then, with grateful acknowledgement of his priestly and academic contribution to the College that we ask Your Eminence to confer on Monsignor Halpin the Boni Consilii Medal.

Helen C. Green Gerety

Helen C. Green Gerety was also awarded the Mater Boni Consilii Medal by Terence Cardinal Cooke at Commencement on June 2, 1969.

Mrs. John Gerety joined the faculty of Good Counsel College in the Commercial Department in the fall of 1944, teaching courses in Business Organization and accounting.

Helen C. Green Gerety graduated from White Plains High School and New York University. She engaged in post-graduate work at Fordham University specializing in accounting.

A faithful and devoted friend she served the College cheerfully and efficiently well beyond the call of duty. Mother Mary Dolores summed up her life of service in the following citation. Nearly a year later Helen Gerety received her eternal reward on May 15, 1970.

Citation

Good Counsel College is happy today to honor Mrs. Helen Gerety for 25 years of dedicated service as a faculty member of the Business Education Department. Devoted to God and to the Church, well-informed and active in civic and political affairs, a competent and valued member of our academic community, charming and gracious in manner, Mrs. Gerety has been for our students a beautiful example of Christian womanhood.

It would be impossible to tally the number of hours in these 25 years that have been given to the College and its interests. In addition to her teaching, Mrs. Gerety has supervised the students preparing to teach business subjects on the secondary level and in business schools. She has served as Director of the Placement Office, starting many graduates in their careers and placing underclassmen in part-time and summer work. She has represented us at meetings and conventions, served on faculty committees, and chaperoned innumerable student social events. And all has been done quietly, efficiently, generously, and graciously.

Together with her husband who lectures at the College in Business Law, Mrs. Gerety has supported all our academic and community activities. The College calendar has been their calendar, the good friends of the College are their good friends. And so it is with sincere appreciation of her great contribution in these 25 years, that we ask Your Eminence to confer on Mrs. Gerety the Boni Consilii Medal.

Sister Marie Therese, R.D.C.

On June 7, 1971, Sister Marie Therese, R.D.C., Professor of French, received the Mater Boni Consilii Medal from President Charles Ford.

Citation

What are the criteria by which, at a given moment in history, we attempt to evaluate a lifetime of consecrated service? Every moment in history is a convergence of past with future, and best understood in its relationship to both. Thus we can most fittingly pay tribute to Sister Marie Therese, whom we wish to honor today, in terms of her relationship to the world of yesterday and the world of tomorrow.

When young people of today dream about tomorrow's world, of what are their dreams made? Are they not dreaming of a world in which there will be more kindness, helpfulness, love and compassion; in which there will be greater respect for the dignity of the human person; in which there will be a stronger fidelity to one's commitments?

These are merely words, for, in speaking of a future which does not yet exist, what have we except words? With the past, it is different. We honor today a woman who, by her years of consecration as a religious and as a professor, projects the past into the future, in that she has already exemplified the realities which our youth hope to find in tomorrow.

Anyone who has been privileged to know Sister Marie Therese as a teacher can testify to her eminent fidelity in the cause of professional excellence. And who knows the number of students or alumnae who have been the recipients of her kindness, helpfulness, love and compassion, quietly and without fanfare. Her respect for the dignity of the human person has been manifested again and again by her active concern for the well-being of each individual student; by her ready gift of self, of time and energy, in helping others to grow intellectually and spiritually.

Sister Marie Therese, as you receive the Mater Boni Consilii Medal today in recognition of your outstanding and consecrated service to this college, may Our Lady of Good Counsel gather up all the good which you have done during these many fruitful years, so that those who follow you may reflect in its richness and beauty. Therefore we ask you, President Ford, to confer on Sister Marie Therese the Mater Boni Consilii Medal.

Sister Mary Liguori, R.D.C.

At the commencement held May 26, 1972, Dr. Katherine M. Restaino, Acting President, was asked to bestow the Mater Boni Consilii Medal on Sister Mary Liguori Mistretta, one of the first members of the faculty who taught the first freshman class on the day the College opened in September 1923, and continued to serve the College for 49 years. Sister Mary Liguori died on November 13, 1985.

Citation

The completion of this college year of 1971-1972 marks the forty-ninth year of Sister Mary Liguori's service to the College. These years have been characterized by enthusiasm for learning, gifted teaching, sincere interest in her students, and generous dedication.

Gifted in classical languages, Sister received her doctorate in Latin from Fordham University. With zeal and enjoyment she taught her subject to successive groups of students whose interest in the classics caught fire from her own. Then as trends in high school moved away from classical languages and there were fewer requests for college Latin courses, Sister prepared very graciously, though with much regret, to teach Spanish. Her proficiency can be demonstrated by the fact that last summer she was by invitation of the Universidad Internacional, Saltillo, Mexico, a faculty member of their summer school. In addition, Sister has placed her knowledge of Spanish at the service of the underprivileged both in Harlem and at the Chicago ghetto. For two summers she served as a volunteer worker, feeling as Terence did when he wrote: "Homo sum; humani nil a me alienum puto." I am a human being, and anything that affects another human being affects me.

Sister has served as President of the Classical Association of Greater New York and is currently a member of the executive board of the Classical Association of the Empire State. She has contributed articles to Classical Outlook and The New Catholic Encyclopedia. She enjoys travel and painting, and follows Horace's dictum: "Dulce est disipere in loco."

In recognition of Sister's forty-nine years of devoted service we request, Dr. Restaino, that you confer on her the Mater Boni Consilii Medal.

Josephine P. Lange

Josephine P. Lange, a graduate of New York University, joined the faculty of Good Counsel in September 1949, to teach courses in the Business Department. For 25 years she served the college faithfully and well.

At the ceremony which took place at Commencement held on Sunday, May 26, 1974, Dr. Katherine Restaino, President of the College, was asked to confer the Mater Boni Consilii Medal on Josephine P. Lange on her silver jubilee of service and the eve of her retirement.

Sister Helen Coldrick, Acting Dean, read the following citation:

Citation

Part of the response of educators to the demand for quality education in America is the expenditure of millions of dollars on computerized learning centers and experimental curricula. But no matter how enormous the outlay of funds, nor how sophisticated the educational technology, the desired results will rarely be achieved unless teachers accept the challenges posed by the continuing quest for improved learning. Teachers still hold the key to quality education. And while the methodologies of education change, the basic qualities of the good teacher do not.

Throughout twenty-five years of service on the faculty of this College, Jo Lange has personified those qualities -- competence in her discipline, concern for her students as individuals with different talents, personalities and interests, and patience and understanding combined with encouragement to students to achieve at their highest level. She is remembered with affection by grateful alumnae as one who exemplifies in her own life commitment to the finest professional and personal ideals.

In addition to the appreciation of her students, Jo Lange has earned the esteem of her colleagues. While, with her friend, Helen Gerety, she was developing the business department according to high standards, she was also enriching the spirit of the faculty with the quiet warmth and gentle strength which marks her personality. Generosity in service and loyal support of every faculty activity are the characteristics combined in the imprint she leaves on the memories of all who shared with her the growing years of the College. It is our experience of those same qualities which make us all look to her now for her continued concern and moral support.

Like most who excel in their profession, Mrs. Lange has garnered much personal satisfaction from her teaching. Among her other activities, the one she probably enjoys most is singing in the White Plains Presbyterian Church Chancel Choir, of which she has been a member since 1962. Therefore, in congratulating her upon her retirement after twenty-five years of dedicated service, it seems most appropriate to invoke the words of the Psalmist:

> Lord, be her secure shelter
>   and a strong fortress to protect her;
> Bless her with your presence;
> Be always ready to help her;
> Treat her according to your constant love.

And as a tribute from the college community, whose members rejoice with her on her silver anniversary of service, we ask Dr. Restaino to confer upon Josephine P. Lange the Mater Boni Consilii Medal.

Sister Rita Dougherty, R.D.C.

Sister Rita Dougherty entered the Sisters of the Divine Compassion in 1953, soon after graduating summa cum laude from the College. Given the name Sister Mary Dolorita, she made her first vows in 1956, and final vows in 1961. Sister Rita served at Good Counsel College from 1955 to 1975, in a variety of capacities: business manager, financial aid officer, treasurer, trustee and Associate Professor, teaching Chemistry, Physics, Earth Science, General Mathematics, Advanced Statistics and Advanced Calculus. In 1975, Sister Rita moved to the American Institute of Banking. Since 1977, she has been at Iona College, as Assistant Dean of Graduate Programs and Director of Graduate Admission of the Hagen School of Business, and currently as Associate Dean of Under-graduate Admissions and International Students Advisor. Sister Rita was awarded the Boni Consilii Medal at Commencement, 1975.

Citation

For nineteen years Sister Rita A. Dougherty has helped guard the first dollar bill received by Good Counsel College when it opened in 1923. Sister Rita has served the College in several capacities as a faculty member, as Assistant Treasurer and later as Treasurer, and as a Trustee. Her responsibilities as Treasurer have been awesome; she has met the challenges of the office in a competent and efficient manner. It is with pride and gratitude that the Trustees of The College of White Plains confer on Sister Rita Dougherty, a summa cum laude graduate of this College, the Mater Boni Consilii Medal.

COLLEGE SONGS

There is nothing that can more strongly unite a group than the singing of the old college songs. Bonds of friendship and love are strengthened, all barriers are broken down. Seniors and sophomores, freshman and juniors, residents and non-residents are all united in bonds of love for dear old Alma Mater and her patron Our Lady of Good Counsel.

Marching Song

As we gaze down the passage of the years,
Memory brings to light our dreams of long ago
As we see through the smiles and the tears
All the friends we used to know.

Though our paths take us far from your side
Constantly we turn to thee,
For you'll always be our guide
Alma Mater, hail to thee.

Life and fame to thee Good Counsel
From loyal hearts and true,
We thy daughters 'neath thy portals
Sing thy praises due.

* * * * *

Alma Mater

Oh, Alma Mater, our voices sound
The depths of love so true;
Loyal daughters within thy portals found
Accept our pledge to you.

Chorus:
Renowned, revered, for e'er be thy name
Renowned with glory, with honor and fame!
Far, far and wide,
Whate'er be the tide
Our voices ring, thy song we sing,
Good Counsel for ever!
Our hearts are linked in friendship strong
Anointed by thy love,
Safe in thy arms from every harm
In quest of Truth above.

Fond mem'ry, you in future may
Remove from eyes the tears
As scenes renew our happy days
With you in bygone years.

Words by Elizabeth Chrystal '28
Music by M. Elizabeth Wilson '28

* * * * *

Alma Mater

With hearts of gold we hail thee,
With joy untold we praise thee,
Our thoughts, our pray'rs with love entwine,
Dearest Alma Mater!

The shady walks wind round thee,
The pine trees whisper near thee
The ivy clings like angels' wings to thee,
Our Alma Mater!

In vale of tears be near us,
With loving care to cheer us,
Our songs of praise and love are thine,
Dearest Alma Mater!

Our happiest days we bring thee,
Our grateful hearts trained by thee,
Our Lady sings as night wind brings us
    thoughts of Alma Mater.

God bless thee, keep thee, guide thee,
Tho' trial, fear, confront thee,
In fond embrace enfold thee,
Dearest Alma Mater!

Our Lady lights the skies for you,
Her starry halo shining through,
A glowing tribute dear to you,
Good Counsel Alma Mater!

Cecily M. O'Connor '34

* * * * *

The Song of the Ivy

When May with her delicate green,
    Has tinted with beauty the scene,
The glad birds are singing,
    The Flowers are springing
Then list'n what the springtime doth say:
    All hail! All hail!
    The Ivy is Queen of the Year,
    Alike in each season is dear.

When summer with roses so sweet,
    Casts perfume and flow'rs at your feet,
On its soft balmy breeze
    As it floats through the trees,
This message you hear it repeat:
    All hail! All hail!
    The Ivy is Queen of the Year,
    Alike in each season is dear

The Green Cathedral

I know a green cathedral,
A shadow'd forest shrine,
Where leaves in love join hands above
And arch your prayer and mine.

Within its cool depths sacred
The priestly cedar sighs
And the fir and pine lift arms divine
Unto the pure blue skies.

In my dear green cathedral
There is a flowered seat
And choir loft in branched croft
Where song of bird hymns sweet.

And I like to dream at evening
When the stars its arches light
That my Lord and God treads its hallowed sod
In the cool, calm peace of night.

* * * * *

Our Senior Walk Farewell

Oh stately pines that heavenward lead
Oh, quiet, peaceful dell,
Where many happy hours we've spent
Farewell, farewell, farewell
Tonight we tread reluctantly
Our last adieu, and tell
Unto the listening heavens
Farewell, farewell, farewell
May Angels hover o'er the pines
and blessings ever dwell
On those whose feet will tread thee, hence,
Oh, Senior Walk, farewell
Farewell, farewell, farewell

This poem appeared in The Prestonian, *May 1950, Graduation Issue, page 6.*

Our Lady of Good Counsel

O Virgin Mother, Lady of Good Counsel,
Sweetest picture artist ever drew,
In all my doubts I fly to thee for guidance --
Mother, tell me, what am I to do?

By thy face to Jesus' face inclining,
Sheltered safely in thy mantle blue,
By His little arms around thee twining
Mother, tell me, what am I to do?

By the light within thy dear eyes dwelling,
By the tears that dim their lustre, too,
By the story that these tears are telling,
Mother, tell me, what am I to do?

Life alas! is often dark and dreary;
Cheating shadows hide the truth from view;
When my soul is most perplexed and weary,
Mother, tell me, what am I to do?

Plead my cause, for what can He refuse thee?
Get me back His saving grace anew,
Ah! I know thou dost not wish to lose me,
Mother, tell me, what am I to do?

Thus alike when needful sorrows chasten,
As amid joy's visits fair and few,
To thy shrine with loving trust I hasten,
O Mother, tell me, what am I to do?

Be of all my friends the best and dearest,
O my counsellor, sincere and true!
Let thy voice sound always first and clearest,
Mother, tell me, what am I to do?

In thy guidance tranquilly reposing,
Now I face my toils and cares anew;
All through life, and at its awful closing,
O Mother, tell me, what am I to do?

(The following lines were composed by Bishop James E. Kearney, to be sung by the graduates.)

These four long years we've nestled 'neath thy mantle
By thy side we've wandered day by day,
Now time has beckoned with his ruthless finger,
And at last our steps are turned away.

Those dear eyes shall follow where we wander,
Those loved arms shall strengthen us anew,
And those fond ears shall listen when we whisper,
O Mother, tell me, what am I to do?

* * * * *

Echoes of Good Counsel

Side 1

Oremus Pro Pontifice Nostro . . . . Cammattari
Asperges Me - Mode 7 . . . . Gregorian
In Monte Oliveti . . . . Martini
Sanctus - "Misa Viscaina" . . . . Duran
Ingrediente Domino . . . . Buff
Veni, Sponsa Christi . . . . Dobbelsteen
Kyrie - "Mass for Three Voices" . . . . Lotti
Easter Hymn . . . . Lyra Davidica

Side 2

Ave Maria . . . . Perosi
Callectis Urbs - Mode 1 . . . . Gregorian
Sanctus - "Mass for Three Voices" . . . . Lotti
Chapel Chimer . . . . Good Counsel Chapel
Folk Music . . . . arr. Shields

Kookaburrah
Go Tell Aunt Rhody
Hey, La-Li
Oh, Mary Don't You Weep
This Land is Your Land

Jubilate Deo .... Aiblinger

Sound Engineer: Mr. Donald Geibel, General Sound and Electric, White Plains, New York

Recording: Capital Records, New York City

Student Enrollment
Fall Term

Good Counsel College
Founded 1923

1923 - 7	1939 - 195	1955 - 280
1924 - 20	1940 - 193	1956 - 304
1925 - 44	1941 - 174	1957 - 321
1926 - 76	1942 - 178	1958 - 376
1927 - 74	1943 - 219	1959 - 420
1928 - 106	1944 - 246	1960 - 463
1929 - 125	1945 - 277	1961 - 518
1930 - 130	1946 - 345	1962 - 494
1931 - 140	1947 - 387	1963 - 496
1932 - 141	1948 - 387	1964 - 508
1933 - 131	1949 - 354	1965 - 514
1934 - 140	1950 - 296	1966 - 506
1935 - 136	1951 - 250	1967 - 501
1936 - 131	1952 - 218	1968 - 501
1937 - 182	1953 - 247	1969 - 461
1938 - 207	1954 - 274	1970 - 433

College of White Plains

1971 - 479	1973 - 667
1972 - 642	1974 - 675

College of White Plains of Pace University

1975 - 791	1978 - 1004	1980 - 1356
1976 - 736	1979 - 1128	1981 - 1551
1977 - 827		

Degrees Issued by Good Counsel College

Year	Date	B.A.	B.S.	BUS.	Total Year	Cum. Total
1927	June 8	11	1		12	12
1928	June 11	12	0		12	24
1929	June 6	21	2		23	47
1930	June 5	17	6		23	70
1931	June 4	17	5		22	92
1932	June 1	24	7		31	123
1933	June 9	28	6		34	157
1933	July 23	1	0		1	158
1934	June 7	27	8		35	193
1934	Aug. 1	1	0		1	194
1935	June 7	28	10		38	232
1936	June 4	27	8		35	267
1937	June 9	22	5		27	294
1938	June 9	20	10		30	324
1939	June 8	24	10	1	35	359
1940	June 7	25	8	9	42	401
1941	June 5	35	10	5	50	451
1942	June 5	28	10	5	43	494
1943	June 3	24	6	6	36	530
1944	Jan.	1	0	0	1	531
1944	June 8	25	10	6	41	572
1945	June 5	20	4	13	37	609
1946	June 6	15	12	9	36	645
1947	June 5	30	19	7	56	701
1948	May 25	34	17	13	64	765
1949	May 31	34	20	18	72	837
1950	May 29	45	14	19	78	915
1951	May 28	35	16	29	80	995
1952	June 2	38	10	22	70	1065
1953	June 4	33	12	5	50	1115
1954	May 27	21	12	12	45	1160
1955	June 3	29	9	9	47	1207
1956	June 6	14	16	13	43	1250
1957	June 1	34	12	11	57	1307
1958	June 4	45	6	7	58	1365
1959	May 30	42	16	12	70	1435
1960	May 26	41	22	5	68	1503
1961	May 31	45	21	8	74	1577
1962	June 1	57	15	15	87	1664

1963	June 7	66	16	10	92	1756
1964	June 5	78	18	10	106	1862
1965	June 4	94	22	4	120	1982
1966	June 3	66	20	6	92	2074
1967	June 2	67	20	4	91	2165
1968	May 30	81	19	4	104	2269
1969	June 2	85	21	20	126	2395
1970	May 25	71	19	8	98	2493
1971	June 7	56	26	13	95	2588

By the College of White Plains

Year	Date	B.A.	B.S.	BUS.	Total Year	Cum. Total
1972	May 26	54	38	6	98	2686
1973	May 28	40	60	8	108	2794
1974	May 26	38	67	10	115	2909
1975	May 23	35	56	22	113	3022

By the College of White Plains of Pace University

1976	May 24	49	79	12	140	3162
1977	May 27	23	54	20	97	3259
1978	May 26	44	45	15	104	3363
1979	May 31	35	40	21	96	3459
1980	May 30	46	51	31	128	3587

Commencement Speakers of Good Counsel College

June 8, 1927 - Honorable Humphrey J. Lynch, Justice of the Supreme Court

June 11, 1928 - Honorable Joseph V. McKee, LL.D., President of the Board of Alderman

June 6, 1929 - Reverend W. Coleman Nevils, S.J., President of Georgetown University

June 5, 1930 - Honorable John P. O'Brien, Surrogate, New York City

June 4, 1931 - Reverend Aloysius J. Hogan, S.J., President of Fordham University, N.Y.C.

June 1, 1932 - Honorable William D. Cunningham

June 9, 1933 - Clare Gerald Fenerty, B.A., LL.B.

June 7, 1934 - Joseph J. Reilly, Ph.D., Hunter College

June 7, 1935 - The Very Reverend Joseph A. Dineen, S.J., President of St. Peter's College

June 4, 1936 - Honorable Frank P. Graves, Ph.D., Litt.D., L.H.D., LL.D., President of the University of the State of New York

June 9, 1937 - Reverend Gerald Walsh, S.J.

June 9, 1938 - Reverend J. Harding Fisher, S.J.

June 8, 1939 - Edmund Borgia Butler, LL.B., M.A.

June 7, 1940 - Robert T. Bapst, Ph.D., LL.D., Superintendent of Schools, Buffalo, New York

June 5, 1941 - The Most Reverend James E. Kearney, D.D., Bishop of Rochester, New York

June 5, 1942 - Honorable Clare Gerald Fenerty, B.A., LL.D., Ph.D.

June 3, 1943 - Reverend William J. McDonald, Ph.D., Catholic University of America

June 8, 1944 - Rt. Rev. Monsignor Patrick J. McCormick, Rector of the Catholic University of America

June 5, 1945 - Reverend Maynard A. Connell, Ph.D.

June 6, 1946 - Reverend Robert J. Slavin, O.P., S.T.L., Ph.D., Catholic University of America

June 5, 1947 - Reverend James A. Magner, Ph.D., Catholic University of America

May 25, 1948 - His Excellency The Most Reverand James E. Kearney, Bishop of Rochester, New York

May 31, 1949 - Honorable Eugene L. Garey, LL.D., New York Attorney

May 29, 1950 - Frank J. O'Brien, M.D., Ph.D., Associate Superintendent of Schools of the City of New York

May 28, 1951 - Rt. Rev. Monsignor Patrick J. O'Connor, M.A., Assistant Professor of Sacred Eloquence, Catholic University of America, National Director of the National Shrine of the Immaculate Conception

June 2, 1952 - George N. Schuster, Ph.D., President of Hunter College

June 4, 1953 - Very Reverend John F. Murphy, C.S.B., Ph.D., President of John Fisher College, Rochester, N.Y.

May 27, 1954 - Reverend John S. Kennedy, M.A., Associate Editor of the Catholic Transcript

June 3, 1955 - Reverend Cyril F. Meyer, C.M., Ph.D., Vice-President of St. John's University

June 6, 1956 - Reverend Thurston M. Davis, S.J., Ph.D., Editor-in-Chief of America

June 1, 1957 - Honorable Mary H. Donlon, LL.B., LL.D., Judge of the United States Customs Court

June 4, 1958 - The Most Reverend Walter P. Kellenberg, Bishop of Rockville Centre

May 30, 1959 - Elbert K. Fretwell, Jr., Ph.D., Assistant Commissioner for Higher Education, New York State

May 26, 1960 - Rt. Rev. Monsignor John J. Dougherty, S.T.L., S.S.D., President of Seton Hall University

May 31, 1961 - Honorable Malcolm Wilson, Lieutenant Governor of New York

June 1, 1962 - Very Reverend Nicholas J. Sullivan, S.J., President of LeMoyne College

June 7, 1963 - Joseph F. Sinzer, Ph.D., Academic Dean, Pace College

June 5, 1964 - Honorable Ogden R. Reid, United States Congressman from New York

June 4, 1965 - Carroll F. Johnson, Ph.D., Superintendent of Schools, White Plains, New York

June 3, 1966 - Rt. Reverend Monsignor Paul Haverty, Former Secretary of Education of the Archdiocese of N.Y.

June 2, 1967 - Thomas R. Horton, Ph.D., Director of University Relations, I.B.M. Corporation

May 30, 1968 - Honorable Everett J. Penny, Vice Chancellor, New York Board of Regents

June 2, 1969 - Honorable Ogden R. Reid, Member of the House of Representatives, Congress of the United States

May 25, 1970 - Honorable Edwin G. Michaelian, The County Executive of Westchester

June 7, 1971 - Joseph P. Cosand, President of the Junior College, District of St. Louis

Commencement Speakers of the College of White Plains

May 26, 1972 - Geraldo Rivera, J.D., Member of the New York Bar Association and ABC Eye Witness News Team

May 28, 1973 - Honorable Edwin G. Michaelian, County Executive of Westchester

May 26, 1974 - Bill Beutel, ABC News Correspondent and Anchorman on the award winning TV news show "Eye Witness News"

May 23, 1975 - Frances A. Keegan, Alumna Class of 1951; Honorable Alfred B. DelBello, County Executive of Westchester

Commencement Speakers of the College of White Plains
of Pace University

May 24, 1976 - Sister Mary Joan Haley, R.D.C., Superior General of the
Sisters of the Divine Compassion
May 27, 1977 - Honorable Alfred B. DelBello, County Executive, the
County of Westchester
May 26, 1978 - Jane Cahill Pfeiffer, Management Consultant
May 31, 1979 - Frank J. Shakespeare, President, RKO General Inc.
May 30, 1980 - Edward B. Kenny, A.B., M.Ed., Ed.D., Vice President
and Dean of the College of White Plains
May 31, 1981 - Basil A. Paterson, Secretary of State of the State of New
York

Honorary Degree Recipients

Awarded by Good Counsel College

Terence Cardinal Cooke   Doctor of Humane Letters
Archbishop of New York   May 1970

Edwin Gilbert Michaelian   Doctor of Laws
County Executive of Westchester   May 1970

Awarded by the College of White Plains

Everett Joshua Penny   Doctor of Humane Letters
Vice Chancellor of the Regents   May 1974
of the University of the
State of New York

Awarded by the College of White Plains of Pace University

Thomas R. Horton   Doctor of Laws
Director of University Relations   May 1976
IBM Corporation

Alfred B. DelBello   Doctor of Laws
County Executive of Westchester   May 1977

Arthur P. Antin
Superintendent of Schools
White Plains City School District

Doctor of Humane Letters
May 1977

Jane Cahill Pfeiffer
Management Consultant

Doctor of Humane Letters
May 1978

William Vincent Cuddy
Attorney, Cuddy & Fedder

Doctor of Laws
May 1978

Mother Mary Dolores Hayes, R.D.C.
General Treasurer
Sisters of the Divine Compassion

Doctor of Humane Letters
May 1979

Frank Joseph Shakespeare
President, RKO General Incorporated

Doctor of Commercial Science
May 1979

Basil A. Patterson
Secretary of State
of the State of New York

Doctor of Civil Law
May 1981

Sr. Mary Joan Haley R.D.C.
Honorary Trustee
Pace University

Doctor of Humane Letters
May 1983

BIBLIOGRAPHY

I

Almanac and Yearbook. Pleasantville, NY: Reader's Digest, 1970.

Bolton, Robert. The History of Several Towns, Manors and Patents of the County of Westchester from its first settlement.

Brady, Sister Mary Teresa, R.D.C. The Fruit of His Compassion. New York: Pageant Press, 1962.

Brann, Henry A. "The Right Reverend Thomas S. Preston, D.D." The Illustrated Catholic Family Annual, 1893.

Ellis, Edward Robb. The Epic of New York City - a Narrative History from 1524 to the Present. New York: Coward - McCann, 1966.

French, Alvah P. History of Westchester County. New York, 1925.

Gannan, Robert I., S.J. The Cardinal Spellman Story. Garden City, NY: Doubleday, 1962.

Heuser, Rev. Herman J., D.D. Mother Mary Veronica, Foundress of the Sisterhood of the Divine Compassion. New York: P.J. Kennedy & Sons, 1915.

Information Please Almanac. Atlas and Yearbook 1966. Dan Golenpaul, Ed. New York: Simon and Schuster, 1966.

Rosch, John. Historic White Plains. The City of White Plains, 1939.

Scharf, J. Thomas. History of Westchester County. Philadelphia 1886.

Sullivan, Mark. Our Times. The United States 1900-1925, Vol. VI, The Twenties. New York: Charles Scribner's Sons, 1935.

Weigold, Dr. Marilyn. "Mapleton." <u>Westchester Historian</u>. Quarterly of the Westchester County Historical Society. Vol. 51, Winter 1975, No. 1.

<u>Who's Who in American History</u>, Vol. I 1897-1942.

II

Alumni News Letters - Good Counsel College

Catalogue of Good Counsel College, 1924, 1925, 1926, 1927.

Faculty Notes - Good Counsel College

News Bureau - Good Counsel College

Newsletter - Good Counsel College

News Releases - College of White Plains

Official Bulletin - Good Counsel College

<u>The Prestonian</u> - Good Counsel College Newspaper:
Oct. 1924, Vol. I, Number 1, to June 1927
Sept. 1927 to May 1934
Oct. 1934 to June 1944
Oct. 1944 to June 1954

<u>Vestigia</u> - Good Counsel College Year Book.

III

<u>Chronicle of Good Counsel College</u>, January 8, 1945 to November 11, 1949. Sister Mary Dolores Hayes. Archives of Good Counsel College.

<u>Chronicle of The Sisters of the Divine Compassion</u>: February 10, 1918 to March 19, 1919; August 21, 1924 to October 31, 1932. Sister Mary Anselm Barry. Archives of The Sisters of the Divine Compassion.

Chronicle. November 10, 1933 to December 31, 1934. Sister Mary
    Ambrose Cavanagh. Archives of The Sisters of the Divine Compas-
    sion.

Chronicle. April 23, 1937 to July 4, 1937. Archives of The Sisters of the
    Divine Compassion.

Chronicle. January 28, 1935 to November 3, 1935. Mother Mary Aloysia
    Kelly. Archives of Good Counsel College.

Chronicle. July 2, 1943 to April 29, 1946; May 2, 1946 to August 31,
    1949; September 1, 1949 to January 29, 1951. Sister Mary Dolores
    Hayes. Archives of The Sisters of the Divine Compassion.

Excerpts from the minutes of the meetings of the Board of Trustees of
    the Sisters of the Divine Compassion regarding the College.
    December 1952 to January 1953. Mother Louise Marie Cutler.
    Archives of The Sisters of the Divine Compassion.

IV

Hartigan, John J. Eulogy for Mother Mary Aloysia, delivered at the
    Requiem Mass, December 31, 1953.

Hayes, Patrick Cardinal - Address Delivered on the Occasion of the
    Blessing of the New Convent Wings and the Commencement of the
    Academy of Our Lady of Good Counsel, June 26, 1923.

Kearney, James E. Bishop of Rochester.
    Sermons delivered at the Tridium in preparation for the Feast of
    Our Lady of Good Counsel on the Silver Jubilee of the College.
    April 23 - 26, 1948.

    Address at the Alumnae Communion Mass on the occasion of the
    Silver Jubilee of the College. April 25, 1948.

    Sermon at the Students' Mass on the occasion of the Silver Jubilee
    of the College. April 27, 1948.

    Address delivered at the Silver Jubilee Commencement. May 25,
    1948.

Eulogy for Mother Mary Aloysia delivered at the Memorial Mass on January 8, 1954.

Kelly, Mother Mary Aloysia, R.D.C. Mary Caroline Dannat Starr, Foundress of the Order of the Divine Compassion. Fordham University, 1926.

Penny, Helen L. Development of the Good Counsel Campus 1890-1961.

Scanlan, Arthur J. Address delivered on the occasion of the Silver Jubilee of Good Counsel College, April 26, 1948.

Spellman, Francis Cardinal.
Letter to the Silver Jubilee Class of 1948, April 20, 1948.

Address at the dedication ceremony of Aloysia Hall, April 26, 1959.

Veronica, Mother Mary, R.D.C. A Brief Review of Seven Years from June 21, 1895 - June 6, 1902.